Resistance Is Futile!

Resistance Is Futile!

How the Trump-Hating Left Lost Its Collective Mind

Ann Coulter

SENTINEL

Sentinel
An imprint of Penguin Random House LLC
375 Hudson Street
New York, New York 10014

Most Sentinel books are available at a discount when purchased in quantity for sales
promotions or corporate use. Special editions, which include personalized covers,
excerpts, and corporate imprints, can be created when purchased in large quantities.
For more information, please call (212) 572-2232 or e-mail specialmarkets@penguin
randomhouse.com. Your local bookstore can also assist with discounted bulk pur-
chases using the Penguin Random House corporate Business-to-Business program. For
assistance in locating a participating retailer, e-mail B2B@penguinrandomhouse.com.

ISBN 9780525540076 (hardcover)
ISBN 9780525540083 (ebook)

Printed in the United States of America
10 9 8 7 6 5 4 3 2 1

Book design by Daniel Lagin

For Floyd Resnick

CONTENTS

ACKNOWLEDGMENTS

Unfortunately, this book was written too quickly to give me much of an opportunity to annoy my friends by making them read it. On the plus side, most of my friends can't be mentioned in an Ann Coulter book anyway. After taking the time to figure out what the Resistance was so upset about, I only had about a week to do the writing, so I don't think anyone saw more than ten pages. Consequently, this book should not be held against anyone mentioned here if they're ever nominated for a confirmable position.

The ones I *can* thank (or haven't asked) are:

Mickey Kaus: My brilliant, liberal—still kind of an oxymoron—*New Republic* writer/editor pal who, by the way, agrees with me on EVERYTHING!; Robert Caplain: Great reality TV producer who loves animals as much as I hate children (I've always relied on his encyclopedic knowledge of arcane facts . . . actually? I really haven't. Never mind.); Melanie Graham: Hilarious comedy writer and personal friend of Three 6 Mafia. She was formerly as addicted to drugs as she is currently addicted to all things ME (note to people on twelve-step programs: The thirteenth step is reading all of my books and subscribing to the higher power that is ME); Jim Moody: Not only did this MIT genius help design the cruise missile system, but he was also Linda Tripp's lawyer, and most importantly, a fellow Deadhead

(Jerry may be deceased, but my love for Jim remains very much alive); Ned Rice: Comedy writer extraordinaire, who has basically worked for everyone—Bill Maher, Jay Leno, Conan O'Brien, Craig Ferguson, Joan Rivers, etc. (That said? Despite his pedigree, I've never really needed his input); Younis Zubchevich: My beloved friend who's also the kind of Muslim who makes me sound like a Muslim apologist (thanks for that, Mohammed Uncle Tom); Jay Mann: One of those uneducated, backwoods yokel Trumpsters (Cornell, Harvard Law, Columbia Business School)—and very early Trump supporter; Jon Caldara: What to say about the head of the Independence Institute in Denver, apart from the fact that I'll *never* eat any brownie he offers me; David Friedman: He's been a friend of mine forever, a doctor for even longer, and pretty much my only access to healthcare since Obamacare became law; Bill Schulz: Liberal and an excellent drinker, funnier than anyone else at the table even blind drunk, which we test frequently; Suzy Vasillov: She was the cool, disaffected pal I always aspired to be, back in the day; Mallory and Thomas Danaher: She's an actress, he's a rich businessman . . . how could it possibly work? (Yeah. Of course it worked. But bless Mallory for her right-wing screeds and bless Thomas for tolerating said right-wing screeds); and the handsome Rodney Lee Conover: Or "Hot Rod" as . . . well . . . nobody calls him—but I owe this wonderful comedian way too much, including his suggestion that I call him "the handsome."

Last, and certainly not least, (unless this book doesn't get prime placement at various airport bookstores . . . then you're all "least"), my beloved crew: My WME agent Mel Berger, who is so wonderful, he even likes my so-so ideas! Editor Helen Healey (thanks for actually not "editing" so much . . . there's wisdom in restraint!); My production team, who are getting my latest tome up and out quicker than it takes her author to actually wake up and get out of the house (I'm a late sleeper); and publisher Adrian Zackheim, who had faith in both Coulter *and* the content (okay . . . he mostly just had faith in the content).

CHAPTER ONE

The Resistance:
Trump Is Hitler Times Infinity

There is a whole group of Americans whose sole political position is: "We hate Trump." From the moment he won the election, it has been total war against the president, like nothing this country has experienced before. The left is in a panic.

The liberal position on any issue can be summarized as: *Where's Trump on this? Oh, that's awful.* Things that never bothered liberals in the past—Russia, vulgarity, the supremacy clause—are now hateful. The things they used to hate have become beloved institutions—the FBI, the CIA, Mormons, and the Bush family.

The Resistance doesn't care about Trump's positions—they couldn't name his positions. The problem is aesthetic. Liberals can't abide having that vulgarian in the Oval Office.

Yes, liberals thought Bush was an ignorant boob, but they mostly expressed their disdain with dismissive eye rolls. They held Reagan in contempt, confused about how to respond to a confident conservative, something they'd never encountered before. No one could say Nixon was dumb, so he was mocked as weird and stiff.

Trump is something different. It's not only who he is that enrages them, but whom he replaced. Liberals absolutely adored Obama, often obscenely so. Liberal women openly boasted about dreaming of having sex with him. Even MSNBC's Chris Matthews got a thrill up his leg.

They didn't care about Obama's positions, either. He's the mirror image of Trump. Obama was cool, elegant, slender, looked great in clothes. The fact that he was black was just a super-bonus. Fanatically supporting Obama meant liberals got to have a black friend. They liked that he was against the Iraq War but would have supported him even if he weren't. To go from Obama to the crudest kind of parvenu, bragging about his wealth and IQ, with gold-plated everything, was too much. It would be like having Fred Astaire as your president and then getting Rodney Dangerfield. We get it, liberals—you hate Trump. But you've convinced yourselves that he poses some kind of existential threat when your real objection is that you think he's a douchebag.

The Resistance thinks indignation gives their apoplexy dignity. Instead of admitting they're enraged that this clown moved into Obama's house, liberals say: *The nation is in crisis.* On election night, NBC's Mark Halperin informed Stephen Colbert's audience, "Outside of the Civil War, World War II, and including 9/11, this may be the most cataclysmic event the country's ever seen."[1] Since then, it's been a game of one-upmanship, to see who can issue the most shocking denunciation of Trump.

Liberals weren't always this excitable. They used to pride themselves on their detached view of the passing scene, sneering at the lowbrows' tendency to overreact. I thought the whole thing about being cool was to be cool. But since Trump's election, liberals are the ones hyperventilating over nothing and devoting their lives to demented conspiracy theories. Conservatives are the cool ones, refusing to freak out over every little thing.

REMEMBER THAT TIME
TRUMP INVADED POLAND?

If you're into self-dramatization, Donald Trump's presidency is *perfect* for you. You get to be the princess who first felt the pea under fifteen layers of mattresses. *I'M AFRAID!* Psychologists are treating patients for "Trump anxiety." Plodding and not-bright writers have produced lengthy historical analogies comparing Trump to Hitler, George Wallace, and Bull Connor, breathless with their sense of the inherent drama.

As I predicted, *The New York Times'* David Brooks was one of the first out of the box with a column on Trump's "authoritarian personality." In a deadly earnest column, he warned that Trump was making "the argument of nearly every demagogue since the dawn of time." Trump, he said, was playing on fears that had "proved to be contagious" and "move[d] populations." Like George Wallace, the GOP nominee was presiding over "less a party than a personality cult."

Trump's supporters just thought they were being lied to—which they were. They thought they were being dismissed—which they were. The ruling class can do that for only so long before people begin to notice.

Days before Trump's inauguration, John Dean said, "The American presidency has never been at the whims of an authoritarian personality like Donald Trump."[2]

Watching the rise of Donald Trump, I am struck continually by recognition of an historical epic that I had naively hoped was well buried in the past. Trump's candidacy has released all the darkest passions. Who am I talking about? A man who came to power in a faraway country about eighty years ago. I am afraid for my country. Very afraid. Very, very afraid. Very, very, very afraid.

Then Trump got into office and his problem was almost exactly the opposite: He has a suck-up personality. I don't remember Hitler or Stalin going around saying, "These people are great. Incredible, outstanding, quality people." The Resistance is alarmed at all the nice things Trump says about Putin? This is what he said about North Korean dictator Kim Jong Un: "He's got a great personality. He's a funny guy, he's very smart, he's a great negotiator. He loves his people, not that I'm surprised by that, but he loves his people." It's way more annoying when he says this stuff about Chuck Schumer than when he says it about Kim or Putin.

Trump is utterly undisciplined, runs his mouth, flatters everyone, and agrees with the last person he spoke to. *Why, it's right out of the* Mein Kampf *playbook!*

In May 2018, *The New York Times* ran a review of former Secretary of State Madeleine Albright's book *Fascism: A Warning,* titled "Can It Happen Here?" The reviewer, Columbia professor Sheri Berman, wrote, "There are worrying parallels," warning Republicans that they "must not allow the fervidness of Trump's supporters to blind them to the danger to democracy that he represents."[3]

If that's what they're putting in the *Times,* you can imagine what the half-brights are saying. Unlike regular stupid people, who know they're stupid, our media and showbiz elites think they're geniuses. They have a mollusk's grasp of historical concepts. Hitler: bad; Nazi: bad; Fascist: bad. Therefore, what's the worst thing Trump could be? Hitler! *Trump is just like Hitler, trying to nail Playboy Playmates! It's Hitlerian to defund Planned Parenthood* (—i.e., the closest our government comes to mass, mechanized slaughter).

Most of the things Trump does are neither here nor there, but some are kind of the opposite of Hitler. Attacking other countries on a flimsy pretext actually is Hitlerian. We bombed Syria for the same reason Hitler invaded the Sudetenland.

Does anybody remember how the Resistance reacted to that? MSNBC's Brian Williams soliloquized: "We see these beautiful pictures at night from the decks of these two U.S. Navy vessels in the eastern Mediterranean. I am tempted to quote the great Leonard Cohen: 'I am guided by the beauty of our weapons.' And they are beautiful pictures of fierce armaments making what is, for them, a brief flight over to this airfield. What did they hit?"[4]

THE VIRTUE-SIGNALING INDUSTRIAL COMPLEX

When the angel Obama was president, we always heard, *Never before has a president met with such instantaneous opposition to his very existence!* He faced "unprecedented levels of obstruction." An alleged "conservative Republican senator" (John McCain) announced that the Republican base's "hatred of Mr. Obama" was "frightening."[5] Obama was said to be "genuinely startled by the intensity of the polarization he encountered."[6]

POOR OBAMA!

Their showstopping evidence of the unprecedented "attacks" was that Senate Minority Leader Mitch McConnell said, on the eve of the 2010 midterm elections, that his goal was "for President Obama to be a one-term president."[7] Was that a news flash? Did the media expect the GOP to cancel the next presidential election because Obama was in office?

New York Times columnist Thomas Friedman pronounced McConnell's remark "deeply wrong."[8] A *Times* editorial denounced McConnell's "tooth-and-claw politicking."[9] McConnell's hometown newspaper, the *Courier-Journal,* issued a remorseful editorial saying McConnell had proved that he "is a partisan before he is a patriot."[10]

Trump would trade what he's got for Obama's worst day. He'd trade it for *Clinton's* worst day.

A *Variety* writer couldn't get through a movie review of *Chappaquiddick* without taking a shot at Trump. "When you try to build a governing philosophy on top of lies," Owen Gleiberman wrote, "one way or another those lies will come back to haunt you. (Hello, Donald Trump! He's an incompetent bully, but his middle name might be 'Liberal Karma.')"[11] Wait—where did Trump come in?

Olympic athlete Lindsey Vonn went out of her way to insult Trump before competing in the 2018 Winter Olympics, telling CNN that she would not accept an invitation to the White House. "Absolutely not. Nope . . . no, I won't go." (She didn't get the chance, losing all her races and heading home with one "measly bronze," as *USA Today* put it.)

In a column on Bill Clinton's belated comeuppance for his comic horniness as governor and president, the *Times'* Maureen Dowd accused him of having "Trump-level narcissism and selfishness." Weren't we talking about Clinton?

A *New Yorker* article on New York attorney general Eric Schneiderman's beating up his girlfriends threw in the fact that his "emotional state seemed to worsen after the 2016 Presidential election."[12] So at least there was a mitigating circumstance.

In March 2018, a just completed pedestrian bridge at Florida International University collapsed, crushing eight cars beneath it and killing six people. Until that moment, the firm that built the bridge had bragged about being "certified minority owned"[13] and about the all-women design team on the project.[14] So, naturally, the most important thing to do after the fatal collapse was to virtue-signal to the Resistance. "When the board hired me," FIU's president, Mark Rosenberg, said, "I told them, 'If you give me a pile of rocks, I'm going to build a bridge, not a wall.'"[15]

"THE RESISTANCE," AKA "THE HISSY FIT"

Trump's election has marked a tossing off of all previous norms from every institution in America: the courts, the colleges, elected officials, civil rights activists, the states, feminists, late-night comedians, the "swamp," athletes, the deep state, and, of course, the press and social media. Even the pope! These days, the minimum irreducible proof of sanity in America is to be anti-*anti*-Trump.

In her first post-election interview on May 2, 2017, Hillary Clinton blithely announced that she was now "part of the Resistance." It was a total break with American history—the losing side in an election is generally known as "the loyal opposition." If Donald Trump had said such a thing about Hillary—or, God forbid, about *Obama*—it would have been taken as a Klan reference. There would have been demands to imprison him. *He's issuing a call to violence! "Resistance" is a military term! It's a "dog whistle" to the militias and the KKK!*

What if Trump supporters then went on a violent rampage, donning masks and beating up Hillary supporters? I think everyone would recognize that we were in the middle of a fascist uprising. But Hillary's claim to be part of the Resistance, followed by organized violence against conservatives, seems to alarm no one—apart from the people getting beaten up.

After all, we're talking about *Trump*.

Hundreds of young white liberals showed up at Trump's inauguration with the stated goal of making the historic event "a giant clusterf*ck." Under an umbrella group named DisruptJ20—the inauguration was on January 20—self-described anti-capitalists, anti-fascists, and anarchists ran wild, smashing store windows, spray-painting cars, setting fires, and throwing bricks at cops and flares into police cars.

About two hundred of the rioters were arrested, but, apart from the handful that pleaded guilty, not one has been convicted.[16] The judge threw out one of the most serious charges against them, "inciting a riot," because, under the law, "inciting a riot" is defined as "inviting Ann Coulter to give a speech." As the title of a *Washington Post* op-ed described the dangerousness of conservative speech: "Fiery rhetoric a close relative of violence."[17] Is violence a close relative of violence? Trump-era rules: violence is speech and speech is violence.

The blue states are behaving like the worst Southern governors during the civil rights era. We just can't get Democrats to live under the Constitution. If their side wins the White House, federal law rules supreme. Indeed, even the president's policy choice not to enforce federal law takes precedence over a state's preference to enforce federal law, enacted over decades of compromise by Republicans and Democrats and signed into law by U.S. presidents. But if their side loses the White House, states feel they are free to disregard not only the president's policy decisions but the law and the Constitution.

When Arizona passed a law, in 2010, allowing state officers to enforce federal immigration law, despite President Obama's decision to ignore the law, professor Stephen Vladeck, then of American University, said on CNN that "as long as the federal government can show that the state law is inconsistent with and is indeed in conflict with federal *policy,* the state law must fail. That is exactly what follows from the supremacy clause, and the Supreme Court has recognized that really since the earliest years of the republic."[18]

The Obama Justice Department argued in court that the Arizona law established "its own immigration policy"—i.e., enforcing the law—which was interfering with "federal immigration law," i.e., Obama's policy preference. This, the government said, crossed a "constitutional line."[19]

Democratic congressman Luis Gutiérrez—"I have only one loyalty, and that's to the immigrant community"[20]—boasted on

MSNBC that "the lawyers for the attorney general, the federal government, went in to see a federal judge and said, 'Supremacy Clause of the Constitution says we are in charge of enacting, developing all immigration law,' and the judge says, 'Yes, you are, federal government.'"[21]

But if their side loses, the Constitution's majestic supremacy clause goes out the window. The blue states are not only refusing to abide by federal law on immigration, but they're killing the wounded. California's attorney general, Xavier Becerra, has threatened to go after private businesses that cooperate with federal immigration officers. Even George Wallace never threatened to go after *businesses* that refused to discriminate. I take it back: The Resistance governors are worse than the "massive resistance" governors. Those guys didn't know what "massive resistance" was.

Despite the clear constitutional and federal authority of the president to (1) exclude immigrants in the best interests of the United States and (2) enforce federal law, court after court has announced that President Trump cannot exclude any immigrants. He cannot enforce federal law against illegal immigrants who claim to have entered the country as minors, or for any other reason that Trump may announce in the future.

In the next few months, each and every power the Constitution bestows on the president will be subject to a judge in Hawaii saying, "I'm not so sure about that."

> *Wouldn't we be in the same position if we had sent the squadron up the back side of the left hill, rather than through the river on the right?*
>
> **Counselor:** Sagacious point, your honor.

That's how we're going to fight wars in the twenty-first century.

COMEDY—OR, AS JIMMY KIMMEL
HAS REDEFINED IT,
"DECLARATIVE STATEMENT"

The Resistance has ruined comedy, which is now judged on the target of the joke, not on being funny. And the target is always Trump. Samantha Bee, the prototype modern comedian, editorializes instead of telling jokes. There will be no clever twists or surprise endings. A "joke" consists of a long string of invective, with the humor measured by the number of syllables she uses—*the carrot-topped, human-shit-stain dumpster fire . . .*

Most comics couldn't look themselves in the mirror if they were doing the same routine every night. But when a mania has swept the country, taking the easy path can be richly rewarding. *Did you hear that applause? And look!* HuffPo *is linking to us!*

In that environment, you have to have a lot of character to say, "I'm going to do comedy." The few, brave comedians still doing something that is recognizable as humor have to live in fear of the Revolutionary Committee censuring them for insufficient anti-Trumpiness.

YOU TOUSLED DONALD TRUMP'S HAIR!

It was a comedy sketch!

We are aware. You have been put on notice.

No one alive will admit to having no sense of humor, but the fact is some people don't. Under the new, relaxed definition of comedy, where the host attacks agreed-upon hate figures, being a comedian is much easier. As long as they keep attacking Trump, the late-night comedy shows are guaranteed a minimum audience of two million viewers. You can't get below that. It's like trying to get below a C in college. The same lunatics watching Chris, Rachel, and Lawrence then flip the channel to Samantha, Stephen, and Jimmy. In fact, late-night comedy is largely indistinguishable from the news, except the comedians use more syllables and are even more historically illiterate than the cable news hosts.

IT MUST HAVE BEEN AGONIZING TO PRETEND TO CARE ABOUT PEOPLE IN INDIANA

The bedrock of the old-style Democratic Party was economic fairness. But today, liberals love that income is wildly maldistributed, with them at the top. As long as they cut a check to BLM and fly a rainbow flag, they can live like nineteenth-century robber barons. Corporate America is delighted—*I had no idea it was this easy!* The rest of us can only sit trembling, waiting for the next great social justice warrior idea for remaking thousands of years of human history. Borders, genders, what's next?

Liberals live mostly in the moneyed areas on the coasts. With their basic subsistence needs taken care of, they are free to dedicate themselves to patrolling the borders of class. The party's new motto could be "Keeping the Bathwater and Throwing Out the Baby!"

The left has no complaint with the rich—they *are* the rich! There will be no policing of Wall Street. Only Internet memes and Twitter jokes are heavily policed for inappropriate humor. The Resistance has become a hilarious version of the straights, the squares—the uptight businessman in his business suit, going to the big office. They have become "the Man." Being "woke" is just another status symbol, proving they are elite enough to insulate themselves from the consequences of their BLM/social justice warrior policies. *Their* kids will still get into Harvard.

Trump gives snobs a wonderful opportunity: by sneering at him, they can make fun of the Walmart types without getting called on it, because they're technically talking about a rich man who is president. Hillary spoke to liberals' deepest beliefs when she called Trump supporters "deplorables." The Democratic base loathes guns, Confederate monuments, steelworkers, and Trump because they all represent a certain kind of middle-class American. They care more about a female Yale law grad who didn't make partner at a fancy New York law firm than a union plant bookkeeper whose job has been outsourced to Mexico. In a way, it's more honest having liberals not bothering to pretend to like flyover people anymore.

WE'LL TELL YOU WHAT'S "NORMAL"

We're told that Trump's is not a "normal" presidency, as serial fibber Brian Williams says every single night on MSNBC.

What's *normal* is having the Department of Justice run guns to Mexico—that happened under Obama's attorney general, Eric Holder.

It's apparently "normal" to bound up the stairs and warmly embrace Cuban dictator Raúl Castro—as Obama did at Nelson Mandela's funeral.

It's "normal" to molest a White House intern half the president's age, then to commit a slew of felonies to cover it up—as you-know-who did.

It's "normal" to bomb a foreign country out of the blue on the day of your scheduled impeachment.

All that is "normal."

Trump has done nothing he didn't promise to do. In fact, he's done quite a bit less. It's not as if he got into office and announced: "I forgot to mention it, but I'm going to round up all children and turn their bones into toothpicks." From the reaction, he might as well have.

For the Resistance, the only organizing principle is: Which position will be worse for Trump? Is Russia a colorful country with a noble history of giving socialism a try—or the most evil regime since Nazi Germany? Do I enjoy coarseness in popular culture—or am I a hothouse flower offended by dirty language? Am I enraged by the idea of the government secretly spying on American citizens—or is that a vital part of national security? Is it outrageous that private communications of the Democratic National Committee were publicly revealed (on WikiLeaks) during a campaign, or is it totally fantastic that a secret recording of Trump (the *Access Hollywood* tape) was blasted all over the world a month before the election? Is transparency in government something that I support, or do I think Trump has got to get off Twitter—a novel and independent thought that has occurred only to me?

In that environment, we may give Trump more than the usual latitude if he acts as if he's under siege. He *is* under siege. Is he unhinged? No, he's hinged, fighting back against the left's infantile, knee-jerk reaction to everything he does.

Instead of governing, Trump is spending his presidency refuting questions like "Did you boil and eat a small child today?" It's one ginned-up, fake story after another. And the people doing this are the most corrupt and conflicted in the history of the world— James Comey, Robert Mueller, Brian Williams, George Stephanopoulos, Nancy Pelosi, Hillary Clinton, and on and on.

NO PUPPET. YOU'RE THE PUPPET.

Nothing the Russians ever dreamed of could compare to what the Resistance is doing to democracy, obliterating the will of Trump voters, who wanted him to get to work on urgent problems.

It is nothing less than a coup.

It may be that Trump is beyond the reach of intelligent people trying to help him. But attacking him the way liberals do is not going to help. It just solidifies his base and leads them to defend everything he does. Liberals might even be right about some of their complaints, but the absurd charges make them sound insane.

If one were inclined to go after Trump, there's no dearth of material. From a certain vantage point, he seems willing to say or do anything for an afternoon of semi-good publicity. It sure looks like he signed a bill that jettisoned his central campaign promise so he could spend the weekend at Mar-a-Lago. One might even say that he's abandoned all the popular issues he ran on. But the Resistance doesn't notice any of that. It's the worst combo platter imaginable for Trump supporters. The Democrats have not suffered at all, but their base is white-hot.

My advice to the Resistance is: Get Trump on the worst thing he's actually done, and stop running off with *Wouldn't it be great if he raped and murdered a nun?* You're right: if Trump had done that, he would be finished, done, put a fork in him. Unfortunately, he hasn't committed that particular crime. What the Resistance is accusing him of is even crazier: *Donald Trump plotted with the Russkies to steal the election from the most qualified person ever to run for president!*

If you'd care to join me here on planet Earth, Trump is practically begging the media to go after him for not caring about any of the issues he ran on. But unfortunately, liberals have lost their minds.

CHAPTER TWO

The Resistance Has Told Thousands of Lies About Trump. Here's One.

Anyone who says Trump admitted on tape to committing sexual assault is a stone-cold liar and should never be trusted to deliver any facts honestly.

The foundational symbol of the Resistance is the pussy hat. This is based on a hot-mic conversation Trump had when taping a TV segment for NBC's *Access Hollywood* eleven years earlier, which miraculously appeared on all our TV sets one month before the election:

"I better use some Tic Tacs just in case I start kissing her. You know I'm automatically attracted to beautiful—I just start kissing them. It's like a magnet. Just kiss. I don't even wait. And when you're a star, they let you do it. You can do anything. Grab 'em by the pussy. You can do anything."

Voters: *Got it. Okay, next.*

Media: WHAT DO YOU MEAN, "NEXT"?

What a threat Trump must be to the combine running our country that they're willing to carefully husband a secretly recorded conversation with him for months and months throughout the primary, producing it only in the eleventh hour as a kill shot. From the moment Trump started talking about the issues that no one else would, the ruling class rose up to try to strangle our movement. MSNBC deployed armies of interns to sit, in real time, listening to every *Howard Stern Show,* hoping for some spicy tidbit from Trump. TV networks searched the files for embarrassing hotmic moments. After going through the vault of his half-century public career, NBC emerged triumphant with the infamous *Access Hollywood* tape. Instead of reporting the news, the news media participated in a stunt.

Oddly, the media barely even noticed the worst part of the tape, when Trump describes his pursuit of a married woman: "I moved on her like a bitch. But I couldn't get there," in his delicate phrasing. The married woman never came forward. *That was you hitting on me? You've got to get your game up.*

Nor did the media highlight the most hilarious part of Trump's seduction technique. He took the lady *furniture shopping.* "She wanted to get some furniture," he says. "I said, 'I'll show you where they have some nice furniture.'" I'm sorry, I love the guy, but who would turn to Donald Trump for decorating advice? *How much for this Taj Mahal–themed bedroom set?*

No, what the stout defenders of family values in the mainstream media were upset about was that Trump had used the P-word. And God bless them—it was the media's titanic overreaction that saved him. Until two seconds before the *Access Hollywood* tape appeared, ex machina, these were the same people telling the rest of us to relax about raw sewage in television, performance art, college curricula the theater, kindergarten classes, museums, fashion, and Hollywood. In a modern miracle, they became Victorian virgins the moment Trump used a bad word. Just a few years earlier, Eve Ensler, authoress of the celebrated *Vagina Monologues,* told MSNBC's Lawrence O'Donnell that thousands of women shouting "vagina" in public was "one of the most thrilling times I've had in the almost fifteen years of V-Day." You can guess what V-Day is.[1] In fact, women shouting about their vaginas had become a big part of our rich cultural tapestry.

Next up: Vogue *magazine reviews the "Iconic Vagina Dress."*[2]

A prime-time ABC sitcom that was on air during the 2016 campaign, *The Real O'Neals,* included this bit of witty repartee:

Mimi: We've been dating for six months and you've never once pressured me to have sex. Which is why I want to have sex.

Mimi hands Kenny a large box of condoms.

Kenny: Wow. 48 condoms!

Mimi: Twelve didn't seem like enough.

* *

Jimmy: What did Mimi do to you?

Kenny: Oh. Just—you know, just . . . all that sex stuff that drives us wild.

Jimmy: No matter what she [Mom] tells you, you're not going to Hell. Trust me. If everything she said was true, I would be so blind by now.

* *

Kenny grabs Mimi's breast and immediately pulls his hand away.

Kenny: Your boobs feel squishy.[3]

In reviews of the show, there was a lot of sniffing about the blue-noses who didn't appreciate the daring wit. *The New York Times'* TV reviewer sarcastically described the show as "Shocking! Or it would be, that is, if this were still the mid-20th century."[4] The *San Francisco Chronicle* touted the show as both "funny and credible," but that "hasn't stopped pre-broadcast protests by conservative groups." As usual, the paper sniffed, "someone, somewhere, somehow, will object—and almost always without having seen the show."[5] *Newsday* sadly remarked, "In a world where everyone's offended by something, 'The Real O'Neals' won't escape unscathed."[6]

NBC News president Andy Lack, the Zelig of liberal sexual abuse, held the network's interview with Juanita Broaddrick accusing Bill Clinton of rape until after his impeachment trial, to protect the president. Lack was also the longtime employer of serial sexual harasser Matt Lauer, whom he paid $25 million a year. But when it came to Trump, it was Lack's network that breached all professional norms, and probably the law, in releasing the *Access Hollywood* tape weeks before the election.

These fastidious cultural commissars were disgusted that Trump had used the P-word in a private conversation. In fact, the ladies of the Resistance were *so* offended, they started shouting "pussy" at the top of their lungs and marching around in "pussy hats." You couldn't get away from all the delicate flowers hollering about their "pussies" and vaginas. This would be like Christians protesting the federal government's funding of *Piss Christ*—a Christ figurine submerged in urine—by waving around even more offensive images of Christ. A normal person would have to wonder, "Were you really that offended?"

Quite obviously, Trump was talking about celebrity culture— and with some degree of disapproval. His whole point was to cite something axiomatically unacceptable—grabbing women by the P-word—in order to say that celebrity culture was so out of whack that a *celebrity* could get away with it. He used the exact same construction when he said he could shoot someone on Fifth Avenue and not lose any of his voters. In both cases, he is using an absurd example of objectionable behavior to illustrate the intensity of either celebrity groupies or Trump fans. That's not a confession; it's hyperbole to make a point.

"THEY LET YOU DO IT." NOT IF YOU'RE TRUMP.

Because everything Trump does must be a crime, journalists went in about ten seconds to *HE'S BRAGGING ABOUT COMMITTING A SEXUAL ASSAULT!* The entire fourth estate pretended to hear something different from what they'd just heard. Trump said, "They let you do it." I don't care how poor your command of English is: "They let you do it" means consent. You could win that case on summary judgment. *Your honor, he said, "They let you do it." By definition, that's not an assault.* Case dismissed.

The media fixed the inconvenient problem of Trump's having said "They let you do it" by simply editing that part out.

Here was MSNBC's Lawrence O'Donnell's clip of the tape:

Donald Trump: When you are a star, you can do anything. Grab them by the [bleep].[7]

And here's Chuck Todd's version on *MTP Daily*:

Donald Trump: You can do anything.

Billy Bush, TV Host: Whatever you want.

Trump: Grab them by the [bleep]. You can do anything.[8]

Here's CNN's version:

Trump: You can do anything.

Billy Bush: Whatever you want.

Trump: Grab them by the pussy.[9]

Suspiciously missing in all of these clips are the words "They let you do it." This allowed commentators to keep announcing, *We all heard the tape of him admitting that he forced himself on unwilling women.*

Can I see the tape again?

No, no—they're all locked up. I don't feel like getting them.

I thought it was only going to be MSNBC and a few of the riper nuts retailing the "sexual assault" nonsense. But noooooooooo—the entire American media has been spreading this deliberate lie since the first journalist thought of it. In fact, Nexis can't perform a search for all publications that have accused Trump of admitting to "sexual assault," because it retrieves too many documents. (Illustrating why *The New York Times* is considered a more serious newspaper than *The Washington Post,* this lie has appeared twice as often in the *Post* as it has in the *Times.*)[10]

You probably don't believe me, so here are a few examples:

"And so we have now heard the Republican nominee for president of the United States bragging about repeated sexual assault."
 —*NEW YORK TIMES* EDITORIAL (FIRST SENTENCE)[11]

". . . a president who admitted to, and boasted about, repeated sexual assault."
 —MSNBC'S CHRIS HAYES[12]

"That is sexual assault. You bragged that you committed sexual assault."
 —MODERATOR ANDERSON COOPER AT THE SECOND
  PRESIDENTIAL DEBATE

"I think, you know, that is a very significant point about where we are as a country, that you can get elected president of the United States after admitting sexual assault."
 —JEFFREY TOOBIN[13]

"Donald Trump was heard on videotape admitting to sexual assault . . ."
 —LAWRENCE O'DONNELL, OCTOBER 10, 2016, AND EVERY
  SINGLE NIGHT OF HIS SHOW[14]

". . . the 'Access Hollywood' video, in which Trump boasts in vulgar terms about sexually assaulting women . . ."
 —*THE WASHINGTON POST*'S DANA MILBANK[15]

". . . Donald Trump could basically admit on tape to committing sexual assault and then win the presidency anyway."
—BRIAN FALLON, CNN POLITICAL COMMENTATOR[16]

"[Trump] even admitted to a pattern of sexual assault on tape . . ."
—*THE NEW YORK TIMES'* CHARLES BLOW[17]

And finally, on September 18, 2017, Hillary Clinton, America's most famous sexual assault defender, cited that "really horrible video of Trump admitting to sexual assault."[18]

HE SAID, THEY LET YOU DO IT!

What Trump actually said was juvenile. That wasn't enough? The media had to accuse him of "admitting to sexual assault"? It would be like attacking Anthony Weiner for being a serial killer.

But he didn't kill anyone.

Yes, but if he were a serial killer, it would be *much* worse!

True, but he didn't kill anyone.

Yeah, it's Trump's fault that no one believes the media. This is how journalists repel people who are perfectly willing to be appalled by Trump. He drives them away, and the media keep pulling them back.

CHAPTER THREE

Bald-faced Lie No. 2: Take a H*cking Joke

The story pops up every few weeks as if it were Alger Hiss's pro-thonotary warbler: *We've got the proof! Trump is on tape asking Putin to hack Hillary's e-mails.*

You'll never hear the tape, only journalists' summaries. So I'll transcribe what Trump actually said: "I will tell you this, Russia: If you're listening, I hope you're able to find the thirty thousand e-mails that are missing. I think you will probably be rewarded mightily by our press."[1]

The resulting hysteria is an example of one of the left's favorite weapons, deployed constantly in the Trump era: Not Getting Jokes. When *The Nation* magazine does it, they probably really don't get it. But I have to believe the rest of the media are using the Not Getting Jokes routine cynically. No one could be that stupid.

In 2008, John McCain showed up at the Sturgis Motorcycle Rally and said, "You know, I was looking at the Sturgis schedule and noticed that you have a beauty pageant. And so, I encouraged Cindy to compete. I told her with a little luck she could be the only woman ever to serve as both the First Lady and Miss Buffalo Chip."

You may not like the joke. You could say it's corny. But it's a joke.

Not to liberals! PBS's Bonnie Erbé grimly informed viewers that in the Miss Buffalo Chip contest, "female contestants are often scantily clad. Whether McCain knew this or not is not known."[2] MSNBC's Rachel Maddow was shocked, saying, "I mean, these are prepared remarks, which means he thought in advance about nominating his visibly horrified wife to take part in a biker beauty pageant."[3] And the biggest girl of them all, Keith Olbermann, spent an entire segment on McCain's joke on his MSNBC show, asking in astonishment: "Was it an off day? Was it a tired candidate caught up in a strange kind of event? Or whatever it was, does this pose a political problem?"

With Trump, the feminists' hostile takeover of the left is complete, reviving the old joke:

Q: *How many feminists does it take to screw in a lightbulb?*

A: THAT'S NOT FUNNY!

The media spent an entire day in 2018 somberly analyzing General John Kelly's remark on his promotion from Homeland Security secretary to White House chief of staff: "I did something wrong and God punished me, I guess." [*Audience laughs*]

Pro tip: When the audience laughs, it was probably a joke.

Liberals are willing to act like naive idiots so they can't be accused of insincerity. *Mick Jagger confessed to killing the Kennedys! I have it on tape right here—*

I shouted out,
"Who killed the Kennedys?"
When after all,
It was you and me.

I don't know who "you" are—but we KNOW Mick Jagger killed the Kennedys.

IN RUSSIA SCANDAL, HACKS E-MAIL YOU!

The Not Getting Jokes strategy has grown into a monster in the Age of Trump.

If you want to annoy a journalist, tell him his problem is that voters take Trump seriously but not literally, whereas the media take him literally but not seriously. *Oh, so we shouldn't take the president of the United States AT HIS WORD???* The Washington *Post*'s Jennifer Rubin has denounced the literally/seriously distinction in forty separate columns, e.g.: "Note to Trump and Thiel: The President Is Always Taken Literally."[4] Throw in columnists James Hohmann and Paul Waldman and the *Post*'s op-ed page spends half its time being angry about not being allowed to take the president's jokes literally.

So let's take Trump literally! When he said he hoped the Russians could "find the thirty thousand e-mails that are missing," he was obviously referring to the e-mails Hillary had scrubbed from her private server. Thirty thousand of Hillary's government e-mails were *missing*. Only twenty thousand of the DNC's e-mails ended up on WikiLeaks and, as indicated, they were not "missing." It was kind of the opposite of "missing": They were all over the Internet.

On July 5, 2016, just a few weeks before Trump's joke, FBI director James Comey had released his report confirming that Hillary's deleted e-mails (1) were unrecoverable and (2) might have been hacked.[5] The hacking, if there was any, was done. It was over. Hillary's thirty thousand e-mails were gone, departed, lost, annihilated—like a Tom Arnold sitcom pilot. It would make no sense for Trump to ask Russia to "hack" her thirty thousand e-mails because they weren't on the private server anymore. There *were* no e-mails to hack. That's why he did not say, "hack." He said, "missing."

What Trump was saying—literally—was: *Hey, Russia, if you have this stolen property that belongs to the American people, please return it to its rightful owners.* In a sane world, Trump would have been honored as Man of the Year at the White House Correspondents' Dinner for demanding the retrieval of U.S. government property.

Trump wasn't even the first one to make this joke. A month after Hillary's private server was revealed, in 2015, Kimberly Guilfoyle said on Fox News: "Maybe Trey Gowdy can cut a deal with the Russians and get all the e-mails and all the correspondence that Hillary conveniently deleted."[6]

In his presidential announcement speech, Governor Bobby Jindal of Louisiana said Russian hackers were more likely to see the secretary's e-mails than the American people were.[7] At the first GOP debate, Governor Scott Walker of Wisconsin said, "It's sad to think right now, but probably the Russian and Chinese governments know more about Hillary Clinton's e-mail server than the members of the United States Congress." *Politico,* the UK's *Daily Mail,* and *The New York Times* all cited that as one of the best lines of the debate.[8]

The press got the joke—until Trump made it.

These dour journalists who claim it is of the utmost importance to take the president literally at all times quoted Trump as saying something he literally did not say: "hack." He said "find." The ubiquity of this mistake is not an accident. It deliberately changes his meaning, from asking Russia to return e-mails that were stolen to asking Russia to hack Hillary's e-mails.

My editor hates when I give eight hundred examples, so you're getting only a few (emphases mine):

> *"Trump called upon Russia to hack his opponent Hillary Clinton's emails . . ."*
> —JONATHAN LEMIRE, ASSOCIATED PRESS[9]

"[Trump] repeatedly praised Russian President Vladimir Putin while urging the country's leaders to hack into his opponent's emails."

—MICHAEL KRANISH, *THE WASHINGTON POST*[10]

"He is the guy that asked Russia to hack into emails and release them for Hillary Clinton."

—AUSTAN GOOLSBEE, ECONOMIC ADVISER TO

PRESIDENT OBAMA[11]

"Trump's call during the presidential primary for Russia to hack Hillary Clinton's emails."

—COLBERT I. KING, *THE WASHINGTON POST*[12]

"[Trump's] public invitation to 'Russia, if you're listening' to hack Clinton's emails at a campaign press conference."

—MICHAEL GRUNWALD, *POLITICO*[13]

"I remember covering Trump's last press conference on the campaign trail in June or July, where he sort of came out and urged Russia to hack Hillary Clinton's emails."[14]

—ASHLEY PARKER, *THE NEW YORK TIMES*

"[Trump's] half-joking call for Russia to hack into Hillary Clinton's emails."

—DAVID FILIPOV, *THE WASHINGTON POST*[15]

"Donald Trump stood up and called on Russia to hack into Hillary Clinton's emails . . ."

—AMANDA CARPENTER, FORMER COMMUNICATIONS

DIRECTOR FOR TED CRUZ[16]

"[Mr. Trump] praised Mr. Putin effusively and exhorted Russia—in what his aides now call a joke—to hack into Hillary Clinton's email."
>—JULIE HIRSCHFELD DAVIS, *THE NEW YORK TIMES*[17]

"Donald Trump himself is saying Russia, if you can hack Hillary Clinton, if you can get her emails, we would love it."
>—JUAN WILLIAMS, FOX NEWS NETWORK[18]

"Trump urged Russia to hack into Hillary Clinton's email account to find the 33,000 emails she deleted . . ."
>—EVAN PÉREZ AND DAN MERICA, CNN[19]

"Trump holds a press conference . . . in which he openly urges Russia to hack into Hillary Clinton's private email server."
>—CHRIS CILLIZZA, CNN WIRE[20]

"When Trump invited Russia to hack Hillary Clinton's email server ('I will tell you this, Russia, if you're listening') . . ."
>—HEIDI STEVENS, *CHICAGO TRIBUNE*[21]

"Donald Trump went out on the podium back in July and called on Russia to hack Hillary Clinton's emails."
>—DAVE JACOBSON, CNN POLITICAL COMMENTATOR AND DEMOCRATIC STRATEGIST[22]

"[Trump] publicly begged Russia to hack into and publish Hillary Clinton's private emails."
>—JAY BOOKMAN, *THE ATLANTA JOURNAL-CONSTITUTION*[23]

"[W]e already know Trump said publicly at a rally, Russia, if you're listening, please hack Hillary Clinton's emails."
—BLAKE HOUNSHELL, DEPUTY EDITOR, *POLITICO*[24]

This isn't paraphrasing. It's lying.

CHAPTER FOUR

Trump Is a Racist—We've Scientifically Proved It!

Every few weeks, David Leonhardt at *The New York Times* or one of the low-testosterone boys at *Vox* produce a scientific proof that Trump is a racist. *We ran the numbers—it's official! Trump is a racist.*

The list of Trump's alleged "racism" is meaningless unless one accepts the input. That's how liberals get stunning figures on things like "white domestic terrorism" compared to Islamic terrorism. White trash degenerates yelling racist insults at a group of African Americans in Douglasville, Georgia (resulting in a combined punishment of nineteen years in prison),[1] counts as one incident of terrorism. Omar Mateen murdering forty-nine people at the Pulse nightclub in Orlando also counts as one incident of terrorism.[2]

Similarly, when it comes to the *Times'* alleged proofs of Trump's "racism," we've looked at the data and we don't agree he said A; you are wrong on B; he meant something else about C.

The list includes, for example, Trump's demand to see Obama's birth certificate. *Everyone knows what that's about!* Not necessarily, any more than it was anti-white for people to question whether John McCain was eligible to be president, having been born in the Panama Canal Zone. In the 1880 presidential election, flinty

Vermonter Chester Arthur was accused of being born in Canada.[3] *RACISTS!* Oh, wait—Arthur was white, too. So is Canada.

The *Times'* litany of Trump's alleged racism also includes his call for the reinstitution of the death penalty after the Central Park wilding attack. Not convinced? The brute *continued* to insist the convicts were guilty "more than 10 years after DNA evidence had exonerated them"—as Leonhardt says.[4] DNA evidence didn't convict them, so it couldn't exonerate them. It was always known that the DNA matched none of the defendants and other attackers "got away," as the prosecutor told the two multi-racial juries that convicted them. The "new" DNA evidence merely identified one of the ones who "got away." The reason Trump continues to say they were guilty is that they were guilty. See *Demonic: How the Liberal Mob Is Endangering America,* chapter 13.[5]

> **David Leonhardt:** Do me a solid, America, and simply agree with my headline. Don't be thinking you're going to be looking at the evidence.

NO NAZI. YOU'RE THE NAZI

For most of the Resistance, all you have to do is say "Charlottesville" to prove that Trump is the leader of the Fourth Reich. The more the rally recedes in time, the fresher a memory it becomes.

In June 2018, film director Spike Lee was still droning on about it—at a meeting of the oppressed: The Cannes Film Festival.

"We have a guy in the White House, I'm not gonna say his [bleep] name, whose defining moment—it was not just for Americans, for the world—and that [bleep] was given a chance to say, 'We are about love and not hate.' And that [bleep] did not denounce the [bleep] Klan, the alt-right, and those Nazi [bleep]."

In fact, of course, Trump has condemned "neo-Nazis" and the Klan until he's blue in the face. He did during the campaign, when he was asked about his feelings toward David Duke more often than he was asked about any policy issue. He denounced them again in his remarks on Charlottesville, a violent melee resulting entirely from the connivance of local politicians and the criminal incompetence of police brass.[6]

Trump's crime wasn't his failure to condemn "Nazis"—there's no such thing—or white supremacists. His crime was saying, "I think there is blame on both sides." The media had been *very clear* that this was NOT what they wanted him to say. But he didn't submit to their will, so they called him a racist.

In his first remarks, Trump condemned "in the strongest possible terms this egregious display of hatred, bigotry and violence on many sides, on many sides."

That statement led to days of hysteria. Trump was condemned by spaghetti-spined Senate Republicans. Executives on his "American Manufacturing Council" resigned en masse. Ivanka was said to "rebuke" her father by issuing the media-approved condemnation on Twitter. *Why wouldn't the president bend to the media's will?* Ivanka, Jared, and chief of staff John Kelly all begged Trump to roll on his back like Fido for the media. Steve Bannon recommended that Trump be kept away from the media altogether.[7]

Trump, according to the moral paragons in the press, had a special obligation to condemn "white nationalists" because of the media's fantasy that Trump is a racist. It gets rather circular. What if the media decided to claim Trump was a child molester? Would he be required to condemn every child molester in the country and then have his words dissected and analyzed by Trumpologists? With more basis in fact, some Americans believed Obama was born in Kenya. Perhaps they should have called on him to condemn the droughts and post-election unrest in that country.

But that didn't happen. Why? Because even birthers are saner than our media.

Let's look at the questions to Trump from the totally objective, fair, unbiased media about Charlottesville. This was at a presidential press conference on *infrastructure*. I've excluded nothing, except the one or two questions on infrastructure, which was—again—the topic of the press conference.

> **Q:** Let me ask you, Mr. President, why did you wait so long to blast neo-Nazis?

> **Q:** Why do Nazis like you?

> **Q:** The CEO of Walmart said you missed a critical opportunity to help bring the country together. Did you?

> **Q:** Nazis were there.

> **Q:** David Duke was there.

> **Q:** Can you tell us how you are feeling about your chief strategist, Mr. Bannon? [In addition to dictating exactly what the president was supposed to say and when, the media had also decided that Bannon was a white supremacist and that Trump had to fire him.]

> **Q:** Can you tell us broadly what your—do you still have confidence in Steve?

> **Q:** Senator McCain said that the alt-right is behind these attacks, and he linked that same group to those who perpetrated the attack in Charlottesville.

> **Q:** Is the alt-left as bad as white supremacy?

> **Q:** Is the alt-left as bad as the Nazis?

Q: How concerned are you about race relations in America? And do you think things have gotten worse or better since you took office?

Q: Mr. President, are you putting what you're calling the alt-left and white supremacists on the same moral plane?

Q: Both sides, sir—you said there was hatred, there was violence on both sides.

Q: The neo-Nazis started this.

Q: You were saying the press has treated white nationalists unfairly?

Q: Will you go to Charlottesville? Will you go to check out what happened?

That last question about Trump going to Charlottesville nearly hijacked the entire press conference by sending the president off on a jag about owning a winery in Charlottesville that was one of the largest wineries in the entire United States: "I own a house in Charlottesville. Does anyone know I own a house in Charlottesville? . . . I mean, I know a lot about Charlottesville. Charlottesville is a great place that's been very badly hurt over the last couple of days. I own, actually, one of the largest wineries in the United States. It's in Charlottesville . . ."

But back to the idiots: *Why do Nazis like you?* Are you kidding? Why didn't any hard-hitting reporters ever ask Obama something like "Mr. President, don't you hate white people?"

Inasmuch as Trump's response to these charming questions still sends the Resistance into paroxysms of self-righteousness, let's look at what Trump said. He began by praising his earlier remarks—always a hit with our media! (Trump has the "best words.") He said his initial response "was a fine statement," adding that his timing "was excellent."

Then he elaborated on the "both sides" point. What about the "alt-left"? Trump asked the press bullies. "What about the fact they came charging with clubs in their hands, swinging clubs? Do they have any problem? I think they do."

"I watched those [videos] very closely, much more closely than you people watched it. And you had a group on one side that was bad, and you had a group on the other side that was also very violent, and nobody wants to say that, but I'll say it right now. You had a group—you had a group on the other side that came charging in without a permit, and they were very, very violent."

A normal person hearing this, who has not been through the left's indoctrination camp, would say, *Wait—I'm sorry, I think this cut off in the middle—where did he praise white supremacists?*

But Trump's remarks were presented as, *Voila! It speaks for itself!*

Asked again and again and again whether he loved Nazis, Trump said:

"I've condemned neo-Nazis. I've condemned many different groups." But he refused to give in to their bullying, adding, "You had some very bad people in that group, but you also had people that were very fine people, on both sides. You had people in that group—excuse me, excuse me. I saw the same pictures as you did. You had people in that group that were there to protest the taking down of, to them, a very, very important statue and the renaming of a park from Robert E. Lee to another name."

Trump said they would know this "if you were honest reporters, which in many cases you're not, but many of those people were there to protest the taking down of the statue of Robert E. Lee."

The media and chicken-hearted Republicans considered it absolutely beyond the pale for Trump to condemn violence on "both sides" and say there were "fine people" on both sides. No, no, no, no, no, no, no! This was NOT acceptable. Masked left-wing hoodlums attacking people with flamethrowers and clubs were 100 percent pure and good. *Aren't you listening? They said they were "ANTI-fascists"!* We have it on the authority of Mitt Romney and Marco Rubio that fascist violence is admirable, *provided* the fascists call themselves "anti-fascist." Hitler's storm troopers must be kicking themselves for not knowing this trick.

Trump was obviously correct that there were Virginians who had no idea who white supremacist showboat Richard Spencer was, but showed up because they didn't want their monuments torn down. No excuse! They were "Nazis," too, and had to be condemned by the president, doxed, and fired.

The incontrovertible proof was the torchlight parade. The rally participants held a torchlight parade! Case closed. They were Nazis. As MSNBC's Chris Matthews explained, "Fine people do not choose to engage in a torchlight parade that echoes the rallies held by the Third Reich in Nuremberg."[8] *Atlantic* magazine readers were treated to an entire essay pointing out that the "Nazi regime began by carrying torches at parades and rallies and, by 1938, burning buildings and Torah scrolls."[9]

Oh, for Pete's sake! Torchlight parades are an American tradition going back to colonial days. Back when we were fighting real Nazis, FDR was greeted with a torchlight parade in Hyde Park. He began his speech by fondly reminiscing about his first torchlight parade as a small child, saying he saw "a queer light outside the window," then peered and saw people "coming down here to have a Democratic celebration."[10] Many towns still continue the tradition, such as Old Saybrook, Connecticut, where the annual torchlight parade, complete with fifes and drums, begins on Coulter Street in

December every year.[11] Torchlight parades are a patriotic American tradition. Liberals have no right to say, "No, that's forbidden because it reminds me of the Holocaust."

Let's review events and see whose remarks stood the test of time.

At college campuses around the country, those noble "antifascists," championed by Romney and Rubio, have continued their violent attacks on conservative speakers—even ACLU members, liberal biology professors, and law professors who happen to believe in free speech. Don't worry, Mitt, the savages threatening to beat up girls are just protesting "fascism"! At Charlottesville, these barbaric thugs were given carte blanche to shut down events, smash windows, and disrupt speakers they don't care for. Everyone called them heroes. Everyone except Donald Trump.

Trump also said:

"So this week it's Robert E. Lee. I noticed that Stonewall Jackson's coming down. I wonder, is it George Washington next week? And is it Thomas Jefferson the week after? You know, you all—you really do have to ask yourself, where does it stop? But they were there to protest—excuse me. You take a look, the night before, they were there to protest the taking down of the statue of Robert E. Lee."

Since then, Confederate graveyards, monuments, fountains, and highway names have been airbrushed out of history from Maine to San Diego. Washington National Cathedral removed the stained-glass memorials to Robert E. Lee and Stonewall Jackson. The Taliban would be proud.

Proving that liberals really do know where the bodies are buried, the city of Memphis removed the statue of Confederate general Nathan Bedford Forrest, dug up his body, and removed it from the park that once bore his name.

We've had to watch in horror as monuments to not only

Confederates but all non-woke American historical figures have been defaced and disappeared.

State leaders in Maryland removed the 145-year-old statue of Roger B. Taney, former chief justice of the United States. He was against the Confederacy and supported President Lincoln, but he authored the infamous Dred Scott decision, continuing slavery.

A few months after Charlottesville, Baltimore's monument to Francis Scott Key, author of the poem that became our national anthem, was spray-painted with the words "Racist Anthem." The third stanza, which no one knows, condemns the British for encouraging slaves to rebel against their masters.

Pittsburgh removed a 118-year-old statue of the great American songwriter Stephen Foster, author of "My Old Kentucky Home," "Oh! Susanna," and "Camptown Races," because the statue includes a figure of a slave playing a banjo at Foster's feet. It will be replaced with a statue of a black woman, to be decided in the future. But definitely a black woman.

Statues of Christopher Columbus were vandalized in Baltimore, Boston, and Houston. Three monuments to the great explorer were damaged in New York City. One was decapitated, and Columbus's head dumped in a nearby garbage can.

Stockton University, in New Jersey, removed a bust of the school's namesake, Richard Stockton, who signed the Declaration of Independence. He owned slaves.

Boston is weighing whether to rename Faneuil Hall, honoring Peter Faneuil, a wealthy colonial merchant . . . who also owned slaves. In Chicago, a bust of the Great Emancipator himself, Abraham Lincoln, was set on fire and defaced. In Ohio, a statue of William Crawford, hero of the American Revolution, was decapitated, apparently because he looked like he could have been a Confederate soldier.

The Thomas Jefferson statue at the University of Virginia has been vandalized so many times, and spray-painted with the words "racist + rapist," that there's a movement to permanently cover the monument to the founder of the university.

It's a game for the left to see how many words and concepts they can anathematize with their intimidation tactics: Pepe the Frog, "illegal alien," "alt-right," two genders, "I.Q.," "chain migration," "bossy," "let's enforce laws on the books about immigration," and so on. *Trump* is the authoritarian? Psychologists refer to this phenomenon as "projection."

The "racism" gag is just a power play by the Resistance against the weak. Bullying people is intoxicating! Trump stood up to them, so they lost their minds. It used to be so easy to scare Republicans! Liddle Marco, Jeff Flake, Ben Sasse—*they'll* say exactly what the media want, when they want it. Maddeningly, Trump isn't any of those guys. This is understandably frustrating for journalists, but it's not "racism."

CHAPTER FIVE

Now They Want to Fight the Cold War?

Trump's election sparked the biggest Red Scare since actual Reds had infiltrated the highest levels of the U.S. government. Russians are more evil than when they were allying with Hitler, annexing Eastern Europe, committing mass murder with forced starvations, sending writers and scientists to gulags, holding show trials, shooting down American planes, and funding terrorists. Liberals were cool with that.

Back when the Soviet Union was actually threatening America with nuclear annihilation and Russian spies were crawling through our government, liberals were defaming Joe McCarthy. Jimmy Carter warned Americans about their "inordinate fear of communism." Sting alerted teenagers to the silliness of the Cold War, singing, "the Russians love their children, too." Dr. Seuss taught little children that the only difference between the USA and the USSR was that we buttered our bread on different sides. (*1984 New York Times Notable Books of the Year!*) (Not a joke.)

As far as liberals are concerned, those were Russia's halcyon days.

The left was already testy with the Red Bear for giving up

Communism. Russia's descent into insanity and madness accelerated when Putin refused to allow LGBTQ marches through Red Square. For having the same position on gays as Obama, circa 2008, Russians were walking on the fighting side of American liberals. But it wasn't until Trump beat Hillary that Russia became the most psychotically evil country in the world, and Putin the mastermind of a malevolent plot to steal the election from the rightful president, Hillary Clinton.

Today, NO fear of Russia is "inordinate." The Russians do not "love their children, too." The entire Democratic Party and two-thirds of the Republican Party are horrified that Trump wants to get along with a nuclear-armed nation that is less corrupt than Saudi Arabia; doesn't steal our technology; fights ISIS; and tried to warn us about the Boston Marathon bombers.

Hating Russia is something new for the left. Does all this high-octane anger about Russia mean that Democrats are finally willing to admit that Alger Hiss was a Soviet spy?

The most fevered fantasies of John Birchers are today the considered opinions of *The Washington Post*'s editorial page. It must be baffling to Putin to be considered the biggest monster ever produced by his nation.

WOULD YOU BUY A USED CONSPIRACY THEORY FROM THIS WOMAN?

A normal person gets an ice cream headache trying to follow the details of the left's Russian conspiracy theory. The basic allegation is that Trump, an incompetent buffoon, managed to engage in a complex international conspiracy with Russian intelligence to steal the 2016 presidential election from Hillary.

In addition to Republicans' generally cynical nature, part of our skepticism stems from the fact that Democrats claim they are robbed *every* time they lose an election, unless it's a landslide.

History, according to Democrats:

- 1968: Nixon won with his racist (and mythical) "Southern strategy."
- 1972: Nixon landslide—no provable cheating.
- 1976: Carter won—FAIR ELECTION, CLEAN AS A WHISTLE!!
- 1980: Reagan won by conspiring with Iranian mullahs to prevent the release of American hostages before the election.
- 1984: Reagan landslide—no provable cheating.
- 1988: Bush won because of his racist Willie Horton ads.
- 1992: Clinton won with 43 percent of the vote—FAIR ELECTION, CLEAN AS A WHISTLE!!
- 1996: Clinton won with 49 percent of the vote—FAIR ELECTION, CLEAN AS A WHISTLE!!
- 2000: Bush won because the Supreme Court stole it for him.
- 2004: Bush won because of Halliburton hacking the voting machines in Ohio.

So we've gotten used to *The New York Times* turning over two-thirds of its op-ed page to Lyndon Larouche–inspired conspiracy theories[1] disputing a Republican's election victory. (Gary Sick: *How Reagan Stole the 1980 Election by Conspiring with Iranian Terrorists to Keep Holding Americans Hostage*.)[2] (Also not a joke.)

2017: *NEW YORK TIMES*, FRONT PAGE, 6 COLUMNS!!!

"All the News That's Fit to Print"

The New York Times

National Edition

VOL. CLXVI... No. 57,470   ©2017 The New York Times Company   SATURDAY, JANUARY 7, 2017   *Printed in Chicago* $2.50

PUTIN LED SCHEME TO AID TRUMP, REPORT SAYS

Never has a conspiracy theory been based on so little and consumed so many. That took the deft touch of the Clintons.

Every sane person knows that Trump did not collude with Russia to sway the election. Even some lefties have had to admit, *I don't want to defend the guy, but this is crazy.* See, for example, the collected articles of Stephen F. Cohen in *The Nation*.[3]

Mark Penn, longtime Clinton pollster, said of the left's Russia neurosis: "Today you can sit down with an impressionable elite—a Harvard-educated lawyer, for example—and they know, with absolute certainty, that somehow Trump was laundering money with the Russians in exchange for help in the election. They have no evidence for these claims and yet they 'know' it, just as strongly as elites once believed the earth was flat."[4]

We've had to restart the Cold War because Hillary Clinton settled on "Russian collusion" as the reason she lost. Inasmuch as Hillary ran against Trump for the same job, one could make the argument that her assessment is not 100 percent objective.

What happened to the anti-war party? Liberals used to be the ones always telling us we have to have a mature relationship with the rest of the world. But today, they're perfectly happy to push us to the brink of war, just to make their Trump hysteria sound high-minded.

Unfortunately, there's zero evidence for any of it. We're still waiting for any evidence that Trump colluded with his own campaign staff.

THEY'RE UNDER THE BED AFTER ALL!

Before we spend months interviewing witnesses who claim to have seen Tiffany Trump talking to Mikhail Baryshnikov at Barney's, we have to ask whether there's any evidence that the Russian government attempted to influence the election—much less that they succeeded.

The claim, as put by Representative Adam Schiff, the West Coast's Chuck Schumer, is the following:

> Last summer [of 2016], at the height of a bitterly contested and hugely consequential presidential campaign, a foreign adversarial power intervened in an effort to weaken our democracy and to influence the outcome for one candidate and against the other. That foreign adversary was of course Russia and it activated through its intelligence agencies and upon the direct instructions of its autocratic ruler Vladimir Putin, in order to help Donald J. Trump become the 45th president of the United States.[5]

First of all, if the Russians did anything that put Trump in the White House, they were *helping* our country, not harming it.

Second, if there were ever an election Russia wanted to affect, it was when Ronald Reagan was running for his second term in 1984. In addition to the obvious reasons for a godless dictatorship to dislike Reagan, the Kremlin had become convinced that he was planning a first strike if reelected. No effort was spared to defeat him. All of the USSR's foreign embassies were instructed to send agents to the United States to help defeat Reagan. The KGB issued talking points to their agents. You can still read them in *New York Times* op-eds from that period: Reagan was accelerating the arms race, he was crushing liberation movements abroad, he was part of the military-industrial complex. Oh, and he was a racist.[6] See, e.g., "If the Reagan Pattern Continues, America May Face Nuclear War," by W. Averell Harriman, in *The New York Times*, January 1, 1984.[7] And also the entire oeuvre of Anthony Lewis.

Reagan won a forty-nine-state landslide. The entire Soviet government, working hand in hand with America's most influential newspaper, couldn't put a dent in a U.S. election in the 1980s—back when the *Times was* influential. But jumping into an exponentially larger media market in 2016, Russia turned the tide with a few Facebook ads! Okay, sure.

Third, what exactly did the Russians do to "influence" the 2016 election?

Four states decided the 2016 presidential election: Wisconsin, Pennsylvania, Michigan, and Ohio. And Iowa—I'll give you Iowa. To become president, you have to win *states.* In order to establish that Russia had any impact whatsoever on the election, much less helped Donald J. Trump become the forty-fifth president of the United States, you would have to prove that about eighty thousand people in those five states saw a particular Russian post on Facebook and then get them to testify, *No, I didn't care about my job being outsourced or Mexican heroin destroying my community. Where'd you get that? The reason I voted for Trump was the Pizzagate conspiracy I saw on Facebook.*

That's the heart of the "Trump colluded with Russia" story. This is what liberals mean when they say Russia "hacked" our election. Not that any voting machines were tampered with or votes changed, but that Internet postings and the WikiLeaks dump of DNC e-mails so mesmerized the electorate that voters had no choice but to vote for Trump.

Obviously, this is stark raving mad.

HUNT FOR RED NOVEMBER

Sure, the Russians would do bad things to America if they thought it would work. But it requires delusional thinking of the first order to imagine that trained spymasters would do any of the things Russia is accused of doing to help Trump.

The original claim—backed by SEVENTEEN INTELLIGENCE AGENCIES (actually, only four[8]) (and three of the four have major credibility problems)—is that Russia hacked the e-mails of the Democratic National Committee and Hillary aide John Podesta, then gave them to WikiLeaks.

Did that help Trump? Maybe. Could anyone have predicted that it would help Trump? Absolutely not. I'd like to be at the meeting where the junior Russian spy says to the head spy, "See, if we leak DNC e-mails showing the party conspiring against Bernie Sanders, it will help Trump!"

Even seasoned campaign veterans have no idea how to affect an election. In 1980, the Democrats *prayed* that the GOP would nominate Ronald Reagan. In 2016, Democrats couldn't believe their good fortune to be running against Trump. Republicans were sure Jeb!'s stupendous fund-raising made him the inevitable nominee. (Ask Mitt Romney.) Reagan won, Trump won, and Jeb! got four delegates.

The Democrats' e-mail leak mostly hurt the DNC chairperson, Debbie Wasserman Schultz, who was forced to resign. But beyond that, no one could have guessed how the e-mail dump would play out.

The Russians—if it was the Russians—may have been trying to save the Democrats. Had they behaved rationally, Democrats would have said: *Hillary is damaged goods. We've got to draft Biden.* This is a party with a history of dumping their candidates late in a campaign—as they did to New Jersey senator Robert Torricelli in 2002. Everyone except Huma Abedin knew that Biden was the better bet. It was an open secret that Obama preferred Biden. Maybe the e-mails were leaked to help Obama. Motives in these cases are always concocted after the fact. Only the media would say, "It would be bad for our country to undermine Hillary!"

The idea that any of the things the Russians are alleged to have done would lead to a predictable and certain outcome is where the Russia conspiracy theory always fall apart.

PAYBACK'S A BITCH

Let's assume MSNBC's most lurid fantasies about the Russians are all true. The next question is: *So what?* Mexico and Israel meddle in our elections all the time. So do the Chinese. Apparently the British do, too. Former British spy Christopher Steele—with ties to MI-6!— tried to sway the 2016 election with his infamous "Russia dossier."

In the early 1990s, the People's Republic of China funneled millions of dollars in illegal campaign donations to Bill Clinton and the Democrats. In addition to the illegality of the donations themselves, there was also evidence of a quid pro quo, which was aggressively covered up by the president and the attorney general.

No independent counsel—and boredom from our media watchdogs.

Antonio Villaraigosa, then–California State Assembly Speaker, thanked the president of Mexico for helping to overturn the will of California voters. After 60 percent of Californians voted in favor of Proposition 187, which would have denied government benefits to illegal aliens, a federal judge overturned it. Celebrating the ruling, Villaraigosa said, "I say President Zedillo had great impact in defeating Proposition 187."[9]

How about the interventions of Mexican oligarch Carlos Slim? In 2008, Slim saved *The New York Times* from bankruptcy. Suddenly the country's most influential newspaper had second thoughts about protecting our southern border.[10] I wonder if there's a way to rank the relative influence of the editorial page of *The New York Times* versus that of Russian bots on Facebook?

Hey—would anyone mind if a Russian oligarch bought a chunk of stock in Fox News?

Since the election, famed Hollywood director Oliver Stone hasn't stopped sneering about the hubbub over Russian interference, saying, "Israel interfered in the U.S. election far more than Russia and nobody is investigating them."[11]

It was openly discussed during the primaries that Trump had lost billionaire Sheldon Adelson's support after vowing to remain "neutral" in negotiations between Israel and the Palestinians.[12] Lickspittle Marco Rubio, hustling for Adelson's money, called Trump "anti-Israel."[13] One month before the election, Adelson gave $25 million to a pro-Trump super PAC.[14] Suddenly, Trump was vowing to overturn long-standing government practice and "recognize Jerusalem as the undivided capital of the State of Israel."[15] PROMISES MADE. PROMISES KEPT! (Sorry about the wall. We just didn't have time to get to it.)

Not that there's anything wrong with that. But liberals have to calm down, step back, and stop acting as if foreigners meddling in our elections is the equivalent of the 9/11 attack.

They do it to us—and we do it to them all day long. Megalomaniac George Soros believes he has a right to go around rearranging other societies because they are displeasing to him. He has been actively interfering in Russia's affairs since the 1990s. Between looting billions of dollars from British pensioners and enriching himself by destroying the economies of Southeast Asia, Soros was part of the Harvard brain trust that robbed Russia blind.

After the collapse of the Soviet Union, President Clinton tapped Strobe Talbott to help rebuild the Russian economy along Western lines. Talbott said, Can I bring my pal George Soros? Following the prescriptions of Harvard professor Jeffrey Sachs—brought in by Soros—the geniuses decided to impose "shock treatment" on the Russian economy. They privatized everything—industries, natural resources, media, technology, and mines. With no normal stock market or private sources of capital, hundreds of billions of dollars in Russian national assets were auctioned off to a small group of cronies at knockdown prices.[16]

In the end, a tiny group of elites who didn't live in Russia owned everything.[17]

Among the billionaire Russian émigrés and their foreign backers was Soros.[18] As Soros bragged to *The New Republic* in 1994, "the former Soviet Empire is now called the Soros Empire."[19] Congressional hearings were convened, but it was too late to do anything. The House Banking Committee chairman, Jim Leach, described what Soros's group had done as "one of the greatest social robberies in human history."[20]

Since then, Soros—often working with the U.S. State Department—has spent about a billion dollars[21] to install governments more to his liking in the former Soviet republics. He didn't care for the pro-Russian candidate who won the 2004 Ukrainian election—the candidate Paul Manafort advised. So Soros used his network of "nonprofits" to claim that the election was stolen. The State Department forced Ukraine to have a do-over. This colossal interference with another country's election was called "the Orange Revolution."

He did the same thing in Georgia in 2003 ("the Rose Revolution") and Kyrgyzstan in 2005 ("the Tulip Revolution"). All three "color revolutions" followed the Soros formula: The winner of an election was immediately accused of fraud by Soros-funded locals, based on Soros-funded "exit polls," and forced to step down as a result of Soros-funded "youth protests."[22] Then our government would muscle the country into holding another election.

If Soros ever did anything like this to Israel, the Mossad would take him out. Putin responds—allegedly—with Facebook ads about the 2016 election and we're supposed to rank him with Adolf Hitler.

Of course, when Americans horn in on other countries' affairs, it is only with the highest moral purpose. As Soros himself says, his meddling is merely intended to defeat "the chauvinistic, xenophobic far right."[23] I guess it's just lucky that he always manages to come out richer.

Although I notice that Soros's butting into other countries' affairs has neither turned out well nor been warmly appreciated by the targeted countries.

The Ukrainian president deposed by Soros in 2004, Viktor Yanukovych, was returned to office by the voters two years later. On the other hand, the Soros-approved leader in Kyrgyzstan, Kurmanbek Bakiyev, was met with violent protests and had to flee the country. In Georgia, the Soros-installed leader, Mikheil Saakashvili, was also forced to flee; he was later stripped of his citizenship and is currently wanted by the government on various criminal charges. Thanks, pompous American billionaire!

Uzbekistan, Tajikistan, and Belarus have ejected Soros's intermediaries from their countries.[24] Malaysian premier Mahathir Mohamad blamed Soros for Asia's economic meltdown in the late 1990s, calling Soros's attacks on their currency "villainous acts of sabotage."[25] China launched an investigation into Soros-backed organizations.[26] At a 2004 press conference, Vladimir Putin denounced Soros's toying with the elections of former Soviet republics.[27] The prime minister of Hungary, Viktor Orbán, won a huge election victory in April 2018, on a platform that consisted, in large part, of denouncing George Soros.

For a guy who loves to run around talking about how President George W. Bush destroyed America's reputation throughout the world with his cowboy diplomacy, Soros is probably more responsible than any other single person for making the rest of the world hate us.

It's taken about half a century, but it's great to get both parties on the record, agreeing that it's an act of the foulest espionage to meddle in another country's politics. I think all Americans would be happy with an agreement that George Soros is not allowed to keep interfering in other countries' elections and they will not interfere in ours.

CHAPTER SIX

Hillary Hatches an Egg

The Russian collusion story was hatched by Hillary Clinton in the summer of 2016, when she needed to neutralize the Democratic National Committee's e-mails showing up on WikiLeaks. It was classic Clinton. Whenever the Clintons were caught in a scandal, they would invent imaginary enemies. Instead of the news being about Hillary's abuse of the long-serving travel office staff, reporters would be forced to run down alleged crimes by the head of the travel office. Instead of talking about Bill Clinton's decades of predatory behavior, "the great story here"—as Hillary told NBC's Matt Lauer—was the vast right-wing conspiracy trying to destroy her blameless husband.

And "the great story" when the Democratic National Committee e-mails started showing up on WikiLeaks was . . . a vast Russian conspiracy!

It had to be something good. The WikiLeaks disclosures were explosive, revealing that DNC head Debbie Wasserman Schultz had plotted to ensure that Hillary won the nomination. This allegedly fair broker spoke dismissively of Bernie Sanders, summarily announcing that he would *not* be president. She called Sanders's campaign manager, Jeff Weaver, "an ASS" and a "damn liar." The e-mails were so appalling that Wasserman Schultz was booed by her own state's delegation and she was forced to resign on the eve of the party's national convention.

Democrats were alarmed. What if WikiLeaks started releasing more e-mails? Desperate measures were called for.

MOOK'S SPOOKS

So on July 24, 2016, Clinton campaign chairman Robby Mook went on ABC's *This Week* and told George Stephanopoulos about the vast Russian conspiracy:

"Experts are telling us that Russian state actors broke into the DNC, took all these emails and now are leaking them out through these Web sites . . . And it's troubling that some experts are now telling us that this was done by—by the Russians for the purpose of helping Donald Trump."[1]

At the time, even fellow liberals were embarrassed by Mook's "eerie suggestion of a conspiracy drawn up in the Kremlin," as *The New York Times*' David E. Sanger and Nicole Perlroth put it. With no evidence, apart from unnamed "experts," the Clinton campaign was accusing a political rival of "essentially secretly doing the bidding of a key American adversary." Even "at the height of the Cold War," they said, this had never happened before.[2] The reporters called Mook's performance on *This Week* "a "remarkable moment."

Another *Times* article on the Russian plot noted that the "Cold War–era intrigue" being pushed by the Democrats "fits with Mrs. Clinton's efforts to establish the idea that President Vladimir V. Putin of Russia wants to see Mr. Trump elected." Noted cybersecurity expert Representative Nancy Pelosi of California told the

Times, "I do know this: that the Russians did the D.N.C. hack." Pelosi knew it, the article added, "not through intelligence briefings, but through other means."[3]

The *Times* was not alone in its skepticism. *Newsday*'s take: "On convention eve, Democrats try to bury new email embarrassment . . . The Russians did it?"[4] The New York *Daily News,* the newspaper that hated Trump with a blind fury, ran the headline "KREMLIN GREMLIN: FBI Probes Russian Hack of Dems Putin Seen Aiding Pal Trump."[5] *We love you, Hillary, but can't we please keep our self-respect?*

The *Los Angeles Times*' story on Mook's conspiracy theory also noticed that he cited only "unnamed experts" with nothing but "circumstantial evidence as backup." It was, Mark Z. Barabak wrote, "one of the most startling turnabouts" to have "the Democrats brandishing fear of Moscow as a club . . . and suggesting that the Kremlin may be interfering in the U.S. election" to help Trump.[6]

The *Dallas Morning News*' headline on the Russian conspiracy theory was *not* "RUSSIANS HACK DNC!" but "Clinton Aides Work to Dampen Email Uproar."[7] The Russia story got equal billing with Ted Cruz's refusal to endorse Trump: "[Clinton aides] argued that Russia seems to prefer Donald Trump as the next U.S. president. They pointed to Ted Cruz's snub of Trump last week as evidence that the Republicans have bigger problems than they do."[8] The alleged Russian hacking was just another talking point.

The *Baltimore Sun* began its article on the Russia story, "The plot seems ripped from the pages of a post–Cold War espionage thriller: Russian spy services hack into the Democratic Party's computers, pilfer reams of data and then leak damaging e-mails in the hopes of helping elect a preferred presidential candidate." But, the *Sun* added, "that is exactly the allegation the FBI confirmed Monday it is investigating."[9]

That was not true: The FBI was not investigating the e-mail

hack, for the simple reason that the DNC wouldn't allow the Bureau anywhere near its computers. The precise reason a number of cyber-security firms questioned whether it was the Russians who did the hacking was that *the FBI never performed its own investigation*. What the FBI was doing could more accurately be described as "giving air cover to the woman it believed would be the next president."

The DNC hired its own firm, and that private firm produced the allegation that forms the entire basis of the Russia hysteria that has roiled this country for the past two years. It raised no red flags that the DNC's chosen investigator, CrowdStrike, is affiliated with a fanatically anti-Russian Ukrainian billionaire.[10]

It's also worth noting that, as a general policy, Julian Assange, the impresario of WikiLeaks, refuses to reveal his sources. But he broke his own rule to say: *The DNC e-mails did not come from the Russians.*[11] You can say Assange is crazy, a zealot, misguided, and reckless, and that he endangers people's lives. But even his enemies don't call him a liar.

An analyst with the cybersecurity firm that made the seminal discovery, Michael Buratowski, explained to *The Dallas Morning News* that "his near-certainty that Russia was to blame was based on evidence such as the hackers using Russian Internet addresses, Russian language keyboards, and the time codes corresponding to business hours in Russia, *as well as the sophistication of the hack*" [emphasis added].[12]

We know it was James Bond because the attacker dropped his wallet, left his fingerprints everywhere, was caught on the security camera—and also because of the sophistication of the attack.

Foreshadowing Trump's response, a *Bloomberg* article quoted cybersecurity expert Bob Gourley saying that, although the hack had "the telltale signs of being Russian," it could be that "some hacker in a garage in Florida found this code and re-used it."[13]

LOOK, RUSSIA!

Undeterred by the skepticism, Clinton partisans barreled ahead with their accusations of a Red Plague. The day after Mook's "remarkable" ABC appearance, Jennifer Granholm, former Democratic governor of Michigan, pushed the Democrats' Conspiracy-So-Immense tale on CNN. She mentioned the nonexistent GOP platform change and Trump campaign manager Paul Manafort's work in Ukraine. As to whether Putin personally ordered the hacks, Granholm said, "I have no idea," but "these are Russian hackers [and] it's not too hard to draw the links."[14] Hillary urgently needed a distraction from the WikiLeaks dump—it's not too hard to draw that link, either.

Clinton campaign chairman John Podesta said Trump and Putin had a "kind of bromance going on."[15] Clinton suck-up Josh Marshall, of *Talking Points Memo*, produced a whole list of Trump's stunning, amazing, unheard-of connections to Russia: His real estate empire was (allegedly) dependent on Russian investors with ties to Putin, campaign manager Paul Manafort was a top adviser to a Russian-backed Ukrainian politician—and what about Carter Page?[16]

Brown-nosing intelligence bureaucrats hoping for a position in the Clinton administration rushed to the press with their personal expertise about a computer hack they knew absolutely nothing about. "I think all signs point to cyber actors with ties to Russian intelligence," said Mike Vickers, a former undersecretary of defense under Obama and a Hillary supporter.[17]

Bewildered Trump spokesmen were asked to respond to the claim of a Vast Russian Conspiracy.

Erin Burnett, CNN Anchor: Why it is so farfetched to blame the Russians and say that the motive was to help you?

Paul Manafort: I mean, it's just absurd. I don't know anything about what you just said. You may know it. Then if you
do, then you ought to expose it. I want to say, you know, I
don't know what you're talking about. It's crazy.[18]

With the Democrats' fear of another WikiLeaks dump only
increasing, they decided, the following month, to claim that not
only was Russia behind the leaks, but Moscow might be altering
the e-mails' content! *Do NOT trust what you read on WikiLeaks,
voters. Politico* reported that on Saturday, August 13, Minority
Leader Nancy Pelosi held a conference call with Democratic leaders on the Hill, instructing them to get the word out that "Russian
hackers" might have inserted false information into the e-mails.[19]

Again, cybersecurity experts scoffed at the claim, pointing out
that if WikiLeaks were ever caught posting fake documents, it
would destroy the credibility of the entire operation.[20] There was
also the problem of there still being no evidence that the Russians
hacked the DNC.

Of course, the Democrats' conspiracy theory didn't change
anything about the DNC's conniving e-mails. As progressive Democrat Dennis Kucinich said, "If the Russians did it, they didn't
write the e-mails. The e-mails were written by Democrats, with
the DNC, that's the problem."[21] But it changed the subject. This
was standard operating procedure for Hillary. Creating imaginary
enemies had been Hillary's go-to move whenever she was caught
in a scandal for the past quarter century. She'd claimed to be under
attack by sexists, political opponents, racists, a vast right-wing
conspiracy—and now the Russkies, conspiring with Trump.

During the 1992 Democratic primary, Jerry Brown raised the
sleazy business of Bill Clinton using his governorship to funnel
state work to his wife's law firm. Hillary's response was to pretend

she was being attacked for being a career woman. "I suppose I could have stayed home and baked cookies and made tea," she said. "But what I decided to do was fulfill my profession."[22]

She blamed rumors of her husband's affair with Gennifer Flowers—which Clinton later admitted to—on a former gubernatorial opponent of her husband, Sheffield Nelson, who was "a very bitter man because my husband beat him, as he well should have, because he was a negative force in Arkansas politics. And he has now spent the last two years doing everything he can to try to get even and it's a sort of sad spectacle."[23]

She blamed the Monica Lewinsky scandal—also later proved true—on a "vast right-wing conspiracy, conspiring against my husband," and urged the press to investigate. "This is the great story here," she said on NBC's *Today* show, "for anybody willing to find it and write about it and explain it."

After losing the 2008 primary to Obama, she blamed her loss on the media's rampant sexism—especially at MSNBC.[24] Let me say that again in case you didn't catch it the first time around: Hillary Clinton blamed her 2008 loss to Obama on the sexism of the media. Her surrogates, like Bill Clinton and Geraldine Ferraro, cried "sexism" directly, while Hillary merely observed that her groundbreaking campaign "certainly has been challenging given some of the attitudes that have been forthcoming in the press."[25]

So the obvious move, when the Democrats needed a distraction from their inept handling of computer servers and their double cross of Bernie, was to accuse Putin of a diabolical plot to elect Trump. Russia had to be made the villain, conspiring against the innocent Clintons.

1998 Flashback:

Judy Woodruff: Wolf, what are they saying at the White House?

Wolf Blitzer: They're making the point . . . that this does confirm what an evil, bad person Linda Tripp was. How she set up someone she claims was her friend and how she betrayed her, stabbed her in the back.[26]

Russia had to become the new Linda Tripp.

At the first presidential debate, on September 26, 2016, Hillary tied the DNC's e-mail dump to Moscow and Trump. "I know Donald's very praiseworthy of Vladimir Putin," she said, "but Putin is playing a really tough, long game here. And one of the things he's done is to let loose cyber attackers to hack into government files, to hack into personal files, *hack into the Democratic National Committee*" [emphasis added].

Trump's reaction was the same as the *Times* reporters' had been when Mook first launched the Russian conspiracy—minus the historical reference. "She's saying Russia, Russia, Russia," but it could be anybody, he said. "It could be Russia, but it could also be China. It could also be lots of other people. It also could be somebody sitting on their bed that weighs four hundred pounds."

This exchange marked not only the wildest Red-baiting since John Birchers accused Eisenhower of being a Soviet agent, but also the first incident of fat shaming during a U.S. presidential debate.

Illustrating how synthetic the Russia story was, Hillary barely mentioned the country during the entire campaign—right up until she needed an enemy to blame for the DNC e-mails spilling out on WikiLeaks.[27] Trump had been going around all year bragging about Putin's having called him "brilliant," denouncing NATO, and pledging to get along with the Russian leader. But Hillary mentioned Russia on the campaign trail only two or three times—usually to remind voters of her vast foreign policy experience. In a January 2016 primary debate, for example, she described her relationship with Putin as "'one, I think, of respect.'"[28]

On June 14, 2016—just a month before the Clinton campaign began pushing the Trump-Russian conspiracy—Hillary brushed off the suggestion that the Russians had hacked the DNC, saying, "cybersecurity will be an issue that I will be absolutely focused on as president." She added, "Whether it's Russia, or China, Iran or North Korea, more and more countries are using hacking to steal our information, to use it to their advantage, and we can't let that go on."[29]

As we will see, it was only after the unthinkable happened—Hillary lost the election!—that the media no longer found Hillary's claim of a vast Russian conspiracy "remarkable." To the contrary, it was a story worthy of congressional investigations, mind-numbing media coverage, and even an independent counsel.

By now, even if the Democratic National Committee went to the media and said, "We beg you—the Trump-Russia stuff is hurting us, please stop," the Resistance wouldn't be able to stop. *The New York Times, The Washington Post,* MSNBC, CNN and late-night comedians will not give it up. Their audience is in a blind rage and won't be satisfied until Trump is impeached on the basis of Rachel Maddow's dream journal. They think Trump is captive to his base? If only! On the other hand, the media's Russia obsession is entirely driven by the left's nutjob base.

There are random conservatives who might believe kooky things from time to time, but conspiracy-mongering is a plant that doesn't fully bloom except in the soil of liberalism. The psychoanalyst Erich Fromm argued that because freedom is terrifying, one way to escape the anxiety is to have a strong belief system, providing a central magnet for all the metal filings to coalesce around. Liberals have no strong belief systems, only status anxieties. This is why their passions must be corralled into conspiracy theories, to bring conformity to their lives. They hate Trump, so everything he does must be on orders from Moscow.

The Resistance has told lie after lie to push the Russia madness, slandering random people connected to Trump, corrupting once respected American institutions, and tying the country in knots. As each lie gets exposed, the circus moves on—*it was a tie, the game was rained out, we'll never know what happened.* They don't get to call the president and his associates traitors for two years and then have the slate wiped clean as they barrel on to some fresh slander. There is a Russia scandal—and it's all theirs. The real story is a blockbuster.

CHAPTER SEVEN

Hillary Finally Runs an Effective Campaign . . . with Our Intelligence Agencies

The Russia conspiracy is classic liberal scandal-mongering. Their plan: Bore us to death. Everyone understands what Bill Clinton did to get himself impeached. Everyone knows that Hillary's ineptitude led to the slaughter of Americans in Benghazi, the cover-up, and her deletion of more than thirty thousand State Department e-mails. We didn't need a flow chart and an index of characters to see that Obama took away millions of Americans' health care, his Justice Department was running guns to Mexico in a boneheaded political stunt, and his IRS was refusing to grant tax-exempt status to conservative organizations for political reasons.

Now: Explain Watergate, Iran-Contra, or Russian collusion.

As is often the case, President Trump's deceptively simple characterization of the Russia panic is exactly correct: It's a made-up story to explain how Hillary lost the 2016 election.

No one is allowed to question whether Russia interfered with our election to help the Trump campaign because, as we are gently hectored, that is the conclusion of SEVENTEEN INTELLIGENCE AGENCIES!

Liberals believe in the January 6, 2017, intelligence report like Christians believe in the inerrant word of God, except liberals are a lot bossier about it. In a new posture, the left deeply trusts our intelligence agencies.

This is the story of how Hillary browbeat our intelligence agencies into producing that report.

At the beginning of September 2016, Obama was under enormous pressure to endorse Hillary's opportunistic conspiracy theory. Even Hillary's campaign aides in the press weren't sold on the Russian hacking story. After the initial shock of the Clinton team's Red-baiting, *The New York Times* did what it could to buttress the Clintonian conspiracy theory, but by the end of the summer even it had to admit that the consensus among government intelligence agencies was that WikiLeaks had no ties to Russian intelligence.[1]

In one last shot to dirty up Obama, Hillary needed him to produce a government report claiming that the Russians had hacked the DNC. It was awkward because, for years, Obama had refused to blame Russia or China for far more serious hacks, either "out of embarrassment or to protect its sources of intelligence," according to the *Times*.[2] Even when a Chinese national was arrested in connection with the hack of millions of the government's security clearance files, the Obama administration did not point the finger at China.

But when *the DNC* was hacked, it was somehow urgent for the Obama administration to get the word out that Russia did it. In early October, the *Times* reported that Obama's aides were "debating whether to openly attribute the cyberattacks to Russia." As late as October 5, the director of the National Security Agency, Admiral Michael Rogers, refused to blame the Russians.[3]

Two days later, John Podesta's e-mails appeared on WikiLeaks. That was a nuclear bomb. Among other things, the e-mails revealed that Hillary had been given an advance copy of one of CNN's debate questions from Donna Brazile—who had replaced Debbie Wasserman Schultz as DNC chair on account of the last round of WikiLeaks disclosures. The entire media-DNC-industrial complex was being exposed, as was the dirty game that had been played against Sanders. The e-mails also strongly suggested that the Clintons' "charitable" foundations were being used as cash cows for the family personally.

Obama still said nothing, but two of the most partisan members of his cabinet, James Clapper, director of national intelligence, and Jeh Johnson, secretary of the Homeland Security Department, issued a joint statement endorsing the Clinton campaign's notion that Russia had hacked the Democrats "in order to interfere with the election."[4]

Russian experts were baffled. Stephen Sestanovich, Columbia professor and George F. Kennan Fellow at the Council on Foreign Relations, questioned the claim, noting the absence of any evidence.[5] President Obama took the alleged Russian hacking so seriously that he did absolutely nothing about it. No sanctions, no rebuke, no retaliation. No—I take that back: He told Putin to "cut it out."[6] That was Obama's response to an attack on our country that the *Times*' Thomas Friedman compares to Pearl Harbor and 9/11.

> Mr. Vice President, Mr. Speaker, Members of the Senate, and of the House of Representatives: Yesterday, October 7, 2017—a date which will live in infamy—the United States of America was suddenly and deliberately attacked by Russia. I believe that I interpret the will of the Congress and of the people when I assert that I will tell Russia to cut it out.

The Clapper/Johnson joint statement was exactly what Hillary needed. It gave her a hook to start lecturing the country about her invented conspiracy. By the third debate, on October 19, she was openly accusing Trump of siding with a foreign power over *the United States of America*. Either you agreed with the Clinton-Pelosi-Mook conspiracy theory—or you were with Putin! Clinton went on and on about the conclusion of "seventeen intelligence agencies"—a conclusion that neither Obama nor his NSA director had been willing to make one week earlier.

Trump wasn't buying it.

Trump: She has no idea whether it's Russia, China, or anybody else.

Clinton: I am not quoting myself.

Trump: She has no idea.

Clinton: I am quoting seventeen . . .

Trump: Hillary, you have no idea.

Clinton: . . . Seventeen intelligence—do you doubt seventeen military and civilian agencies? . . .

Trump: And our country has no idea. Yeah, I doubt it. I doubt it.

Clinton: Well, he'd rather believe Vladimir Putin than the military and civilian intelligence professionals who are sworn to protect us. I find that just absolutely . . .

Trump: She doesn't like Putin because Putin has outsmarted her at every step of the way.

This was the first appearance of the SEVENTEEN INTELLIGENCE AGENCIES. It was not the Word of God report that would come out on January 7, 2017, but a precursor. Sort of a John the Baptist SEVENTEEN INTELLIGENCE AGENCIES report. Factcheckers throughout the media ruled Hillary's nutso claim "TRUE," citing the "Joint Statement" of Clapper and Johnson, which had very clearly referred to "the U.S. Intelligence Community," and, if you counted them all up, there are seventeen. That's how Clapper and Johnson's political document became SEVENTEEN INTEL-LIGENCE AGENCIES.[7]

PolitiFact
"We rate Clinton's statement True."[8]

USA Today
"Yes, 17 intelligence agencies really did say
Russia was behind hacking."[9]

As much fun as it was to rate Hillary's statement "TRUE" and call Trump an idiot, the media were still not sold on the Russian conspiracy theory.

A week after the mighty "Joint Statement" from Clapper and Johnson (SEVENTEEN INTELLIGENCE AGENCIES!), *Bloomberg* columnist Leonid Bershidsky wrote that, "instead of variations on 'the Russians did it' theme," the Clinton campaign needed to make "a clear statement" that "they failed and that they are taking lessons in basic cybersecurity."[10] But mostly the media protected Hillary by ignoring her conspiracy-mongering entirely. A few days after the debate, *The New York Times* put a story about a private security group concluding that Russians hacked the DNC on page A-14.[11]

ANOTHER BAD JOKE
THE PRESS TOOK SERIOUSLY

It was only after Hillary lost the election that her Russian conspiracy theory was taken *very* seriously by the fourth estate. As described in the book *Shattered: Inside the Doomed Campaign of Hillary Clinton*, within twenty-four hours of Clinton's concession speech, campaign chair John Podesta and manager Robby Mook met with the communications team "to engineer the case that the election wasn't entirely on the up-and-up. For a couple of hours, with Shake Shack containers littering the room, they went over the script they would pitch to the press and the public. Already, Russian hacking was the centerpiece of the argument."[12]

Obviously, Democrats would have preferred to claim that Trump was conspiring with North Korea or ISIS. But unfortunately, Trump had no business with those entities. He had some vague dealings with Russia, so they went with Putin.

Our goal is to undermine Trump—what do we have?

Not much. He had a Miss Universe pageant in Moscow—

Fantastic! So I guess we have to gear up for another cold war!

Well, if that's what we have to do . . .

If Trump's only interests abroad had been in Canada, the Democrats would have had to convince Americans that Canada was the most evil country on earth.

Having once described Robby Mook's Russia conspiracy as "remarkable," after Hillary lost the election, *The New York Times* was convinced! In an article titled "How Russian Cyberpower Invaded the U.S.," *Times* reporters—including Sanger—somberly reported that there was "no way to be certain of the ultimate impact of the hack." But Russia had found "the perfect weapon: cheap, hard to see coming, hard to trace."[13]

Really, really great idea, *New York Times*—to be getting your

Trump attacks from America's biggest liar. We'll definitely stop calling you "fake news" now.

By early December, headlines like these began appearing on the front pages of newspapers throughout the country:

The Denver Post
"CIA: Russia Intervened"

The Houston Chronicle
"CIA: Russia Backed Trump"

The Los Angeles Times
"2016 Election Hacking Faces New Scrutiny"

The New York Times
"Russian Hackers Acted to Aid Trump, U.S. Says"

The New York Times
"Hacking the Democrats"

About a week later, Hillary met with her donors, telling them, "The press is finally catching up to the facts." As she often did, Hillary imagined a media that was wildly biased against her. "We desperately tried to present [the Russia hacking story] to them during the last months of the campaign," she complained.[14] But underdog Hillary could not catch a break from the media—a media in which only two of the one hundred largest newspapers in the country endorsed her opponent.[15]

Liberals with any self-respect ridiculed the press's instant embrace of "intelligence" claims about Russia interfering with our election, pointing out that a few years earlier, these same intelligence agencies had assured us that there were WMDs in Iraq. As

Rolling Stone's Matt Taibbi said, "We ought to have learned from the Judith Miller episode."[16]

AGENCIES EVERYWHERE BUT NOT A DROP OF INTELLIGENCE: THE JANUARY 6, 2017 REPORT

To silence the pesky naysayers, on January 6, 2017, the director of national intelligence released a more strongly worded report. This time, there were *four* agencies on board: the Central Intelligence Agency, the Federal Bureau of Investigation, the National Security Agency, and the Office of the Director of National Intelligence. In other words, SEVENTEEN INTELLIGENCE AGENCIES! (™ Hillary Clinton).

So it's kind of important that three of the four agencies attesting to Russian interference were led by men not known for their absolute devotion to the truth: CIA director John Brennan, national intelligence director James Clapper, and FBI director James Comey. The fourth man to lend his name to the report, NSA director Michael Rogers, confessed to only "moderate" confidence in the report's conclusions.[17]

Here's a brief review of the men's history.

JOHN BRENNAN—IT'S JUST BEYOND THE SCOPE OF REASON!

As Obama's chief counterterrorism adviser, Brennan gave a speech in June 2011 claiming that U.S. drone strikes had not killed a single civilian. As was later proved, Brennan had actually been receiving reports confirming that civilians had been killed.[18]

Also in 2011, Brennan fabricated details about the most celebrated military operation in half a century: the Osama bin Laden raid. Brennan rushed to the press to tell them that Bin Laden had been armed—and he had used his wife as a human shield! Both claims had to be corrected the next day by White House spokesman Jay Carney.[19]

Most seriously, in 2014, as Obama's CIA director, Brennan hotly denied Senator Dianne Feinstein's accusation that the agency was hacking into computers being used by the Senate to investigate the CIA. "Nothing could be further from the truth," Brennan told NBC News' Andrea Mitchell. "I mean, we wouldn't do that. I mean, that's just beyond the scope of reason in terms of what we would do." Once the "facts come out," he said, Feinstein would be proved wrong.[20]

A few months later, the inspector general concluded that the CIA had been hacking into the computers of Senate staffers investigating the agency.[21]

Democrats and commentators demanded Brennan's head.[22] But in a fairy-tale ending, he won them back by becoming a hero of the Resistance. Not only did Brennan sign the report of SEVENTEEN INTELLIGENCE AGENCIES, but today he tweets perfectly rational and normal things like this to the president:

"When the full extent of your venality, moral turpitude, and political corruption becomes known, you will take your rightful place as a disgraced demagogue in the dustbin of history. You may scapegoat Andy McCabe, but you will not destroy America . . . America will triumph over you."[23]

In an instant, Brennan became "one of the finest public servants we have" (CNN)[24], "a straight shooter" (CNN)[25], and a "straight arrow" (MSNBC)[26]. It's a Cinderella story!

JAMES CLAPPER—THE "LEAST UNTRUTHFUL" ANSWER

James Clapper lied under oath at a 2013 Senate hearing:

> **Senator Ron Wyden:** Does the NSA collect any type of data at all on millions or hundreds of millions of Americans?
>
> **Clapper:** No, sir . . . Not wittingly.

A few months later, WikiLeaks posted Edward Snowden's documents invalidating that claim—as Clapper himself admitted, calling his answer "clearly erroneous" and the "least untruthful" answer he could give.[27] If it seems like he was on the spot, desperately trying to avoid revealing important national security secrets in a public forum—he was warned in advance about Wyden's question.

Are we getting Clapper's "least untruthful" answer on whether Russia hacked the Democrats' e-mails to help Trump?

JAMES COMEY—HIS OWN BOSWELL

Finally, there is Mr. North Star, James Comey. Leave aside his refusal to prosecute Hillary Clinton for the mishandling of classified documents and his decision to outsource the FBI's investigation of the Trump campaign to the Clinton campaign. If his book tour demonstrated nothing else, it clearly shows that Comey has an uncanny ability to interpret any remark, grimace, or raised eyebrow in the worst possible light for Trump. (And the best possible light for himself!)

Those are the SEVENTEEN INTELLIGENCE AGENCIES vouching for the claim that the Russians hacked the DNC e-mails to help

Trump: three wildly partisan members of the Obama administration trying to curry favor with the woman they believed would be the next president—and "moderate" support from the NSA's Mike Rogers.

Even a district court judge in Hawaii wouldn't accept that as evidence.

CHAPTER EIGHT

Intelligence Agencies: *You* Tell Her We Can't Game the Electoral College

We keep asking for evidence of Russian collusion and all we get back is SEVENTEEN INTELLIGENCE AGENCIES AGREE! Aren't you listening? Not twelve—*seventeen!* Whenever liberals start citing meaningless large numbers, they don't have a real argument.

> *President Trump has made 3,001 false or misleading claims.*
>
> *97.3 percent of scientists agree on global warming!*
>
> *Robert Mueller has racked up nineteen indictments!*
>
> *Seventeen intelligence agencies conclude that Russia hacked the election!*
>
> *I'm citing a surprisingly large number, and not going into any detail about what it means.*

The average person doesn't care if it's a single agency's conclusion, provided the evidence is credible. For one thing, there's generally a lot of overlap in the experts. It's not that impressive to say: Chris Hayes, Rachel Maddow, Ari Melber, and Lawrence O'Donnell ALL agree! Moreover, no one knows who counts as an "expert."

Global warming "scientists," for example, always seems to include a lot of lawyers.

As indicated by the killjoys questioning the findings of SEVENTEEN INTELLIGENCE AGENCIES, the authors of the famed January 6 report decided that, in lieu of evidence, they would simply assert top-line conclusions. That's always more persuasive.

Here is a full and accurate summary of the report:

> We assess with high confidence that Russian President Vladimir Putin ordered an influence campaign in 2016 aimed at the US presidential election, the consistent goals of which were to undermine public faith in the US democratic process . . .
>
> We assess Putin, his advisers, and the Russian Government developed a clear preference for President-elect Trump over Secretary Clinton.
>
> Putin most likely wanted to discredit Secretary Clinton because he has publicly blamed her since 2011 for inciting mass protests against his regime in late 2011 and early 2012, and because he holds a grudge for comments he almost certainly saw as disparaging him.[1]

Spookily, that was *exactly* how Hillary Clinton had explained her loss to donors just three weeks earlier. She said that Vladimir V. Putin launched the attacks "to undermine our democracy," because "he has a personal beef against me." Putin, she explained, "publicly blamed me for the outpouring of outrage by his own people, and that is the direct line between what he said back then and what he did in this election."[2]

In fact, despite the very serious-sounding title, "Assessing Russian Activities and Intentions in Recent US Elections," take out the spy jargon and the report is nothing but Hillary's talking points against Trump.

The report may as well have read:

The mission of the Intelligence Community is to seek to determine if this is the president we want for our daughters.

Key Judgments

We assess that president-elect Donald J. Trump has said degrading things about women in the past. All three agencies agree with this judgment. CIA and FBI have high confidence in this judgment; NSA has moderate confidence.

We assess that President-elect Trump's goals were to undermine young girls' self-esteem and to silence women's voices. All three agencies agree with this judgment. CIA and FBI have high confidence in this judgment; NSA has moderate confidence.

President-elect Trump's approach evolved over the course of the campaign. When it appeared to Trump that Secretary Clinton was likely to win the nomination, the campaign began to focus more on lifting up his racist, sexist, homophobic, xenophobic, Islamophobic supporters. All three agencies agree with this judgment. CIA and FBI have high confidence in this judgment; NSA has moderate confidence.

We further assess president-elect Trump will continue to develop capabilities to fat-shame women in the United States, judging from past practice and current efforts. All three agencies agree with this judgment. CIA and FBI have high confidence in this judgment; NSA has moderate confidence.

Trust us. Trump is a dickweed.

FOGGY WITH NO CHANCE OF EVIDENCE

Proving that no one who cites the report actually read it, fully eight of the report's fourteen pages consist of an already published analysis of RT, an utterly irrelevant Russian TV network available on channel one million of your TV. The RT analysis was originally published by the CIA back in 2012 but got stapled to the Russian hacking report, like a homework assignment you forgot to write and had to quickly assemble at midnight the day before the paper was due, hoping the teacher wouldn't notice. (You're paying taxes for this crap.) It's a real mystery why intelligence professionals were not blown away by the Russian hacking report.

Consider the reactions of a few liberals who went the extra mile and read the report.

The Atlantic's Russian émigré writer Julia Ioffe tweeted about the report:

> @juliaioffe 1:23 PM–6 Jan 2017
> A lot of this #DNI report seems to work off the (false)
> assumption that anyone watches RT, a channel that fudges
> its ratings.

> @juliaioffe 2:46 PM–6 Jan 2017
> It's hard to tell if the thinness of the #hacking report is because
> the proof is qualified, or because the proof doesn't exist.

> @juliaioffe 3:36 PM–6 Jan 2017
> Have to say, though, I'm hearing from a lot of Russia
> watchers who are very skeptical of the report. None like
> Putin/Trump.[3]

The Intercept's Glenn Greenwald complained about those "blindly and uncritically" accepting "provocative claims about a foreign adversary." The problem with the report's key claims, he said, is that "there is no evidence for it . . . just CIA assertions over and over, and that just simply isn't enough."[4]

The Atlantic's David A. Graham's summary of the report was that the "intelligence community is in effect telling readers, 'trust us.'"[5]

Brookings Institution fellow Susan Hennessey tweeted:

> @Susan_Hennessey 1:12 PM–6 Jan 2017
> The unclassified report is underwhelming at best. There is essentially no new information for those who have been paying attention.

> @Susan_Hennessey 4:14 PM–6 Jan 2017
> Once report was gutted of classified info, the dumb move was to try to bulk it up with old Open Source reports.

> @Susan_Hennessey 4:49 PM–12 Jan 2017
> I think this dramatically misreads the report. It was top line conclusions, not a presentation of evidence.[6]

(Further proof that we're not working together in the era of Trump: I'd never heard of Ms. Hennessey until I saw references to her tweets about the intelligence report and tried to look them up . . . "You are blocked from following @Susan_Hennessey and viewing @Susan_Hennessey's Tweets.")

Veteran Intelligence Professionals for Sanity (VIPS) wrote an open letter to Obama about the report, asking him to "authorize public release of any tangible evidence that takes us beyond the unsubstantiated, 'we-assess' judgments by the intelligence agencies."

You're probably thinking VIPS is some right-wing hate group, but it's well respected by the mainstream media. Members of VIPS have been fawningly interviewed on CNN and MSNBC and cited in *The New York Times* and *The Washington Post*. The head of the group, Ray McGovern, has no trouble getting his letters published in journals of elite opinion.[7]

Make that: VIPS *was* well respected. That was back when the group was questioning the intelligence on Iraq's WMDs. Now that the group is questioning the intelligence on Russia hacking the DNC, only one news source on Nexis has published the group's letter to Obama: the *Yerepouni Daily News,* an Armenian newspaper. The *Yerepouni* has a smaller audience than any other news outlet, apart from Russia Today.[8]

FIRST THEY IGNORE YOU, THEN THEY LAUGH AT YOU, THEN THEY DESPERATELY SPREAD YOUR CONSPIRACY THEORY BECAUSE YOU LOST

Remember that headline, the one from the list of harebrained excuses for why they lost election?

The *Times*' headline about the 9/11 attack was more laid-back.

Unfazed by the report's regrettable shortcoming of having zero evidence, the *Times* described it as "extraordinary," "damning," "unanimous," "a political blow to Mr. Trump."[9] The three men vouching for the report, John Brennan, James Clapper, and James Comey, had certainly come a long way since the media wanted them boiled in oil and fed to the dogs.

Maybe government officials are rolling in proof that they're refusing to show us. But they have to understand that what would be even more persuasive than their nagging is evidence.

And yet, nearly two years after the SEVENTEEN INTELLIGENCE AGENCIES! released their high-handed report, there was still not a speck of substantiation for any Russian interference. There had been high hopes for this or that Trump adviser being the Russian collusion mastermind, but it all came to nothing. Mueller's showboating indictment of Russians was a joke.

With everything else falling apart, the Resistance was holding on to that intelligence report like a drowning man to flotsam. On May 18, 2018, Trump's secretary of homeland security, Kirstjen Nielsen, was ambushed by CNN's Manu Raju and asked, "Do you have any reason to doubt the January 2017 intelligence community assessment that said it was Vladimir Putin who tried to meddle in this election to help President Trump?"

It's all the poor devils had left.

Nielsen gave a noncommittal response, so CNN's Kate Bolduan was forced to scrap all other news at the top of her show and report on this "stunning development." The Homeland Security secretary would not admit that the Russians hacked the DNC to help elect Trump![10]

Who can blame the Resistance for having blind faith in our intelligence agencies? They've got a spectacular track record!

- Five months before the Iranian Revolution toppled the shah, the CIA concluded, "Iran is not in a revolutionary or even a pre-revolutionary situation." Four months before the shah's downfall, the Defense Intelligence Agency assessed that the shah would "remain actively in power over the next 10 years."[11] One month before the shah was fleeing for his life, CIA analysts assessed that the shah's hold on power was secure.[12]
- In 1982, five years before Gorbachev began dismantling the Soviet Union, the CIA concluded that "the U.S.S.R., far from being on the verge of collapse, has experienced major growth."[13] Four years before the USSR's economic disintegration, the CIA assessed that the Soviet economy was "without danger of collapse."[14] Months *after* President Reagan drove a stake through the heart of the Soviet economy by refusing to give up Star Wars at Reykjavík, the CIA concluded that the Soviet economy had "significantly improved" in the previous year.[15]
- The day before Iraq invaded Kuwait in 1990, leading to the Gulf War, our intelligence services were still exchanging information with Iraq,[16] in the belief that "dialogue" and "mediation" would continue.[17]
- And, of course, the CIA assessed in 2002 that "Iraq has continued its weapons of mass destruction (WMD) programs."[18]

The problem with the CIA began about fifty years ago when the off-the-charts left-wing, post-Watergate Congress gleefully set about dismantling this nation's intelligence operations. They can't do any of the dirty stuff, so today the only job of a CIA officer is to read foreign newspapers and leak classified information to the press. It's like an organization of clandestine newspaper readers. The reason no one at the CIA saw 9/11 coming was that there was nothing about it in *The Islamabad Post*. It's amazing we even won the Cold War. While the Soviets were stealing us blind, our guys were out having long expense-account lunches and thinking about writing their memoirs.

Since then, the CIA hasn't been able to find enemy spies in its own agency. Larry Wu-tai Chin sold vital defense documents to the Chinese for *thirty years* before the agency caught up with him. Aldrich Ames, whose betrayal led to the execution of ten Soviet sources, was a drunk, lived well beyond his means, and failed a polygraph test. But the CIA couldn't figure out who the spy was.

In 1999, NATO forces bombed the Chinese embassy in Belgrade by mistake, based on CIA intel.

Of course, the trillions of dollars we've spent on "intelligence" were all worth it when these bloodhounds sniffed out and prevented the 9/11 attack. No—I'm sorry. That didn't happen. Ditto on the Boston Marathon bombing, despite repeated warnings about the bombers from Russia, our most hated international foe.

Moral: When the intelligence community says, "Trust us," we should trust them! Cable news nitwits have every right to throw a hissy fit if we don't all swear fidelity to the January 6 report.

Thanks to Trump, the U.S. intelligence community has sprung to life again! The sleeping giant awoke just in time to push a Hillary Clinton conspiracy theory on the nation. Their mission: Take out Trump. The good news is, the last time the CIA tried to bump off a newly ensconced leader was in the early 1960s. Fidel Castro went on to be the longest-serving head of state in the world.

CHAPTER NINE

Different Strzoks for Different Folks

Would there be a Russia investigation if Hillary had lost?

(That's a rhetorical question—of course not. Trump and all his supporters would simply be locked up for micro-aggressions.)

Would there be a Russia investigation without FBI agent Peter Strzok?

Would there be a Russia investigation without FBI consultant Christopher Steele?

Every place you look in the FBI's Russia investigation, the same two names keep popping up: Peter Strzok and Christopher Steele. Steele is the author of the preposterous dossier that sparked the FBI investigation, and Strzok is the FBI agent who started it.

So it's rather important that both of them are Trump-hating fanatics.

Strzok cleared Hillary of wrongdoing for using a private server as secretary of state to hide her e-mails from the American people, thereby mishandling classified material and exposing government e-mails to hacking. It was also Strzok who instigated the investigation of Trump's alleged collusion with Russia, apparently based on . . . Christopher Steele's "Russia dossier." It was Strzok who interviewed Trump national security adviser Michael Flynn about his perfectly legal conversation with the Russian ambassador—which the FBI was listening to—leading to one of Mueller's prized indictments: Flynn was charged with lying to investigators. It was also Strzok who got the FISA warrant on Trump aide Carter Page, based on the Steele dossier.

These are a few of Strzok's most famous text messages to his equally Trump-hating mistress, FBI agent Lisa Page, sent during Strzok's investigation of the Trump campaign:

> Trump is a disaster. I have no idea how destabilizing his Presidency would be.

> . . . And F TRUMP.

> OMG did you hear what Trump just said?

> Just went to a southern Virginia Walmart. I could SMELL the Trump support . . .

> I am riled up. Trump is a f***ing idiot, is unable to provide a coherent answer.

> God Hillary should win 100,000,000–0.

He also chatted about "the absolute bigoted nonsense of Trump," called him an "enormous douche," and said, of the possibility that Trump might win, that he was "Panicked."[1]

In August 2016, a few months into the Trump investigation, Strzok and his mistress, Lisa Page, exchanged the following texts:

> PAGE: he's not ever going to become
> president, right? Right?!
>
> STRZOK: No. No he won't. We'll stop it.

This guy was the lead investigator on the Trump probe.

The Resistance was thrilled that the inspector general's report concluded that there was no "documentary or testimonial evidence" that political bias "directly affected" any "specific" decisions.

See? No evidence! No story!

New York magazine quickly put up an article titled "DOJ Report Confirms That the President Is a Dishonest Conspiracy Theorist."[2]

Is there ever "documentary or testimonial evidence" that bias "directly" affected "specific" decisions? We couldn't have any discrimination laws if that were required. Just because your boss goes around making racist jokes doesn't mean his bias directly caused your firing, you conspiracy theorist! Unless a cop writes in his diary or expressly tells investigators, "Oh yeah, I arrested this guy because I hate n#gg@rs," there is no "documentary or testimonial evidence" that his feelings "directly affected" your arrest.

In what other circumstance would the left conclude that a law enforcement agent's gigantic personal bias was benign? It's a pretty big elephant to ignore when the lead investigator tells his girlfriend, that the possibility of the target being elected president was "f---ing terrifying," and assures her, "He won't [be president]. We'll stop it."

Strzok also told Page that the Russia investigation was an "insurance policy" on the off chance that Trump actually won the election:

> I want to believe the path you threw out for consideration—
> that there's no way he gets elected—but I'm afraid we can't

take that risk. It's like an insurance policy in the unlikely event you die before you're 40 . . .

The media have tied themselves in knots trying to explain away this text, but all their alternative interpretations are inane. *The Washington Post*, for example, points out that even with an insurance policy, YOU STILL DIE![3] The solace is, your loved ones get an insurance payout. Similarly, even with the Russia investigation, Trump is still president. But the solace is, you get to shackle him, throughout his presidency, with a phony investigation.

The Wall Street Journal's rationalization is even dumber—evident in the fact that *The New York Times* cited it with approval. The *Journal* explained that, "in the full context," Strzok was merely "'reacting to the argument that there was no point getting worked up because Trump was bound to lose."[4] Yes, exactly. Strzok was saying: *Get worked up—he might win!* How does that make the text sound any better? As long as there are words on the page, journalists think they've made a point.

Everyone understands what Strzok meant when he said the Russian investigation was an "insurance policy"—except reporters.

After covering itself with glory by "clearing" Hillary Clinton (lead investigator: Peter Strzok) by announcing that she hadn't *intended* to commit various crimes—crimes for which intent is not an element—the FBI leapt on the Russia dossier about Trump. (Lead investigator: Peter Strzok.)

The creator of the dossier was Christopher Steele. In addition to being paid by the Clinton campaign and the DNC, Steele told Department of Justice official Bruce Ohr that he was "desperate that Trump not get elected and was passionate about him not being president." Ohr might not have noticed the problem there, inasmuch as his wife also worked at Fusion GPS, hired by Hillary for dirt on Trump. The FBI—presumably Strzok again—proposed to pay Steele to continue compiling his Russia dossier on Trump.

And that's how the FBI signed on to do opposition research for the Clinton campaign. It's almost as if the top brass wanted to get off on the right foot with the woman they assumed would be the next president.

The FBI has been leaking like mad, trying to convince the public, first, that the Russia dossier was of monumental importance, and then—scratch that—it was NOT the basis for anything they did. But it's difficult to claim that the dossier wasn't a big part of the FBI's Trump investigation. The Bureau's other scrolling list of excuses—*Carter Page went to Russia! George Papadopoulos talked about Hillary's e-mails! Roger Stone tweeted something mean about John Podesta!*—have all fallen flat.

The New York Times did what it could to pretty up Steele's dossier, but even it had to admit: "The material was not corroborated, and *The New York Times* has not been able to confirm the claims."[5] This being the *Times,* it had to explain to angry readers why they couldn't read the dossier, in its full glory, on the newspaper's Web site. The newspaper's answer: "Because the 35 pages of memos prepared as opposition research on Mr. Trump contain detailed claims that neither the intelligence agencies nor *The Times* has been able to verify, *Times* editors decided to briefly summarize the claims and not publish the document."[6]

Despite the dossier's having been widely distributed to the entire Washington media since around July 2016, not one of its claims about Trump has ever been verified. "A year and a half later, no public evidence has surfaced connecting Mr. Trump's advisers to the hacking or linking Mr. Trump himself to the Russian government's disruptive efforts"—as *The New York Times* admitted in paragraph 3,000 of a May 16, 2018, story on the FBI's investigation.[7]

It's one thing for the FBI not to be able to corroborate something. These days, FBI headquarters couldn't corroborate the location of its ass. But Pulitzer Prize–winning investigative reporters haven't been able to confirm any of the dossier's claims, either.

Most of the claims were wild allegations that couldn't be proved one way or the other. But to give you a sense of Steele's ability to evaluate information, in February 2018, he leaked one of his post-election bombshells to Jane Mayer at *The New Yorker*. According to Steele, Trump rejected Mitt Romney for secretary of state—because of the Russians! This claim was so important that Steele *wrote it in a memo to himself after the election.*

"If what the source heard was true," Mayer said, "then a foreign power was exercising pivotal influence over U.S. foreign policy." It may sound "crazy," she admitted, but "subsequent events could be said to support it."[8] The Russians-blocked-Romney story was treated as major breaking news almost everywhere. White House press secretary Sarah Huckabee Sanders was asked about it at the daily press briefing. The New York *Daily News* ran an editorial titled "The Russia House," citing the claim and concluding, "Sure enough, Russia-friendly Rex Tillerson, of ExxonMobil, got the job."[9] Case closed. (*The New York Times* didn't mention the retarded claim. David Leonhardt was off that day.)

Hey—were you any of you guys in the country in 2016? Remember the speeches Romney gave about Trump, calling him a "con man," "a fake," talking about his "bullying, the greed, the showing off, the misogyny"?[10] You can say that the president should be a bigger man, but you can't say Trump was *dying* to make Romney his secretary of state and only Russian intervention could explain why he didn't.

As I recall, MSNBC lavished attention on Romney's comments at the time, but the memory of them seems to have vanished. They were blown away by Steele's report. *Obviously, Trump wanted Romney, so that raises the question: Why was he not made secretary of state? I brought articles proving Romney wanted the job, and we know that Trump wanted him—that's a given. The only question is why Romney didn't end up as secretary of state?*

Chris Hayes called the Romney yarn "the biggest story in politics today." MSNBC's prototype Republican Steve Schmidt responded, "If that's true—those are the grounds necessary to remove this president from office beyond any discussion, beyond any doubt."[11] On *MTP Daily,* Katy Tur asked Senator Ben Cardin about Steele's claim. Senator Cardin: "Well, we would not be surprised."[12]

Could Trump be a reincarnation of Hitler, Senator?

Cardin: *We would not be surprised.*

Obviously, MSNBC'S Rachel Maddow[13] and Brian Williams led their shows with the momentous news.[14]

It might work, it might work!

But what if someone remembers what Romney said in 2016?

Yeah, but let's try it. It might work.

A sensible law enforcement agency would have dropped Steele's dossier after about six seconds and found a different angle for attacking an icky Republican presidential candidate. That's not our can-do FBI! In the hands of Trump obsessive Peter Strzok, wholly uncorroborated accusations by anonymous foreigners, collected by another foreigner, were used to launch a madcap investigation of a candidate in the heat of a presidential campaign. The dossier was even used to obtain a warrant under the Foreign Intelligence Surveillance Act against one of Trump's "foreign policy advisers," Carter Page.

Forget about Omar Mateen—the most qualified person ever to run for president needs our help!

WE'RE WITH HER

If they couldn't charge Trump with a crime, they could at least dirty him up. But, frustratingly, none of the dossier's claims were leaking. As *The New York Times* said, "Remarkably for Washington," Steele's memos had been in the hands of "many reporters for competing news organizations" for months, but the dossier's allegations had never leaked.[15]

With Trump's inauguration weeks away, FBI director James Comey, CIA director John Brennan, and National Security Agency director Michael J. Rogers made the "extremely unusual" decision—in the words of the *Times*—to widely publicize the dossier. They explained that its claims were "so potentially explosive" that they had to tell everyone about it. Manifestly, the dossier wasn't exploding anywhere—until the intelligence agencies decided to circulate it. They gave it to President Obama, President-elect Trump, and Democratic and Republican leaders in Congress.[16] As everybody knows, the way you keep something quiet in Washington is to tell a lot of politicians.

To be distributing a raw intelligence file on anyone is a shocking abuse of power. *The New York Times* sees "echoes of Watergate" in everything Trump does. Well, here's an "echo" for you: Nixon aide Chuck Colson went to prison for disseminating *a* FBI file to the press. The *Times'* Echoes-of-Watergate meter must be on the blink.

FBI raw intelligence reports are notoriously unreliable. Ask anyone who's ever requested a copy of his own security file about the bizarre gossip and hearsay that turns up in these things. As *The New York Times*' David Wallis described the reports, "Imagine a federally financed version of the National Enquirer with J. Edgar Hoover as its editor-in-chief."[17] (He cited the left's leading bogeyman, so it must be really bad.)

In the 1990s, Craig Livingstone, the Clinton White House's director of personnel security, improperly acquired FBI background files on hundreds of people, including former Bush administration officials and Republican Party leaders—and all hell broke loose. FBI director Louis Freeh denounced the White House. There were congressional investigations and private lawsuits. An independent counsel was appointed.

The Atlanta Journal-Constitution editorialized: "Of all the scandals and reports of scandals that have touched the Clinton White House, the one that sends cold chills up our spines is the still-developing story of official snooping into the personal FBI files of potential enemies."[18] The *Journal* was not alone. It was such a shocking abuse of power for the White House to be pawing through FBI background reports that it took several years of intensive investigations by Congress, the FBI, and the special counsel to get an answer to the most important question resounding throughout the country: *Who hired Craig Livingstone?* It was, naturally, Hillary Clinton.[19]

The FBI's background reports are compiled by federal agents, talking face-to-face to real people—not the scribblings of a foreigner recounting gossip he's heard from Russians. That's the file on Trump that U.S. law enforcement and intelligence agencies decided to hand out to nearly a dozen politicians.

G-MEN FOR HILLARY

The real horror of the FBI's anti-Trump operation isn't the left's gigantic hypocrisy, or even the sleaziness of the FBI spying on a presidential candidate for political reasons. The main problem isn't even the FBI's proclaiming itself above the law, beyond the reach of legislative or executive oversight. No, the main takeaway from the Bureau's Trump investigation is how utterly useless our FBI is.

When do we reach the point where disbanding the FBI is redundant? At least under J. Edgar Hoover, the FBI was competent. Today, the Bureau is the social justice warrior version of the Keystone Cops. One has only to look at their interview of Hillary Clinton, not recorded, not conducted under oath, and performed *after* Comey wrote his draft memo finding her innocent. Pure corruption, pure incompetence. But don't take my word for it. Just ask D. B. Cooper.

Which of these is your favorite FBI moment?

Shooting dead a dog, a fourteen-year-old boy, and a woman holding her baby at Ruby Ridge?

Incinerating more than eighty men, women, and children to death in Waco, Texas?

Blowing off a Phoenix agent's warning about a lot of Muslims taking flight lessons two months before the 9/11 attacks?

Announcing that Hillary had done nothing wrong before completing the investigation?

Clearing terrorist Omar Mateen shortly before he slaughtered fifty people at an Orlando nightclub?

Refusing to follow up on repeated warnings about Parkland shooter Nikolas Cruz?

On July 10, 2001, two months before the 9/11 attack, Phoenix FBI agent Kenneth Williams sent a memo to FBI higher-ups that was so prescient, it sounds like a joke. The memo described a "coordinated effort" by Osama bin Laden to place operatives in U.S. flight schools. He said there were an "inordinate number" of Arabs taking flying lessons, noting their anti-American views and heightened interest in airport security. He linked some of the students to an Islamic extremist group in London.

Williams sent his memo to the "Radical Fundamentalist Unit" and the "bin Laden desk" at FBI headquarters, in Washington. The FBI did nothing—for fear of being accused of "racial profiling."[20] If only the 9/11 terrorists had been Trump supporters, our FBI might have stopped them.

The FBI took out four FISA warrants on Carter Page, but not one on Pulse nightclub killer Omar Mateen, despite multiple warnings from his co-workers, as well as his known association with an al-Qaeda suicide bomber. Asked about the Bureau's monstrous ineptitude in the Mateen case, James Comey said: "I don't see anything, in reviewing our work, that our agents should have done differently."[21] (One thing we do *not* have to worry about with Comey is a lack of self-esteem.)

The outline of the problem begins to come into focus. Agents in the field are trying to protect the country, while back at FBI headquarters in Washington, the brass is concentrating on getting good write-ups in *The New York Times*. "Deep Throat," Bob Woodward and Carl Bernstein's secret source for their Watergate exposé, was an FBI guy, Mark Felt, bitter that Nixon had passed him over as director. Today, the FBI probably teaches classes on Felt at Quantico: *How to take down a duly elected Republican president.*

Now we know: The Obama administration weaponized not only the IRS, the DOJ, and the EPA against conservatives, but even the police-state branch of government. A gigantic surveillance apparatus was commandeered by disreputable men to smooth Hillary's path to the presidency. In this one case, we can be thankful that the FBI brass is so utterly incompetent.

CHAPTER TEN

James Comey: *Please Fire Me!*
Oh My Gosh, I'm Being Fired!

Everyone forgets this now, but the only reason we have a special counsel is that the FBI director spent much of the administration's first year wildly hinting that Trump was under investigation. As a result, when Trump finally fired Comey, the president appeared to be firing *the man investigating him*! By intentionally misleading Congress and the public, Comey created the circumstances that seemed to demand an independent counsel.

Only after he was fired, and an independent counsel safely appointed, did Comey finally admit: Trump was never under investigation in the first place.

Trump was trying to run the country, he knew he wasn't under investigation, and the head of the FBI knew he wasn't under investigation, but Comey obstinately refused to tell the American people that the president of the United States was not under investigation.

In fact, you might say the FBI director left the distinct impression that Trump *was* under investigation.

The New York Times, March 20, 2017:
"F.B.I. Is Investigating Trump's Russia Ties, Comey Confirms"

The New York Times, March 20, 2017:
Editorial: "Comey's Haunting News on Trump and Russia"

The New York Times, March 21, 2017:
"The F.B.I. Is Scrutinizing Trump's Russia Ties.
How Will That Work?"

As we now know, behind closed doors, Comey was repeatedly assuring the president that he was not being investigated. But the director wouldn't say that in public. Comey's entire career consists of his betraying his bosses, then documenting for history how he alone acted heroically. He's his own Boswell. *Hmmm . . . who should I cast as the hero in this story? I know—ME!* [Comey rides in to *Bonanza* music.]

Is there, oh, I don't know, a terrorist threat, a school shooting, or a heroin epidemic this guy might have been working on?

If you've been told you're not a subject of the investigation, why not ask for that to be announced publicly? *Can you please tell someone this? I'm trying to be president here—if I'm not a target, it would be really helpful for you to tell the public that.* It's one thing not to talk about an investigation when no one knows there is an investigation. But the media were ablaze with accusations that Trump had colluded with Russia. Trump wasn't just an ordinary citizen living under a cloud of suspicion, which would be bad enough. He was the president.

What was the huge problem with the FBI director saying, "Contrary to runaway speculation by the press, the president of the United States is not a subject of our investigation"?

Soon Trump would launch his much-maligned tweet of May 12, 2017, implying that he might have taped his conversations with Comey. That, finally, would force the director to stop blackening

Trump's name. But first, there was more taunting from the FBI chief.

Throughout his May 3, 2017, Senate testimony, Comey pregnantly stated that he could not comment on whether the president was under investigation. This wasn't an incidental point: he was asked the same question over and over and over again. A year later, as the more sordid aspects of the FBI's Trump investigation came to light, the media were sick with worry about the president's "attacks" harming morale at the Bureau. Yes, it must be awful to be threatened with an investigation! I wonder if having the head of the nation's premier law enforcement agency running around intimating that you're a criminal suspect would be at all demoralizing?

Knowing what we know now—that Trump was *not* under investigation—Comey's testimony at the May 3 hearing was unconscionable:

> **Senator Richard Blumenthal (D-CONN.):** And you have not, to my knowledge, ruled out anyone in the Trump campaign as potentially a target of that criminal investigation, correct?

> **Comey:** Well, I haven't said anything publicly about who we've opened investigations on, I briefed the chair and ranking on who those people are. And so I can't—I can't go beyond that in this setting.

> **Blumenthal:** Have you ruled out anyone in the campaign that you can disclose?

> **Comey:** I don't feel comfortable answering that, Senator, because I think it puts me on a slope to talking about who we're investigating.

Blumenthal: Have you—have you ruled out the president of the United States?

Comey: I don't—I don't want people to over-interpret this answer, I'm not going to comment on anyone in particular . . . [1]

**

Senator Al Franken (D-MN): Would President Trump's tax returns be material to such an investigation—the Russian investigation—and does the investigation have access to President Trump's tax returns . . . Is it that you can't say or that you can't say in this setting?

Comey: That I won't answer questions about the contours of the investigation. As I sit here I don't know whether I would do it in a closed setting either. But for sure—I don't want to begin answering questions about what we're looking at and how. [2]

Trump's taxes? The clear implication was that the president of the United States was suspected of receiving payoffs or paying for Russian interference in the election. Comey wouldn't even answer that.

On May 9, 2017, Trump fired Comey, in a letter that said, "While I greatly appreciate you informing me, on three separate occasions, that I am not under investigation, I nevertheless concur with the judgment of the Department of Justice that you are not able to effectively lead the Bureau."

Guess what this reminded *The New York Times* of? That's right! Watergate! In the considered opinion of the *Times,* the firing had "echoes of Watergate." [3]

As for Trump's claim that he was not under investigation, the Resistance was not buying it. Senator Chris Coons said Trump "seems to protest too much."[4] Representative Elijah Cummings said, "It is not normal for one who is under investigation" to "stand in the way of that investigation."[5]

On CNN, Jeffrey Toobin dismissed Trump's declaration that he was not under investigation as "goofy," saying it proved the opposite: "It just shows that he knows he's under investigation." He also said, with fresh originality: "It's not normal."[6]

An hour later, on the same network, Toobin said, "Never in history have we had an FBI director fired by a president who was under investigation by the FBI."[7]

Strangest of all was MSNBC's Chris Matthews. Even after hearing his own news reporter, Pete Williams, clearly state that "the FBI told [Trump] three times he was not under investigation," the *Hardball* host said of the Comey firing: "He's under investigation. He fires the investigator."[8]

All this had the effect of creating the impression that the president was firing the man who was investigating him. And who had created that impression? That's right: James Comey. Bitter about his firing, he had no reason to correct his own insinuation that the FBI was hot on Trump's trail.

On the bright side, Comey's firing led to one of *The New York Times*' most precious editorials—an "open letter" to deputy attorney general Rod Rosenstein:

> Dear Deputy Attorney General Rod Rosenstein:
>
> It's rare that any single person has to bear as much responsibility for safeguarding American democracy as you find yourself carrying now. Even before President Trump's shocking decision on Tuesday to fire the F.B.I. director, James Comey, a dark cloud of suspicion surrounded this president, and the very integrity of the electoral process that put him in office.

At this fraught moment you find yourself, improbably, to be the person with the most authority to dispel that cloud and restore Americans' confidence in their government. We sympathize; that's a lot of pressure.

The media can get an independent counsel on anyone if all it takes is a "dark cloud of suspicion." In fact, the *Times*' specialty is creating "dark clouds of suspicion." In this case, they had the FBI leadership as partners in the creating dark clouds of suspicion business.

When accused felonious leaker Andrew McCabe, then acting director of the FBI, testified to Congress two days after Comey was fired, he continued the defamation by innuendo, calling the Russia investigation "highly significant" and refusing to confirm Trump's claim that Comey told him he was not under investigation. "I will not comment," he said. He also agreed with a senator's point that an innocent man doesn't "typically need to be reassured that they're not the subject of an investigation."[9]

Adding fuel to the fire, the day of McCabe's testimony, Trump gassed on to Lester Holt that it was *his* decision to fire Comey.

To remind everyone of whom we're talking about, this is a man who has bragged:

"I'm the biggest developer in New York by far. There's nobody even close."

"Nobody has ever had crowds like Trump has had."

"My IQ is one of the highest."

"Nobody in the history of this country has known so much about infrastructure as Donald Trump."

"The best taco bowls are made in Trump Tower Grill."

"Nobody loves the Bible more than I do."

"I write a book called *The Art of the Deal*, the number-one-selling business book of all time."

"There's nobody who's done so much for equality as I have."

"I have the best words."

"There is nobody more conservative than me."

"We have, by far, the highest IQ of any cabinet ever."

"There is no one who respects women more than I do."

"Never has there been a president, with few exceptions . . . who's passed more legislation, who's done more things than what we've done."

"I can be more presidential than any president that's ever held this office."

"Enemies of mine are saying it was the greatest speech ever made on foreign soil by a president."

(I know the Resistance is aware of these quotes because they're the ones obsessively compiling them.)[10]

What were the odds that Trump was going to go on national TV and admit that he had submissively accepted the recommendation of some petty little Bureaucrat on a major personnel change? Trump would admit to shooting JFK if he thought it would make him sound cool. *People are telling me—good people, great people—I am the best shot.*

But inasmuch as Trump had just gone through a huge production of accepting Rosenstein's recommendation that he fire Comey, his boastful impulse was not the exact thing that was needed at that moment. The media insist that Trump *admitted* to NBC's Holt that he had fired the FBI director because of the Russia investigation. In fact, by my count, Trump gave about half a dozen reasons. The main point was that it was *his* decision.

Among Trump's reasons:

1. Comey was a "showboat. He's a grandstander."
2. The FBI "was in virtual turmoil—less than a year ago. It hasn't recovered from that."
3. Rosenstein was "highly respected. Very good guy . . . [and] he had made a recommendation."
4. "I just want somebody that's competent."
5. "He's the wrong man for that position."

Trump also said that he might expand the Russia investigation, but he just wanted it done right.[11] It didn't matter. "Russia" was all anyone in the Resistance heard. Reporters rushed to Wikipedia to look up "Saturday Night Massacre." I'll save you the trouble: President Nixon—whose White House really *was* under investigation—ordered his attorney general and then his deputy attorney general to fire the independent counsel investigating him, and they both resigned instead. More on this in the next chapter, for the utter illiterates in our media.

Nixon would be a great analogy—if Trump were under investigation, which he was not. But no one knew that yet, because Comey refused to say so.

On May 17, 2017, one week after the director's firing, Robert Mueller was appointed independent counsel. Again: At this point, the American people still thought the FBI was investigating Trump. It would be another month before we found out that that was not true.

Irritated by the media's continued insistence that he was the target of a criminal inquiry, the next day Trump tweeted: "James

Comey better hope that there are no 'tapes' of our conversations before he starts leaking to the press!" The media were indignant that Trump would produce proof of something that they were wildly speculating about. Why, oh why, couldn't they make their reckless accusations in peace?

Thanks to that tweet, a few weeks later, on June 8, Comey *finally* told the public the truth: the president wasn't under investigation.

> **Senator James Risch (R-ID):** I gather from all this that you're willing to say now that, while you were director, the president of the United States was not under investigation. Is that a fair statement?
>
> **Comey:** That's correct.[12]

Was that so hard?

Specifically regarding the "obstruction of justice" accusations, Senator Susan Collins asked the director:

> And was the president under investigation at the time of your dismissal on May 9?
>
> **Comey:** No.

The president had not fired the man who was investigating him after all. Please disregard the media's previous month of frenzied comparisons to Nixon and demands for impeachment hearings.

In addition to finally telling the truth about Trump's not being under investigation, the bulk of Comey's opening statement at the June 8 hearing consisted of his descriptions of Trump's badgering him to tell the public that he wasn't under investigation. Trump, he said, called it "a cloud" that was "impairing his ability to act on behalf of the country." The president "repeatedly" told him, 'We need to get that fact out.'"

Normal people: WOW! He really wasn't under investigation! Anybody would be frustrated by that!

The media: This just shows how self-obsessed Trump is.

CNN, June 7, 2017:

Ryan Lizza: I think one thing that the testimony shows is that Trump was obsessed with himself. Is he under investigation and why wouldn't Comey go out and say that he wasn't? That seems to be a major factor leading up to the firing, if you read the testimony . . .

Wolf Blitzer: He was really concerned.[13]

A year later, when Rudy Giuliani stated the obvious—that Trump fired Comey primarily because the director refused to say the president wasn't under investigation—everyone acted as if this was a wacky alibi dreamed up after the fact by a team of high-priced lawyers.

It was "odd," Chris Cillizza wrote in *The Washington Post*.[14] *Slate* magazine's William Saletan exulted: "That's not what Trump said" when he called Comey a "showboat"![15] *The Washington Post*'s Amber Phillips said that Giuliani's "admission" made Republicans "look, well, a little foolish"—because they "publicly took Trump at his word that the firing was about something else."[16]

You can't win with these lunatics. When Trump says he's not under investigation: *He's lying! We need an independent counsel.* When Comey admits Trump wasn't under investigation: *Trump is self-obsessed for wanting people to know that.* When Trump says he fired Comey because the director refused to tell the public he wasn't under investigation: *TOO LATE! You called him a showboat!*

It's heads, they win; tails, Trump loses.

Unfortunately, by the time Comey finally announced that Trump wasn't under investigation, Mueller had already been appointed. And why was he appointed, again? I forget. *He was appointed because of the false impression intentionally created by James Comey that the president was under investigation.*

CHAPTER ELEVEN

A Tale of Two Dicks

Still bitter over Bill Clinton's impeachment, journalists lift phrases from the Monica Lewinsky scandal and claim that Trump is doing the *exact same thing*—only worse. They'd say Trump is worse than Nixon, but *nothing* could be worse than Nixon. Liberal hatred of Nixon is out of all proportion to the crime. Our side doesn't care anymore, but their side is still lining up every Saturday outside the National Archives, in College Park, Maryland, to listen to the Nixon tapes. Please. It's 2018. Join Match. Do some gardening. Call your mother. Something.

Reporters seem to recall nothing about Clinton's impeachment and Nixon's near impeachment, other than the words "obstruction of justice." They act as if everything Trump does is "obstruction" and then, in a Perry Mason moment, point out that CLINTON WAS IMPEACHED FOR OBSTRUCTION OF JUSTICE!

I think we're done here.

MSNBC'S Chris Hayes gleefully presented a clip of attorney general Jeff Sessions saying about Clinton, "No one is above the law, even the president."

No sh*t, Sherlock. But Hayes acted as if he were holding a signed confession: "That was Senator Jeff Sessions in 1999, talking about possible obstruction of justice by President Bill Clinton. He was unequivocal. So, if we reach a place in which a sitting president is found to have committed obstruction of justice or another crime, just remember where Jeff Sessions stands."[1]

Yes, and "if we reach a place" where Chris Hayes is found to have committed obstruction of justice, I think I know exactly where Jeff Sessions stands! Unfortunately, there's no more evidence that Trump obstructed justice than that Hayes did.

MSNBC's Rachel Maddow led off her show by portentously announcing: "Famously, the first article of impeachment against Richard Nixon was about obstruction of justice. The first article of impeachment against Bill Clinton was obstruction of justice. So one thing that's very important about obstruction is that it's illegal. You can get caught for it. You can get impeached for it."[2]

If Trump ever commits obstruction of justice, no one at MSNBC is going to get caught sleeping.

Clinton and Nixon were accused of crimes that fall under the rubric of "obstruction," but there are specific elements to those crimes. Obstruction isn't just a hunch of *The New York Times*' editorial board. Thus, for example, Clinton was impeached for perjury and subornation of perjury, proved by tape recordings of the woman whose perjury he suborned, and DNA evidence proving his own. Nixon wasn't impeached at all; he resigned. (And if he had been impeached, the main article against him would have been "Exposing Alger Hiss as a Soviet spy in 1948.")

Liberals think that because they find Trump distasteful, anything he does must be "obstruction of justice." Election night was traumatic enough. For Trump to have the audacity to exercise the powers of the president is a bridge too far. It's like saying that because 100,000 pussy-hat-wearing women claim that Trump "terrifies" them, then—QED—Trump is a "terrorist." No. There has to be an actual crime. No one gets charged with obstruction except by interfering with the investigation of a civil or criminal offense—otherwise nothing has been obstructed. It would be hard enough to prove that Trump obstructed justice by exercising his constitutional powers if he had been under investigation. But he wasn't.

It used to be Trump out there alone claiming he was not being investigated. But ever since the public found out about the FBI siccing spies—I mean "confidential informants"—on the Trump campaign, it's the FBI wildly backpedaling, insisting that not only was Trump personally not under investigation, but neither was his campaign. It was a counterespionage investigation! They were protecting the Trump campaign!

In any event, he's allowed to be president.

The constitutional result of that very, very bad election night is that Trump has authority to fire any political appointee he wants, for any reason at all. He can have multiple reasons—or no reason. He can fire his employees for incompetence, insubordination—or because if he doesn't like the cut of their suits. The president can certainly fire an FBI director who—to take an utterly random, made-up example off the top of my head—repeatedly and falsely insinuates that the president himself is under investigation. He'd be an idiot not to fire that guy.

A president can even shut down a probe. He might believe that a particular inquiry is a waste of time or resources, or that more important matters need investigating. In the '90s, for example, while al-Qaeda was furiously planning the 9/11 attack, President Clinton directed his FBI to throw enormous resources into tracking possible abortion clinic bombers.[3] That decision may have cost thousands of Americans their lives. And it was the president's to make.

It wouldn't be unreasonable for Trump to decide that the FBI's time could be more wisely spent investigating psychotics like Nikolas Cruz, the Parkland school shooter, or Omar Mateen, the Pulse nightclub shooter, than to continue working up Peter Strzok's "insurance policy" against the Trump presidency. A lot of people with dead kids dearly wish FBI agents had shown a little more interest in running down the leads they got on those guys, rather than doing oppo research for the Clinton campaign.

What a president cannot do is interfere with an investigation by saying to his secretary, a potential grand jury witness, "I was never alone with Monica, right?" knowing full well that they both knew that he was, and that it was relevant evidence in a lawsuit against him. He cannot instruct a former intern to lie in an affidavit. He cannot ask the CIA to tell the FBI not to investigate the Watergate break-in for national security reasons, when the real reason was that it might expose the president's connection to the burglars.

An otherwise lawful act can be obstruction, but only if done to thwart the administration of justice. If Trump realized that Jared Kushner was ruining his presidency and shot him, and then he fired the U.S. attorney investigating the crime, *that* would be a textbook case of obstruction of justice, even though the president has the right to fire U.S. attorneys. If he offered to pardon witnesses in exchange for their agreement to lie and blame Steve Bannon for shooting Kushner—again: excellent example of obstruction of justice, even though the president has the power to pardon.

But Trump hasn't shot Kushner, and he probably won't, since he doesn't even realize that Kushner is wrecking his presidency.

Unless he has a corrupt purpose, the president is allowed to do his job. It is not obstruction to interfere with the liberal sport of annoying the president.

Journalists simply assume that Trump colluded with Russia, and therefore firing Comey was his attempt to prevent anyone from finding out. On CNN, legal analyst Jeffrey Toobin claimed that Trump's statement to NBC's Lester Holt that he fired Comey because "this Russia thing with Trump and Russia is a made-up story" constituted "very substantial evidence of obstruction of justice." (He helpfully added that "obstruction of justice is a crime that has often been associated with presidential scandals, whether it's Richard Nixon or Bill Clinton."[4] Wow, what a scoop!)

Media analysis in the Trump era consists of liberal daydreams foisted on the public. *What if Trump robbed a bank? Then we could impeach him?*

On MSNBC's *MTP Daily,* Nick Confessore, of *The New York Times,* mocked conservatives for their defense of Trump as compared with Bill Clinton, smirking, "Look, I think it's obvious that lying about a consensual affair in the White House is a lot worse than lying about colluding with a foreign adversary."[5]

While it's great to see a *New York Times* reporter adopting the Larry Flynt standard on sexual harassment, Clinton's hilarious crime of "lying about a consensual affair" was considered so destructive to our legal system that, for the first time in history, all nine Supreme Court justices boycotted his next State of the Union address—even the justices Clinton had appointed.

You know what would be even funnier? If Confessore had said, "Lying about a consensual affair is a lot worse than lying about MURDER!" The problem is, Trump hasn't committed murder. He also hasn't "collud[ed] with a foreign adversary"—whatever crimes that phrase is supposed to encompass.

At this point—after two years of the best minds in law and journalism determinedly searching for evidence of Russian collusion—the Resistance has a better chance of getting Trump on murder. That's an accusation that hasn't already been thoroughly investigated, and produced goose eggs.

AT LEAST THEY'RE FINALLY ADMITTING CLINTON WAS A CROOK

To defend Mueller's continued employment despite the noticeable absence of any Russian collusion, the Resistance claims that independent counsel Ken Starr was asked to investigate Whitewater—a "failed land deal"—and then, for no reason whatsoever, veered off into Clinton's sex life. With no one allowed on their airwaves to contradict them, journalists have created a fantasy version of Clinton's impeachment.

> **MSNBC's Chris Hayes:** Ken Starr started on a land deal in Arkansas, and he ended up with a White House intern which, to me, illustrates the way these things can kind of mushroom.[6]

> **CNN's Don Lemon:** [The investigation of Bill Clinton] started with Whitewater, ended up with Monica Lewinsky.[7]

> **CNN's John Berman:** Look, President Clinton was impeached for things that were not about Whitewater originally.[8]

> **MSNBC's Lawrence O'Donnell:** We ended up with Monica Lewinsky and a perjury charge and all sorts of testimony about sex because that stuff arose, as it were, while Kenneth Starr was investigating completely unrelated matters.[9]

Just in case anyone had missed this important point, six months later, *The New York Times*' Bret Stephens thought the dead horse still needed some beating, saying on MSNBC, "People on the right say, 'This has nothing to do with the Russia collusion story, allegations of collusion with Russia . . . Bob Mueller is on a fishing expedition'—I would remind these same people that Monica Lewinsky had nothing to do with Ken Starr's original agreement and these are the same people who went for Bill Clinton and in fact impeached him in 1998."[10]

Touché, Mr. Stephens!

What we have here is the problem of surrounding yourself with fellow zealots. There's no one in the room to tell you when you're full of sh*t.

Ken Starr didn't just lurch off into a probe of Clinton's sex life when he was supposed to be working on Whitewater. By the time the attorney general requested an independent counsel for the Lewinsky scandal, the president had committed at least a half-dozen felonies in office. The following day, he would commit dozens more.

Paula Jones's private lawsuit against the president and Starr's investigation of the Clintons' Arkansas cronies proceeded along completely separate trajectories for three years. As Starr was racking up convictions against the Clintons' business partners and associates—for actual, pre-existing crimes, not process crimes, like "lying to investigators"—Jones's lawsuit was being tied up in court with Clinton's frivolous appeals.

Under our new Trump-era theories of criminal law, Clinton's attempt to block Jones's lawsuit by appealing her case to the Supreme Court would constitute "obstruction of justice." His legal argument was utterly specious—as the Supreme Court ruled, 9–0. But appealing a case, even on absurd legal grounds, is not obstruction. Clinton had a right to appeal, just as President Trump has a right to fire anyone who works for him or shut down any investigation he thinks is a waste of time.

Eventually, Clinton lost his dilatory appeals and Jones's lawyers began collecting evidence. This involved taking the testimony of other women Clinton had lewdly propositioned on the job, to the extent that that many women could be rounded up and questioned before Clinton's term expired. The existence of other female victims was crucial evidence in Jones's case, in order to prove intent, a pattern or practice, or absence of mistake. *I didn't intend to expose myself to Miss Jones—my pants just dropped!*

You can say, as Harvey Weinstein, Larry Flynt, and Nick Confessore do, that there should be no legal prohibition on powerful men using female underlings as sex toys. But if we're going to have laws, people need to be able to collect evidence to prove their cases, and what Clinton did to Jones was against the law. Indeed, Jones's lawsuit was based on the statute liberals consider more sacrosanct than any other passed in the twentieth century: the 1964 Civil Rights Act. That law prohibits discrimination on the basis of sex, including sexual harassment.

There is no point in having laws if people feel free to perjure themselves, hide evidence, and suborn the perjury of others. Go ahead: dump toxic chemicals in a lake, steal money from your investors, refuse to hire black people. If you get caught, you can just lie about it under oath!

That's what Clinton decided to do, opting to prevent Jones from collecting relevant evidence by perjuring himself and suborning the perjury of women he had molested.

As soon as Lewinsky's name appeared on Jones's witness list on December 5, 1997, Clinton began a frantic campaign to ensure that she would not tell Jones's lawyers the truth. He coached her on what lies to put in her affidavit. He had his secretary pick up gifts he'd given her, to prevent them from being subpoenaed by Jones's attorneys. He helped arrange a lawyer for her. He asked his powerful friends to get her a job in New York City, resulting in interviews at MacAndrews & Forbes, Burson-Marsteller, American Express, and—the job she accepted—Revlon. Why, it was almost

as if justice itself were being—what's the word I'm looking for?—
OBSTRUCTED!

The president himself aggressively, unmistakably committed
perjury. Asked in an interrogatory to name every state and federal
employee he'd propositioned since 1986, Clinton answered, "None."[11]

That's already about half a dozen felonies the president had
committed before Ken Starr had ever heard the name Monica Lewinsky. Or, as Clinton later described that sequence of events, he was
"defending the Constitution!"

Starr found out about Clinton's obstruction of justice on January 12, 1998, when Linda Tripp showed up in his office with tapes
of Lewinsky discussing her agreement with the president to commit perjury in Jones's case. Starr investigated, got a clean wiretap
on Lewinsky, and, two days later, presented the tapes to the attorney general, Janet Reno.[12]

The shock of the president's flagrantly suborning perjury in a
private citizen's civil rights lawsuit against him was so great that
even *The New York Times* briefly suspended its denunciations of
the "far right" to editorialize, "It is not the legality of anyone's sexual behavior that is at issue here. The legal questions before Mr.
Starr are obstruction of justice, perjury and suborning of perjury."
If the charges were true, the *Times* said, Clinton's presidency "will
be thrown into a disabling political crisis."[13]

Reno could have requested a new independent counsel. She
was asking for a new special counsel investigation, one way or
another. As NPR reported, "it was pretty clear that they were fac-
ing a crisis."[14] Starr's office was already up and running. *The New
York Times* reported that Reno took the case "seriously enough to
deliberate only 24 hours" before asking a court to expand Starr's
mandate to include Clinton's obstruction of justice in the Jones
case.[15] A Justice Department official told *The Washington Post,* "It

was really a situation where people were floored." Reno made her decision "right away."[16]

Starr was later excoriated for having requested the expanded mandate, rather than, one surmises, handing it off to DOJ lawyers and saying, *It's your problem, I'm going back to Pepperdine Law School.* Perhaps his reasoning was the same as Reno's.

Unbeknownst to anyone, including the president, Starr's mandate was expanded on January 16, 1998. The next day, January 17, 1998, Jones's lawyers took Clinton's deposition, where he proceeded to commit scores and scores more felonies.

E.g.:

Q: At any time were you and Monica Lewinsky alone together in the Oval Office?

A: I don't recall.

Q: At any time have you and Monica Lewinsky ever been alone together in any room in the White House?

A: I have no specific recollection.

Q: If she told someone that she had a sexual affair with you beginning in November of 1995, would that be a lie?

A: It's certainly not the truth. It would not be the truth.[17]

It's not perjury to say under oath that you don't recall something—if you don't recall it. It *is* perjury to claim to have "no specific recollection" of ever being alone with someone who repeatedly performed oral sex on you, whom you sodomized with a cigar on Easter Sunday, and who serviced you as you chatted on the phone with congressmen about sending troops into battle.[18]

Clinton, you will recall from a few paragraphs back, had induced

Lewinsky's perjury, by direct request, as well as with gifts, private meetings, and job offers from bigwig Democrats.

Clinton deposition:

Q: Have you ever talked to Monica Lewinsky about the possibility that she might be asked to testify in this lawsuit?

A: I'm not sure . . . [19]

These perjuries were committed in a case having nothing to do with the independent counsel's investigation—it wasn't "lying to investigators." None were legitimate functions of the president. They were serious crimes—serious enough for the entire Supreme Court to sit out the president's next State of the Union address.

That's not the same as Mueller's realizing there's nothing to the Russian collusion story and then deciding to set off into an investigation of Trump's business affairs.

IT'S JUST LIKE THE SATURDAY NIGHT MASSACRE!

After Trump fired his FBI director, James Comey, the air rang with comparisons to the Saturday Night Massacre, in which President Nixon fired special prosecutor Archibald Cox, who was investigating the Watergate burglars, and also effectively fired his attorney general and deputy attorney general for refusing to fire Cox.

The New York Times editorialized about the "obvious historical parallel" to the Saturday Night Massacre, concluding that "the country has reached an even more perilous moment."[20] There were "Echoes of Watergate" and "Flashbacks" to the Saturday Night Massacre.[21]

The Washington Post's Dana Milbank referred to the "obvious comparisons" to the Saturday Night Massacre, in an editorial titled "Trump, Like Nixon, Will Fail."[22] On MSNBC, wise man Tom Brokaw stepped in to say, "The one thing I learned during Watergate: Everybody take a deep breath." The Saturday Night Massacre recollections poured out in such profusion that the Richard Nixon Presidential Library and Museum tweeted: "FUN FACT: President Nixon never fired the Director of the FBI."[23]

Within twenty-four hours of Comey's firing, Nexis records more than two hundred comparisons to the Saturday Night Massacre. That's not including words like "Nixonian" or "Watergate."[24]

One rather important difference is: Archibald Cox was investigating actual crimes tied to the president's staff, not wishful thinking about ex–campaign aide Carter Page being Trump's secret conduit to Putin.

Let's review the events that led to Cox's appointment as special counsel to investigate the Nixon White House.

The night of the Watergate break-in, June 17, 1973, police discovered that one of the burglars had the phone number of Nixon aide Howard Hunt in his address book. The day after the break-in, Hunt's White House office was searched by the FBI.

Six weeks later, on August 1, 1973, investigators found a cashier's check for $25,000 in one the burglars' bank accounts, made out to "the Committee to Re-elect the President"—or CREEP, as it was derogatorily known. By the end of January 1974, the burglars, Hunt, and G. Gordon Liddy, finance chairman of CREEP, had all been convicted or had pleaded guilty to criminal offenses—actual crimes like burglary and wiretapping, not lying to investigators or registering under the wrong lobbying law.

In March, one of the burglars, James McCord, wrote a letter to the judge from prison, informing him that, contrary to press speculation, the break-in was not a CIA operation, but that "others involved in the Watergate operation were not identified during the trial."[25]

Around this same time, FBI director L. Patrick Gray told a Senate committee that White House counsel John Dean had "probably " lied to FBI agents when he said he didn't know if Hunt had an office at the White House. (That was a good guess, in light of the fact that Dean had overseen the search of Hunt's office the day after the break-in.)[26] The following month, Gray admitted that, soon after the break-in, he had destroyed documents from Hunt's White House safe at the request of Dean, who told him they were "political dynamite" and "should never see the light of day."[27]

Dean began cooperating with Senate investigators, at which point the president accepted resignations from his chief of staff, two White House counsels, and his attorney general.

As historian Paul Johnson has said, wiretapping political opponents had a long and distinguished history. Presidents Franklin D. Roosevelt, Lyndon B. Johnson, and John F. Kennedy deployed wiretaps, dawn raids, and IRS audits against their political enemies, as well as members of the press.[28] But Republican presidents can't do what Democrats can. The Watergate break-in may have been standard political fare, but these were *Nixon's* people, and they got caught.[29]

Within eight months of the break-in, seven men with close connections to the Nixon White House had been convicted of espionage crimes against the opposing party in a presidential campaign. One of them had his own office at the White House, and one had been the finance chairman of the president's reelection committee. Top administration officials resigned en masse, and John Dean, the White House counsel who had ordered documents destroyed, was cooperating to save his own skin.

It was only then that a special counsel was appointed to investigate the Watergate break-in and its connection to the White House. By contrast, the decision to assign a special counsel to Trump was made sometime around midnight, November 8, 2016.

To be anywhere in the ballpark of Watergate, we would need something like the following:

1. In the summer of 2016, five Russians are caught red-handed by security guards breaking into Democratic headquarters to steal e-mails. When the Russians are patted down, the police find that one of them has Steve Bannon's Trump Tower phone number on him.

2. The FBI finds checks from Sheldon Adelson made out to the "Trump for President" PAC, deposited into the Russian hackers' bank accounts.

3. The five Russians, Bannon, and Adelson plead guilty or are convicted of breaking into the DNC to hack e-mails.

4. FBI director James Comey testifies that Jared Kushner gave him documents from Bannon's safe and told him to destroy them, saying they were "political dynamite."

5. One of the Russians writes to the judge from prison to say that "others" were involved in the DNC e-mail hack.

6. Three of Trump's closest White House aides resign on the same day. (We have to pretend this would be something unusual in the Trump White House.)

7. Kushner begins cooperating with congressional investigators.

ONLY AT THAT POINT is Mueller appointed special counsel.

So Trump's firing of his FBI director was just like Watergate in the sense that the president fired someone.

CHAPTER TWELVE

Mueller's the Russian!

If liberals are looking for Soviet-style corruption of American democracy, they couldn't do better than the office of Robert S. Mueller. The special counsel is our leading import from Russia. The very nature of Mueller's probe is Soviet justice. He has an open-ended commission to look for any crimes committed by anyone connected to the Trump campaign.

When Trump vowed during the campaign to reopen the investigation into Hillary's handling of her state department e-mails, the air crackled with phrases like "banana republic" and "tin-pot dictator." Bringing criminal charges would be in clear violation of the well-established law that the Clintons are immune from prosecution!

This exchange at the second presidential debate in October 2016 nearly sent the governing class after Trump with a butterfly net:

Clinton: You know, it is—it's just awfully good that someone with the temperament of Donald Trump is not in charge of the law in our country.

Trump: Because you'd be in jail.

President George W. Bush's attorney general, Michael Mukasey, told *The Washington Post*, "Putting political opponents in jail for offenses committed in a political setting, even if they are criminal offenses—and they very well may be—is something that we don't do here." Obama's attorney general, Eric H. Holder Jr., tweeted, "In the USA we do not threaten to jail political opponents." Bush's secretary of homeland security, Michael Chertoff, told *The New York Times* that Trump's remark "smacks of what we read about tin-pot dictators in other parts of the world, where when they win an election their first move is to imprison opponents."[1]

Trump wasn't threatening to prosecute Hillary because she was his political opponent! He was talking about reopening an FBI investigation into actual crimes—an investigation that the Office of the Inspector General later found had been led by agents wildly rooting for Hillary's campaign. What if she robbed a bank? Would the fact that she ran for president immunize her from prosecution?

Everything these hysterics falsely accused Trump of proposing is exactly what federal law enforcement has done to him: Trying to put him in jail simply for being Hillary's political opponent.

With no evidence of a crime, deputy attorney general Rod Rosenstein appointed Mueller special counsel, giving him limitless authority to search for some criminal or administrative offense committed by Trump or anyone associated with him.

A special counsel with a roving mandate to investigate Trump is thwarting the will of the people, robbing him of a critical window to get things done. It's said so often that it's a cliché: presidents have a one-year honeymoon to accomplish anything. After that, they're mere administrators. Trump never got the "honeymoon" part. Imagine how useless his post-honeymoon will be with a limitless investigation into everyone around him.

Mueller is running a star chamber, answerable to no one,

furiously charging Trump associates with crimes that have nothing to do with Russian interference in our election and even less to do with right and wrong. When the entire apparatus of the government, with a limitless checkbook, is against you, you're probably pleading guilty to something. In the real world, you might get some maniacal super-rich guy determined to destroy you. But the government can really do it.

That's how we ended up with dozens of completely innocent day care operators rotting in prison in the 1980s and '90s, convicted of committing nonexistent crimes. Interestingly, almost all of the phony childcare sex abuse cases were brought by grandstanding liberal prosecutors—Janet Reno (Grant Snowden), Ira Reiner (McMartin preschool), and Scott Harshbarger (the Amirault family). Show-off prosecutors, thinking only about their own political futures, are never going to say, *Yeah, I was wrong about that one and ruined someone's life. The guy turned out to be completely innocent.* Fortunately, most prosecutors have real crimes to investigate and are not out charging innocent people based on the neurotic fantasies of liberal women. But an independent counsel doesn't have anything else to do but obsessively fixate on one man.

Looking at Mueller's indictments so far, it would appear that his assignment was to search the *Federal Register* and enforce every technical violation he can find. It's like a law school exam, where you try to tick off as many legal issues as possible in a short time frame. Except Mueller has no time limit. If you parachute in fifteen prosecutors to examine a specific person, they are going to find the elements of *some* crime. How far down the road to a banana republic do we want to go?

There are tens of thousands of federal crimes on the books— no one knows how many, despite periodic attempts to count them. Every year, Congress adds about sixty new crimes to the *Federal*

*Register.*² Attorney Harvey Silverglate's book *Three Felonies a Day* argues that the ordinary law-abiding citizen could be innocently committing—as the title suggests—three felonies a day. There's a Twitter page, @CrimeADay, that simply tweets federal criminal laws you might be inadvertently breaking—though inadvertence will be no excuse if Mueller ever comes after you.

Among them:

> @CrimeADay–Feb 26
> 43 USC §1733, 50 CFR §§100.27(b)(6) & 100.8 make it a federal crime to use a fish wheel on public lands in Alaska to catch fish for subsistence use if you don't legibly write your first initial, last name, and address on the side of your fish wheel that faces midstream.

> @CrimeADay–Feb 24
> 49 USC §5124, 49 CFR §173.54(i) make it a federal crime to transport a toy torpedo bigger than 23mm in diameter.

> @CrimeADay–Feb 22
> 21 USC §§331, 352 & 21 CFR §801.430(e), (g) and (h) make it a federal crime to sell tampons without saying how absorbent they are, unless they are vending machine tampons.

The tampon law is more threatening to the public welfare than the ones Mueller has won any convictions on.

While the media wildly speculate about the raft of criminal charges Mueller might bring, nothing of any importance ever happens. We just keep hearing: *The noose is tightening!* At a certain point, it has to be tightened.

Maybe—as "legal analysts" say 1,700 times a night on cable

TV—Mueller is starting with small fish and working his way up to something HUGE. Maybe he's getting witnesses to "flip" and tell him all about Trump's secret meetings with Vladimir Putin. Maybe all these petty little indictments for "lying to investigators" will eventually add up to a real crime. *See, you start with the little fish* . . . Maybe it will even have something to do with Russia!

But no one knows that. These are liberal dream sequences. What's known is: we have indictments and plea bargains on the sorts of crimes ridiculed in *Three Felonies a Day*. Everything else is the product of hardworking journalists' imaginations.

WANT US TO KEEP CALLING YOU "HONORABLE"?

Hope breathes eternal in the liberal heart. *Mueller is still investigating!* they keep telling us. That's true, but, as long as we don't know what Mueller is doing, can we stop talking about how honorable he is? People who had never heard of him until ten minutes ago assure us that he is hardworking, honest, meticulous, a pillar of integrity, great dancer—makes his own clothes!

If we don't know what he's doing, how do we know he's doing a good job?

We're told that we can't say there's no Russian collusion, because we don't know what Mueller has found yet. But whatever he's doing, he's doing a heckuva good job!

For all we know, Mueller is like Jack Nicholson in *The Shining*, maniacally typing, "All work and no play makes Trump a dull boy."

The only thing we can truly be sure of is that there is not the remotest possibility that Mueller will conclude his investigation by announcing: TRUMP IS IN THE CLEAR! However honorable he is, Mueller knows that if he doesn't get Trump on something, he'll wish he'd never been born. Rachel Maddow will call for a FISA warrant on him. Mueller's best play is to get himself fired, so he can be a Resistance Hero like James Comey.

Ken Starr is the only independent counsel in U.S. history whose investigation caught a president dead to rights committing felonies in office. They were serious crimes, too, like perjury and subornation of perjury, proved by DNA evidence and an FBI wiretap.

The usual track record of independent counsels is not so impressive. Their main job is to be political hit men against Republican administrations, to the delight of the press.

There was lunatic Patrick Fitzgerald, who knew that no crime had been committed about five minutes after he was sworn in, but instead of quitting and going back to Chicago, he decided to stick around and put a bunch of people under oath. Eventually, he charged Scooter Libby with perjury for remembering a conversation differently than *Time* magazine's Matt Cooper remembered it. Fittingly, Fitzgerald is now James Comey's lawyer.

Perhaps the most notorious special counsel was Lawrence Walsh, who investigated "Iran-Contra" for five years, then dropped an indictment of former defense secretary Caspar Weinberger, implicating the sitting president, *four days before a presidential election*. Bush lost his reelection, and two months later the indictment was dismissed.[3]

Robert Mueller may be as pure as driven snow. But before his sainthood is confirmed, let's look at the full record. Even the Catholic Church has a devil's advocate.

The Americans falsely accused by Mueller's FBI probably don't think the special counsel is all *that* honorable. He was director for the Bureau's two most famous screw-ups since Richard Jewell, the innocent man falsely accused by the FBI of committing the 1996 bombing of Centennial Olympic Park, in Atlanta. Steven Hatfill and the late Senator Ted Stevens were both innocent men, relentlessly pursued by agents who refused to budge from an idée fixe about the men's guilt. Sounds familiar, no? DOJ lifers, like Mueller, Comey, and Rosenstein are swamp creatures. As the stories in the sidebar illustrate, they have lost sight of the whole innocent/guilty thing, and see themselves as some combination of St. George the dragonslayer and Moses the lawgiver. Both, you will recall, acted under direct divine guidance.

MUELLER'S CABIN FEVER!

Eight days before the 2008 election, the government convicted Senator Stevens of a crime. The longest-serving Republican in Senate history lost his reelection by less than 2 percent of the vote. Just like Mueller's indictments against Michael Flynn, Rick Gates, George Papadopoulos, and Alex van der Zwaan, Stevens was charged with lying—because they couldn't prove the actual crime of bribery, with no evidence of a quid pro quo.

The big case that absolutely had to be brought right before an election was that Stevens had failed to disclose on his Senate financial forms the "gift" of cut-rate renovations on his Alaska cabin. According to prosecutors, Stevens had paid $160,000 for renovations worth $250,000. On the other hand, independent appraisers valued the work at $125,000, which would mean Stevens had overpaid.

Months later—after the election—Obama's attorney general, Eric Holder, moved for a dismissal of all charges against Stevens, after discovering that the government had failed to turn over crucial exculpatory evidence.[4] When the trial judge, Emmet G. Sullivan, found out about the withheld evidence, he not only threw out the charges but angrily ordered an independent counsel to investigate the investigators.[5]

In addition to "honorable," another way of describing Mueller is: "too corrupt for Eric Holder."

Was Mueller aware of the Bureau's malicious pursuit of Stevens? Either he was, which would be bad, or he wasn't, which would be worse. He didn't notice that his agents were assembling a baseless criminal case against a sitting U.S. senator, on the eve of an election?

TIP OF THE HATFILL

In Steven Hatfill's case, we don't have to guess about Mueller's personal involvement. He was involved. It was Mueller who recruited the lead investigator, Richard Palmer, from the San Diego office and allowed him to monomaniacally pursue Hatfill to the exclusion of all other suspects—including the guy who did it. Mueller worked "in lockstep" with Palmer on the anthrax investigation, demanding constant briefings, according to a book on the case, *The Mirage Man* by David Willman.[6]

Following the FBI's utter failure to anticipate the 9/11 attack, the anthrax mailings a few weeks later were an opportunity for the FBI to shine. The anthrax had killed five people, sickened seventeen, and shut down large parts of the government. It was only the second biological attack on U.S. soil since immigrants with the Rajneeshee commune sickened 751 Oregonians in 1984.

Instead of proving themselves, Mueller's FBI spent six years hounding an innocent U.S. Army biodefense researcher. They searched Hatfill's home and his father's storage locker, brought in anthrax-sniffing dogs, followed him twenty-four hours a day, and trained surveillance cameras on his girlfriend's townhouse. If this had ever been done to Syed Rizwan Farook and

Tashfeen Malik in San Bernardino, we'd be having war crimes trials for FBI agents.

Hatfill was always an unlikely suspect. His specialty was viruses, not bacteria like anthrax. But the FBI had gotten a tip. Hatfill was a "flag-waving" patriot.[7] He fit the FBI's profile.

Nothing could shift Palmer's gaze from Hatfill.

As we have seen with Mueller's special counsel investigation, everything leaked. Almost immediately, Hatfill was publicly named as a suspect. When agents showed up to search his home, reporters were waiting for them, news helicopters whirling overhead. Agents complained to Mueller that the constant leaks showed bad faith toward a cooperating witness and requested an internal probe to find the leaker. But Mueller refused, saying it would be bad for "morale."[8]

No trace of anthrax was ever found anywhere near Hatfill. The only evidence against him came from bloodhounds brought in from California by Palmer. Their handler claimed the dogs went wild when they sniffed Hatfill. Hatfill says he petted the dogs and they liked him.

For both Mueller and then–deputy attorney general James Comey, the bloodhounds were the *"slam dunk"* proof that they had the right man. So let's look at the bloodhound evidence.

The bloodhounds also led the FBI to a pond a few miles from Hatfill's home. There, agents found a glove box that they believed could have been used for handling anthrax microbes.[9] The FBI proceeded to drain the pond, at a cost of nearly half a million dollars. No anthrax was found. The "anthrax box" turned out to be a makeshift turtle trap.[10]

A few years earlier, a man had been jailed for rape in California after one of the bloodhounds used in Hatfill's case led investigators directly to his front door. Four months later, the suspect was released when DNA evidence proved someone else had committed the rape. In another case, a California judge threw out a murder conviction based on the unreliability of the bloodhound evidence, saying the dog's handler was as "biased as any witness this court has ever seen."[11]

And yet, Director Mueller assured attorney general John Ashcroft and Senators Tom Daschle and Patrick Leahy that Hatfill was their man—staking his claim on the bloodhounds. Presciently, deputy defense secretary Paul Wolfowitz asked James Comey if he was sure Hatfill wasn't another Richard Jewell. Comey replied that he was "absolutely certain that it was Hatfill," citing the bloodhounds.[12]

Seven years after their pursuit of Hatfill had begun, in February 2008, federal judge Reggie B. Walton issued a scathing opinion, saying the government had not found "a scintilla of evidence" against Hatfill. A few months later, the government quietly settled with the researcher for $5.82 million. At long last, Mueller's FBI turned its attention to a more likely suspect, Bruce Ivins, a bacteriologist with a history of mental illness, who had much to gain by helping to develop an anthrax vaccine. As soon as agents began to focus on Ivins, he committed suicide.[13]

Far from apologizing, Mueller said of the Bureau's relentless pursuit of an innocent man, "I do not apologize for any aspect of this investigation." He said it would be incorrect "to say there were mistakes."[14]

Maybe he can get that line copyrighted for the Russia investigation.

IMPEACH OR DIE TRYING

In addition to "honorable," it is apparently part of Mueller's contract with the media that he must always be described as a "lifelong Republican." *You can check Wikipedia! It says so right there.* Oh, well, in that case, I take back everything I said. I had no idea Mueller was a "lifelong Republican." Why, he's just like dyed-in-the-wool conservatives Rick Wilson, Charlie Sykes, Richard Painter, Jennifer Rubin, David Brooks, and Steve Schmidt. They're so hardcore, they supported Christie Todd Whitman!

The media's "lifelong Republicans" typically must meet three requirements: (1) They are technically, in some sense, "Republicans," so the media aren't total liars; (2) They are willing to be nastier about Trump than any liberal would be; and (3) They are physically repulsive, to remind the audience: *This is the face of a typical Republican.* Either they look like the ticket counter guy at Allegheny Airlines in Cincinnati, or you think they should be petting a Persian cat and shouting "YOU HAVE FAILED ME, NO. 7!"

Long-serving Trump campaign spokesperson Hope Hicks could have handed Putin a suitcase full of money, with a written request that he hack our voting machines. The media couldn't have reported it. They do NOT want people looking at Hicks and thinking: "Trump voter."

If it matters that Mueller is a "lifelong Republican," then I guess it matters that he's hired a team of left-wing zealots. Of the seventeen lawyers in Mueller's office, fourteen are registered Democrats. Not one is a registered Republican. In total, they have donated more than $60,000 to Democratic candidates.[15]

At a December 2017 House hearing, Representative Steve Chabot named nine of Mueller's straight-shooting, unbiased staff attorneys:

First, Greg Andres gave $1,000 to the Democrat running to hold the seat—the Senate seat previously held by Barack Obama. He gave $2,600 to Democrat senator Gillibrand, who just this week led the charge of Democratic senators demanding that President Trump resign. And, yeah, Mr. Andres gave zero to the Trump campaign, or to any Republican, for that matter.

Next, again, in alphabetical order, Rush Atkinson. He donated to the Clinton campaign last year. Again, zero to the Trump campaign.

Third, Kyle Freeny contributed to both Obama campaigns and to Hillary Clinton's campaign; zero to the Trump campaign.

Next, Andrew Goldstein—he donated $3,300 to both Obama campaigns; again, zero to the Trump campaign.

Fifth, Elizabeth Prelogar, who clerked for liberal Supreme Court Justices Ginsberg and Kagan, contributed to both the Obama and Clinton campaigns, and zero to Trump.

Next, James Quarles—he's contributed to the Democratic presidential campaigns of Dukakis, Kerry, Obama and Hillary Clinton, and Gore as well. He did contribute to former congressman Chaffetz and Senator Allen, but he contributed over $20,000 to Democratic House and Senate candidates, and again, gave zero to Trump.

Seventh, Jeannie Rhee—she actually represented, as was previously mentioned, Hillary Clinton and the Clinton Foundation in several lawsuits. She's donated $16,000 to Democrats, contributed $5,400 to the Clinton campaign and zero to the Trump campaign.

Eighth, Brandon Van Grack contributed to ActBlue, the fund-raising outfit organized to elect Democratic congressional candidates, contributed to the Obama presidential campaign, and of course, gave nothing to Trump.

And, finally, Andrew Weissmann—he contributed $2,000 to the Democratic National Committee, $2,300 to the Obama campaign, $2,300 to the Clinton Campaign, and zero to Donald Trump. He's also the guy who praised the holdover acting attorney general, Sally Yates, for defying President Trump on the travel ban.[16]

The Resistance brushed off the conspicuous anti-Trump bias in Mueller's office with platitudes about how prosecutors are "allowed to have political opinions," as Jeffrey Toobin said on CNN. We were assured by deputy attorney general Rod Rosenstein that their "views are not in any way a factor in how they conduct themselves in office."[17]

Obviously, no one believes this, otherwise "lifelong Republican" wouldn't be spot-welded to Mueller's name.

But, more important, Mueller doesn't seem to appreciate that an independent counsel investigation isn't the kind of job where you want the hungriest prosecutors. You want DEA agents who are hungry to bust up drug cartels. You want organized-crime prosecutors who are hungry to take down the mob. You want your maid to be hungry to clean your house. But lawyers on a special counsel's investigation of the president aren't supposed to be hungry. They're supposed to be fair.

Inasmuch as Mueller's Russia investigation seems to be running out of steam, why not have him do crimes of government officials chronologically, one a year:

2018: Mueller investigates the Clinton Foundation, and Bill's million-dollar speeches preceding favorable action by the secretary of state, his wife.

2019: Mueller investigates the classified national security information that ended up on the computer of Anthony Weiner, convicted sex offender.

2020: Mueller pursues the criminal contempt resolution against Eric Holder, approved on a bipartisan House vote of 255–67 during the Fast and Furious investigation.

2021: Mueller investigates former IRS official Lois Lerner's political targeting of conservative groups.

2022: Mueller investigates Hillary Clinton for lying under oath about Benghazi, as well as her destruction of government e-mails in violation of 18 U.S.C. 2071.

2023: Mueller investigates the private meeting between Bill Clinton and Loretta Lynch when Bill's wife was under investigation.

The Russia investigation is going nowhere. After more than two years of obsessive searching by the nation's top investigative reporters and "as many as 100 FBI agents,"[18] no one associated with Trump's campaign has been charged with any crimes involving Russian collusion. It's impossible to prove a negative, but when two years of dedicated investigation by fanatics fails to produce evidence of a crime, we're getting pretty close to saying: Trump is 100 percent crime-free! Unless you count the gold fixtures. Which I do.

Instead of "firing" Mueller, how about simply recognizing that the job for which he was hired has ended? *Great, great job, Bob. I don't know what you've done, but thank you so much. You've done an incredible job.*

When you hire a nanny for your toddler and the toddler goes

off to Harvard, you're not "firing" the nanny. The purpose of her job is gone. When I get out of my Uber, I'm not "firing" the Uber driver. His task has been completed. I know we don't like to admit that government jobs are ever done, but even EPA cleanups eventually come to an end.

CHAPTER THIRTEEN

Bonfire of the Nonentities

It ought to be difficult to write a book about current affairs, since the news changes every day. But with the Resistance, it's actually surprisingly easy, because it's the same stories over and over and over again. You feel like a time traveler on an endless loop. Time passes, but it's always the same "breaking news." Liberals allow no one who disagrees with them to come on their networks, so there's never anyone on the panel to point out that they are building an enormous edifice, with balustrades, cupolas, and gables, on a faulty assumption. The networks can't find a single Trump supporter to put on their airwaves—and, to be fair, there were barely enough of us to elect him president.

It's wall-to-wall Trump haters, so the Resistance is free to create fantasy scenarios, until a fact appears contradicting their theory. Then they say: *TRUMP LIED TO US!* No, he didn't lie. You've been analyzing a story that existed only in your heads. Any sane person could have told you that at the time, but putting sane people on your shows would be a buzzkill for the viewers.

Not only is there, so far, zero evidence that the Russian government tried to meddle in our election to help Trump, but all the "collusion" parts of the story have collapsed spectacularly.

The basic problem the Russia conspiracy theorists keep running up against is that Trump didn't really have a campaign. Trump's game plan: Fly all over the country giving stem-winder speeches to ten-thousand-person crowds every day for eighteen months. You'd probably have to go back to the Johnson administration to find a president who spent less money getting to the White House. Trump's devious strategy was to propose ideas that were wildly popular. (Something about a wall?) How could Russia collude with an organization that didn't exist?

It would be harebrained enough to accuse Marco Rubio of collaborating with a foreign power to steal the election. But at least Rubio had a real campaign, with strategists, pollsters, and consultants. Trump didn't have any of those things and was annoyed when he was forced to start hiring them. He didn't even have a "campaign manager" in any traditional sense of the word. The "campaign" was Trump. He was his own counsel. The press might remember that: they endlessly mocked him for it.

That's why the media keep fixating on this or that campaign "adviser" as the secret Russian link, and then come back a week later admitting that the "adviser" never actually talked to Trump. Of all the contrived crimes, the idea that a nonexistent campaign plotted with the Russians has to be the most preposterous conspiracy Hillary has ever concocted. But that's the one she was pushing, so the Resistance complied.

Early on, the media settled on the key members of the Russian conspiracy. They were: Michael Flynn, Paul Manafort, Carter Page, Roger Stone, and Jeff Sessions. (The Resistance didn't discover poor George Papadopoulos until August 2017.) It was "odd," "strange," "bad judgment" that all these men had some connection to Russia.

In March 2017, that was all we heard. On CNN, for example, Representative Eric Swalwell said it was "just bad judgment that

you would have so many connections as Russia is attacking us"—
citing "Roger Stone, Paul Manafort, Carter Page, Michael Flynn."[1]
Representative Jim Himes explained at a committee hearing on
Russia, "The people around the President, Michael Flynn, Jeff Sessions, Rick Gates, Carter Page, Paul Manafort, have an odd connection to Russia."[2] MSNBC's Chris Hayes described the "widening
circle of associates of President Donald J. Trump" mixed up in the
Russian investigation—Michael Flynn, Roger Stone, Paul Manafort,
Carter Page, and Jeff Sessions.[3]

These were the hordes of people around Trump who had mys-
terious connections with Russia—except, oops, they didn't. The
so-called odd connections between the Trump campaign and the
Russians turned out not to be odd at all. On closer examination,
scratch the part about it being odd; that was not remotely true. In
fact, it was kind of the opposite of the truth. The Russian connections could more aptly be described as "drearily ordinary."

There were heated accusations against attorney general Jeff
Sessions, but this turned out to be another liberal brain aneu-
rism. The Resistance ended up having to pretend they'd never said
anything about the attorney general being a felon. The slanders of
Sessions were so spectacular, they'll get their own chapter. Papadopoulos got drunk and claimed to have secret inside information
about something known to every newspaper reader in the world.
He eventually pleaded guilty to lying to the FBI. We'll get to him in
another chapter, too. Periodically, longtime Trump friend Roger
Stone pops up as the mastermind of treasonous collusion with the
Red Menace, but Stone is practically begging to testify, dampening
the Democrats' enthusiasm.

That leaves Flynn, Manafort, Gates, and Page as the evil geniuses
of the Trump campaign's criminal collusion with Russia.

MICHAEL FLYNN, SECRET AGENT

Trump's short-lived national security adviser Michael Flynn was treated like Alger Hiss—assuming liberals had been upset about a Soviet spy sitting at FDR's elbow at Yalta, which they weren't. Flynn was investigated for a phone call with the Russian ambassador during the transition. This allegedly violated the Logan Act, a 218-year-old law that has never been enforced.[4] For months, we heard about the beloved Logan Act—as soon as journalists had looked it up on Wikipedia.

The never-enforced Logan Act prohibits private citizens from negotiating with foreign governments. In the 1980s, at the height of the Cold War, Senator Teddy Kennedy was wildly trying to conspire with Soviet leader Yuri Andropov against the sitting president of the United States, Ronald Reagan. In his mash notes to Andropov, Kennedy belittled Reagan and asked for the Communist leader's help in undermining America's "belligerent" president. The senator proposed setting up a U.S. media tour for Andropov, including interviews with Walter Cronkite and Barbara Walters.[5] Thirty years later, when the Soviet Union was no more— despite Kennedy's best efforts!—General Flynn talked to the Russian ambassador on behalf of the incoming administration. Liberals think Flynn should go to prison, but Teddy was the "conscience of the Democratic Party."

Soon there were darks rumors that, in his private-sector work, Flynn had registered under the *Lobbying Disclosure Act,* instead of the *Foreign Agents Registration Act.* FARA is a law so important that (1) compliance is "voluntary"; (2) it doesn't apply to the media; and (3) criminal charges have been pursued under the law only seven times in the past half-century.[6] (Some media outlets, such as

Russia's RT network, are required to register under FARA—but only since the inception of the modern Red Scare.)

Eventually, it was determined that Flynn had committed no crime, so he pleaded guilty to lying to the FBI about his perfectly legitimate conversation with the Russian ambassador. In an act of mercy, Mueller dropped the count of "failing to offer an FBI agent a beverage during the interview."

PAUL MANAFORT AND RICK GATES: SOME STORIES DON'T GET BETTER WITH RETELLING

Paul Manafort and his fellow political consultant Rick Gates may or may not have committed crimes. But so far, none of their alleged crimes has anything to do with Trump. The original charges against them were under the same unenforced lobbying registration law that Flynn was initially charged with violating. Since then, Manafort has been charged with setting up offshore accounts to avoid taxes, which is fantastic news. Surely this means Mueller will soon be getting around to George Soros's offshore accounts. His tax shelters have more to do with Russian interference in our election and undoubtedly contain a lot more loot.[7]

To people outside of Washington, Manafort's and Gates's work in foreign countries sounds shady. Washingtonians must be laughing their heads off. You can't throw a rock in that town without hitting someone who is—as Freedom House puts it—"willing to argue the case for just about any aspiring dictator."[8] American political consultants have advised campaigns in more than half of the countries in the world.[9] Domestic campaigns provide status and name recognition, but the money is in foreign campaigns. As

James Carville says, "Why go to New Jersey and lose for 100 grand when you [can] go to Peru and lose for a million?"[10]

Lanny J. Davis, chief counsel to President Clinton, and Mike Espy, Clinton's agriculture secretary, represented Laurent Gbagbo, president of Côte d'Ivoire, who was later tried by the International Criminal Court for murder, rape, persecution, and "other inhuman acts."[11] Another valued client was Teodoro Obiang Nguema Mbasogo—described in *The New York Times* as "the ruthless, longtime dictator of Equatorial Guinea."[12]

Tony Podesta—brother of Hillary's campaign chairman—has represented Colonel Muammar Qaddafi.[13] In 2008, White & Case, a prominent New York law firm, was so eager for Qaddafi's business that it offered him "a special 15 percent discount off of our standard rates."[14]

Israel's 2015 general election was chockablock with former Obama campaign advisers—David Axelrod, Jim Messina, and Jeremy Bird, as well as Democratic pollster Mark Mellman.[15] A few years earlier, the Israeli newspaper *Haaretz* ran an article about American political consultants Arthur Finkelstein and Stanley Greenberg's work on that year's election, titled "Forget About Bibi and Shelley, It's Really Finkelstein vs. Greenberg."[16]

Former representative and Democratic presidential candidate Dick Gephardt has lobbied American officials on Middle Eastern policy on behalf of Turkey.[17] Top aides to both Obama and Howard Dean, David Axelrod and Joe Trippi, had clients in the 2015 presidential election in *Nigeria*.[18] That was probably much cleaner than an election in Ukraine.

The Ukrainian election Manafort and Gates worked on was bristling with American political consultants—including Obama pollsters Joel Benenson and John Anzalone. Tad Devine, chief strategist for Bernie Sanders's 2016 campaign, worked for the same candidate as Manafort and Gates. Is he being investigated? Are any of them? In October 2017, this headline ran in *Politico*: "I've Covered Foreign Lobbying for 20 Years and I'm Amazed Manafort Got Busted." The author, Washington reporter Ken Silverstein, wrote, "I can say with certainty that the law, which Manafort is accused of violating, known as the Foreign Agents Registration Act, or FARA, is a complete joke."[19]

Imagine—as you are reading this paragraph, there could be men walking our streets who registered under the Foreign Agents Registration Act instead of the Lobbying Disclosure Act. Or was it the Lobbying Disclosure Act instead of the Foreign Agents Registration Act?

NO PAGE TURNER

For most of Trump's first year in office, Carter Page was the central figure in the Russia conspiracy theory.

Page's importance to the Trump campaign was dubious from the start. The only reason the candidate felt compelled to blurt out Page's name was that the "foreign policy community" was threatening to anathematize anyone who went near Trump. As Danielle Pletka, of the "conservative" American Enterprise Institute, snootily informed *The New York Times*, "It's always surprising when a member of our relatively tightly knit community is willing to sacrifice their reputation to stand with someone like Donald Trump."[20]

The blacklisting worked! Trump attracted no big names, allowing the media to chuckle about the absence of foreign policy advisers on his campaign. In response, he told *The Washington Post* in March 2016, "If you want, I could give you some of the names . . . Carter Page, Ph.D"—reading Page's name off a piece of paper. It was perfectly obvious that Trump had thrown out Page's name not to get through the end of the week, or even through the end of the interview, but just to get through the end of his sentence.

The next day, *The New York Times* ran an article titled "Top Experts Confounded by Advisers to Trump," noting that "even Google offered little but outdated biographies of Mr. Trump's new cast of experts." None, the *Times* reported, had spoken to Trump.[21]

But with nothing else to back up the Russian collusion story, the media went with Carter Page. On April 11, 2017, *The Washington Post* broke the news that the FBI had gotten a FISA warrant on Page, as "part of an investigation into possible links between Russia and the campaign."[22]

The FISA warrant against Page was doted on, speculated about, lovingly presented as the Fabergé egg of Russian collusion for most of 2017.

The news was *not* that the U.S. government was spying on Americans—but the ultimate, slam-dunk, smoking-gun proof that the Trump campaign had colluded with Russia.

Senator Mark Warner explained that "if a FISA warrant has been issued, it is a very, very serious matter."[23] On MSNBC, intelligence analyst Malcolm Nance said the existence of the FISA warrant meant they "must have had some significant intelligence about Carter Page and his links to Russian intelligence."[24] MSNBC's favorite Republican, Rick Wilson, said, "Obviously, Page is now—he's now dead to rights."[25]

> *If Alfred Dreyfus has been accused of treason, they must have some very significant intelligence. Obviously, Dreyfus is now—he's dead to rights.*

While it's wonderful to see liberals become such staunch defenders of our boys in blue, I notice that their vaunted concern for the rights of the accused vanished pretty quickly. I hope they apply the new rules next time a cop shoots a black kid. *He wouldn't have shot him if he didn't have a darn good reason!*

This went on all year, with the FISA warrant against Page cited as Exhibit A in the case against Trump for colluding with Russia.

The Resistance positively reveled in the government's spying on an American citizen. Here's MSNBC's Nance issuing a warning to Page back in March 2017:

"I have a message for him, all right? U.S. intelligence is not going to be coming at him like a lawyer, right? We will turn on the entire power of the U.S. collection system. And if he is lying, it is going to become very well known very quickly . . . If there's a FISA warrant out there . . . we have the ability to collect anything on him, including all of his finances and every relationship he has with anybody in this world."[26]

I don't remember this attitude when Ken Starr was wiretapping Monica Lewinsky. In fact, I don't remember this attitude when the FBI was investigating actual Soviet spies.

To the contrary, one of the left's most celebrated victories in the twentieth century was the Church Committee, exposing the government's espionage against American citizens. As a result of the hearings, led by Idaho senator Frank Church, severe restrictions were imposed on our spying agencies. When some of these constraints were lifted after 9/11, *The New York Times* sounded the alarm, warning that a failure to respect the rights of international terrorists would "do enormous damage to what is left of America's standing in world opinion."[27]

Yes, the 9/11 attack had harmed our nation. But think of the damage Carter Page could do!

The *Times* has gleefully exposed perfectly legitimate government surveillance programs just for fun. One Bush administration program silently tracked terrorists' finances. No American's civil liberties were at stake. The government was peeking at the banking records of entirely foreign suspects. It was nonviolent. There was no possibility of collateral damage, no starving Iraqi women and children, no innocent Afghan civilians being droned. The Bush administration begged the *Times* not to run the story and destroy the usefulness of the program. Other media outlets had the same information but they complied. Only the *Times* refused. Exposing government surveillance was too important! But when it comes to harassing Trump's campaign aides, no undercover operation goes too far. No government black ops raise any civil liberties concerns.

After nearly a year of feverish speculation about Carter Page, the House Intelligence Committee released a memo in early 2018 (the "Nunes memo"), revealing that the basis for the FISA warrant against Page had been the Hillary-funded Russia dossier, uncorroborated to this day.

I have no illusion that the government's maniacal pursuit of Page, Flynn, Manafort, and Gates will give pause to the Goebbels-like liars, determined to expel Trump and his supporters from the body politic at any cost. But it ought to make a fair-minded person wonder why we have an FBI and Department of Justice in the first place. We know what we *want* them to be doing: arresting drug dealers, terrorists, gangsters, bank robbers, kidnappers, and so on. If, instead, what federal law enforcement does is spy on political opponents and convene star chambers to bring petty prosecutions against the left's political enemies, it's not clear why taxpayers should be paying for it.

CHAPTER FOURTEEN

Jeff Sessions Is a Felon!
Oh, Okay, Never Mind.

On September 12, 2017, Rachel Maddow uncorked one of her interminable mockathons about Attorney General Jeff Sessions.

> Someday, I swear, we are going to run down all of the cover stories and excuses and denials that have come out of the Trump administration and Trump campaign over the last nine months, just on the issue of their contacts with Russians.
>
> Someday, I'm telling you, we're going to cancel all other news and I'm just going to spend the whole hour on the show listing all of the times that various members of the administration and transition and campaign said something denying contacts with Russians that was later proved to be untrue.[1]

During Senator Jeff Sessions's nomination hearing in January 2017, disgraced groper Senator Al Franken asked a long, rambling question that went on for thirty-two and a half minutes, about "a continuing exchange of information" between the Kremlin and the Trump campaign, citing a CNN report that claimed the Russians had "compromising" information on Trump.

Franken's gaseous question is rarely provided by the news media in its full glory, so here it is:

Franken: OK. CNN has just published a story, and I'm telling you this about a news story that's just been published. I'm not expecting you to know whether or not it's true or not. But CNN just published a story alleging that the intelligence community provided documents to the president-elect last week that included information that "Russian operatives claimed to have compromising personal and financial information about Mr. Trump." These documents also allegedly say, "There was a continuing exchange of information during the campaign between Trump's surrogates and intermediaries for the Russian government." Now, again, I'm telling you this as it's coming out, so you know. But if it's true, it's obviously extremely serious, and if there is any evidence that anyone affiliated with the Trump campaign communicated with the Russian government in the course of this campaign, what will you do?

Sessions: Senator Franken, I'm not aware of any of those activities. I have been called a surrogate at a time or two in that campaign and I didn't have—did not have communications with the Russians, and I'm unable to comment on it.[2]

A few months later, Democrats were *sickened* to discover that, as a senator, Sessions had met with Russian ambassador Sergey Kislyak.

Senator Claire McCaskill tweeted: "I've been on the Armed Services Committee for 10 years. No call or meeting with Russian ambassador. Ever."[3] This set off a week of howling as politicians, reporters, prosecutors, and concerned "citizens" accused Sessions of perjury.

On *CNN Tonight,* justice correspondent Evan Pérez said Sessions's meeting with Ambassador Kislyak was "raising concerns," because U.S. intelligence considers Kislyak Russia's "top spy in Washington."[4] (You'd think they'd hide their spies a little better.)

Republican CNN contributor Margaret Hoover agreed, saying that "you can't have the head of the Justice Department that oversees the department that's in charge of investigating domestic espionage somehow have met with the top Russian spy twice during the campaign when we know that that government was trying to intervene in U.S. elections."[5]

The only part of that sentence that was true was that Sessions was the head of federal law enforcement.

A senator's meeting with the Russian ambassador was "not a normal activity," according to CNN contributor Bakari Sellers. He said Sessions had to be "deliberately" lying to forget that "he literally met with someone who was deemed by our national intelligence community to be a Russian spy and the number one recruiter of spies."[6] To illustrate the unprecedented nature of these meetings, Sellers added, "We also *know* that the 25 or 25 other members of the armed services committee, *none of them met with the Russian ambassador*" (emphases mine).[7]

MSNBC's Rachel Maddow claimed that the FBI "knew" Sessions had "contacts with the Russian government." And yet, Sessions "apparently just bluntly lied to the Senate about it under oath."[8] A week later she cited "the worry" that Sessions's meeting with the ambassador at the Republican National Convention was "not a coincidence."[9] According to Maddow, then-Senator Jeff Sessions was tapped to be Trump's secret conduit to the Russians— and it was so secret that he met with the Russian ambassador at the convention in front of thousands of people! *(You see—that's just the cover you'd expect him to use!)*

MSNBC's Lawrence O'Donnell dedicated an entire show to Sessions's "perjury," somberly announcing, "The attorney general of the United States is now a suspect in a perjury investigation."

Sessions's "perjury" was treated as a fact. *That much we know. Now we just have to see if perjury is a serious crime.*

After a little legwork, the Resistance discovered: Perjury is a *major* crime! A *Washington Post* article by Aaron Blake proclaimed, "Six Times Jeff Sessions Talked About Perjury, Access and Recusal—When it Involved the Clintons."[10]

House minority leader Nancy Pelosi announced that Clinton had been *impeached* for less than what Sessions had done. (We know that God was on vacation in the Bahamas that day, or Pelosi's head would have exploded.) *The Washington Post's Fact Checker* said of Pelosi's idiotic claim: "too early"![11] Yeah, that was the problem. We just needed a tiny bit more evidence to nail it down.

Graduate of the James Comey School of Pomposity and former prosecutor John Flannery proclaimed on CNN, "I'm saying perjury, yes . . . Why do you think people lie about things? Because they are conscious of the guilt of something they did wrong. Shakespeare said guilt spills itself for fear of being spilt."[12]

The American Civil Liberties Union filed an ethics complaint against Sessions in Alabama, saying he had engaged in "conduct involving dishonesty, fraud, deceit or misrepresentation." So did an outfit called Lawyers for Good Government—signed by two thousand lawyers.

Twenty-three "citizens," including three doctors and a pastor, from California, Maine, Massachusetts, Oregon, and Vermont, filed a complaint with the Department of Justice demanding a criminal inquiry into Sessions's lie. "We feel there is probable cause to charge him with a crime," attorney J. Whitfield Larrabee explained. "We want indictments in the case. We want Attorney General Sessions to be treated just the same as anyone else."[13]

More than a dozen Democratic members of Congress called on Sessions to resign, including Senators McCaskill and Dick Durbin and House minority leader Nancy Pelosi.[14]

And then the facts came out.

FRANKEN'S KARMA

It turned out that—so sorry, our mistake—senators meet with ambassadors *all the time.* The very senators howling the loudest about Sessions had themselves met with Ambassador Kislyak repeatedly. On reconsideration, they probably shouldn't have said things like, "I've been on the Armed Services Committee for ten years. No call or meeting with the Russian ambassador. Ever."

That was Senator McCaskill, who had memorialized one of her meetings with the ambassador in a tweet on January 30, 2013: "Off to meeting w/Russian Ambassador . . . "—AKA RUSSIA'S TOP SPY AND RECRUITER OF SPIES! (™ CNN)

Senator Durbin had repeatedly boasted about his meetings with Ambassador Kislyak. Less than a year before he was calling on Sessions to *resign* for not mentioning such a momentous confab, Durbin had said at a Senate Appropriations Committee hearing, "I called the Russian ambassador . . . Several times, I've had this conversation with the Russian ambassador . . . "[15] In 2012, Durbin announced on MSNBC, "I have met with the Russian ambassador here in my own office, with several other senators." (Durbin is *very* important.)

In a televised Senate hearing less than a year before Sessions's hearing, Senator Barbara Boxer talked about a group of Democratic senators meeting with Kislyak: "Senator Durbin called a bunch of us together to meet with the Russian ambassador . . . "[16]

At about the same time Sessions was meeting Kislyak at the Republican Convention, *Foreign Policy* magazine reported on a meeting of *thirty Senate Democrats* with the Russian ambassador and other foreign diplomats. The purpose of the meeting was to allow the diplomats to lobby them to support Obama's Iran deal.[17]

Russia's "top spy and recruiter of spies" had been to the Obama White House at least twenty-two times. His last visit was right before the election, when he met a slew of aides with suspicious names—Alexander Ermolaev, Alexey Lopatin, Vyacheslav Balakirev, and Sergey Sarazhinskiy.[18] Rachel Maddow would be forced to make a citizen's arrest if people with names like that worked in the Trump White House.

Obviously, the only "lie" surrounding Sessions's testimony was the ludicrous claim that it was unusual for a U.S. senator to be meeting with a foreign ambassador. If Sessions had mentioned his customary senatorial duties in response to a question about Moscow conspiring with the Trump campaign, the entire hearing room would have laughed at him. His nomination would have had to be rejected on the grounds that he was a blithering idiot.

At least Sessions's accusers admitted error when it became clear that members of Congress regularly meet with ambassadors. No—my mistake: they never acknowledged that they were wrong. There was no apology for spending weeks falsely accusing the sitting attorney general of a felony. The defamers just moved on to their next victim.

Indeed, Sessions's name was soon slipped back into the list of Trump associates with Suspicious Russian Contacts. Having never admitted, *Yeah, we got that one wrong,* liberals began casually citing Sessions's "lie" again.[19] When it comes to the Russian collusion story, there are no strikeouts. There are only ties, rained-out games, and "Mueller is still investigating!"

Whatever happened to that "citizens'" complaint with the DOJ? Who knows! *The Washington Post* never mentioned it again. And what about Maddow's claim that the FBI "knew" about Sessions's contacts "with the Russian government"? Had some government official actually told a credulous reporter that the FBI was investigating a senator *for meeting with an ambassador*? Can we get that official's name? The media might finally have produced a crime having something to do with Sessions.

The Russian collusion story isn't a narrative at all, but a constantly changing kaleidoscope with the same glass panes appearing, disappearing, and then reappearing, under the same headline: RUSSIAN COLLUSION PROVED! Each time, we're supposed to pretend it's an all-new "breaking news" story that hasn't been disproved six times already.

Thus . . .

SESSIONS OBSESSION

On May 25, 2017—two months after we found out that there's apparently no one in Washington who hasn't met the Russian ambassador—CNN released a bombshell:

"First on CNN
AG Sessions Did Not Disclose Russia Meetings
in Security Clearance Form, DOJ Says."

(The telltale sign that this would turn out to be another nonsense story: "By Manu Raju and Evan Pérez.")

There was excitement in the land:

Politico, May 24, 2017
"Sessions' Background Check Form
Omitted Meetings with Russian"

ABC News, May 24, 2017
"Sessions Did Not Disclose Meetings with
Russian Ambassador on Security Clearance Forms"

Newsday, May 25, 2017
"CNN Reports Attorney General Jeff Sessions Failed to
List His Russia Contacts on a Security Clearance Form."

Helpful as always, the FBI "refused to comment." That's what "legal experts" are for! "Legal expert" Albany Law School grad Mark Zaid told CNN that "a member of Congress would still have to reveal the appropriate foreign government contacts notwithstanding whether it was on official business." There was, he said, "no exception."[20]

Naturally, no one was more excited about Sessions's security clearance form than MSNBC's Rachel Maddow. She announced that Sessions had "lied by omission" in "sworn paperwork."

The Justice Department tried to explain that Sessions was merely following FBI instructions, but Rachel wasn't falling for it. That was an "alibi," worthy of a full Maddow mockathon on September 12, 2017.

> The attorney general's explanation for why he didn't disclose his multiple meetings with Russian officials during the campaign on his application for a security clearance is

because he now says the FBI told him not to. Of course he would have. He would be happy to disclose those things, even though he lied about it to newspapers for weeks afterwards.

He was happy to disclose it. The FBI told him not to. He's just following FBI advice.

That's his excuse/alibi. That is checkable . . .

And, you know—benefit of the doubt—maybe the FBI did tell Jeff Sessions he didn't have to disclose his meetings with Russians when he was applying for a security clearance. Maybe they gave him that explicit instruction, which is what he says happened.

If so, the FBI ought to be able to prove that relatively easily and that will turn out to be a strange piece of advice they gave him, but at least, if that's true, Sessions will get shored up in terms of his excuse why he filed that false paperwork.

If it turns out, though, that the FBI didn't give him that instruction and his excuse is false, what will the consequences of that be?

And then Rachel launched her stunning crescendo, claiming she would have a full show someday—No commercials! Cancelling all other news!—so she could "spend the whole hour on the show listing all of the times that various members of the administration and transition and campaign said something denying contacts with Russians that was later proved to be untrue.[21]

CNN, six months later: "FBI Email: Sessions Wasn't Required to Disclose Foreign Contacts for Security Clearance[22]

Hey—what ever happened to that full show Rachel promised us—no commercials!—where she'd go through all the "cover stories and excuses" from the Trump administration that were later proved untrue? How about an apology? Maybe not a full show, but at least half a show—or as long as her sneering accusation about Sessions's flimsy "alibi/excuse." Nope. She never mentioned Sessions's absolutely hilarious "alibi" again.

Rachel's amnesia when the truth came out is a perfect example, because it's symbolic. The fact is, this has happened to the Resistance about three million times since November 8, 2016. Most of what the media sells isn't news, but smirking certitude. Total confidence is very impressive to people who can't be bothered to check the facts. So it's important to point out that these sages, these guardians of all that is true and holy, are always, *always* making it up.

Incidentally, where was the FBI during the six months of Sessions being raked over the coals for meetings so insignificant that *the Bureau doesn't want them listed on security clearance forms*? Comey, Brennan, and Clapper were in the hot tub together, clinking Bellinis over the worldwide hysteria about an apocryphal conspiracy they pushed to dog the Trump presidency.

Over and over again in the Russia conspiracy, wild allegations are made, hyperventilated over, finally proved false—and then never heard about again. If you only count balls and not strikes, you can prove anything.

CHAPTER FIFTEEN

Don Jr. and Hillary: Both Wear Pants. One of Them Colluded with Russia.

The single most famous line in the Russian collusion story is Donald Trump Jr.'s response to an e-mail offering him dirt on Hillary: *I LOVE IT!* That quote is on the blotter of every desk at CNN. It's on the MSNBC company mugs. It's the unofficial motto of the Resistance, taped on the ceilings above liberal beds. This is the biggest, blackest, most incriminating item in the Russian collusion story.

> "Russian Dirt on Clinton? 'I Love It,' Donald Trump Jr. Said"
> —*THE NEW YORK TIMES*, JULY 11, 2017

Don Jr. was responding to an e-mail from British publicist Rob Goldstone, who claimed to have "official documents and information that would incriminate Hillary and her dealings with Russia," which would be "very useful to your father." Goldstone said the offer was "part of Russia and its government's support for Mr. Trump," encouraged by Goldstone's client, the Russian singer Emin.[1]

In fact, Don Jr. did not e-mail back like a big dope, saying, "I LOVE IT!" He replied in a roundabout, friendly way, saying he was on the road, suggesting he call Emin himself, and adding, "If it's what you say I love it especially later in the summer."[2]

I'm sorry, but that's not "I LOVE IT!"

Weirdly, the singer Emin was never available for a phone call with Don Jr.—he was always "on stage." But according to the publicist, Emin wanted Don Jr. to meet with a lawyer who was heading to the United States. The Russian lady who showed up at Trump Tower had no information whatsoever about Hillary. She just wanted to lobby Don Jr. on Russian adoptions.

It's almost as if the publicist's claim about valuable information on Hillary was just a ruse. Too late! Don said "I love it"—that's all that matters.

As *everyone* knows, if someone from Russia offers you dirt on a political opponent, the first thing you do is CALL THE FBI. We've been told so by congressmen, senators, Obama economic adviser Austan Goolsbee, disgraced news reader Dan Rather, CNN's Ron Brownstein, and Gloria Borger. Everybody knows!

It was confirmed by the highest authorities. Here's Neal Katyal, former acting solicitor general under Obama:

> If one of us were, you know, in the campaign and got a call from the Russians saying, hey, we have dirt on your opponent, I think our first reaction would be, oh, I got a call on the other line. We'd hit hold, and call the FBI.[3]

And here is Richard Painter, Mr. Ethical:

> Well, let's cut the bologna here. We know what the Russians have been doing . . . And when the Russians call or someone calls on behalf of the Russians and offers derogatory information about a former secretary of state who is a presidential candidate, the first person you call is the FBI. I

don't care if you're a Republican as I am or a Democrat. You call the FBI. The last thing you do is go meet with the Russians to try and get the derogatory information.[4]

Even incoming FBI director Christopher Wray said so—under the deft cross-examination of Senator Lindsey Graham:

> **Graham:** Let me ask you this: If I got a call from somebody saying the Russian government wants to help Lindsey Graham get reelected, they've got dirt on Lindsey Graham's opponent, should I take that meeting?
>
> **Christopher Wray, FBI Director Nominee:** Well, Senator, I would think you'd want to consult with some good legal advisers before you did that.
>
> **Graham:** So, the answer is, should I call the FBI?
>
> **Wray:** I think it would be wise.[5]

Okay. Got it. Call the FBI if you're offered Russian dirt on your opponent. But as I recall, when Christopher Steele offered Hillary Clinton Russian dirt on her opponent, she said *I love it!* The Democratic National Committee said *I love it!* Even the FBI said *I love it!* Why didn't the FBI call the FBI?

If Don Jr. was supposed to call the FBI when he was sitting around, minding his own business and, out of the blue, a British guy offered him damaging information on his father's political opponent, how much worse would it be if Don Jr. had paid Goldstone $12 million to go and dig up Russian dirt on Hillary? That's what Hillary did to Trump. In fact, that's what the FBI did, offering Steele $50,000 to continue collecting Russian gossip about Trump.[6] Oh, those Russians! They're archfiends undermining everything that is good and true—unless they're working with the Democrats and the FBI to take out Trump.

DON JR. THINKS. HILLARY ACTS.

Hillary's campaign and the DNC hired Steele, using a Seattle law firm as a cutout. The law firm hired Fusion GPS, which in turn hired the British spy, who paid current and former Russian government officials for incriminating information on Trump. Say, do any TV lawyers know if it's against the law to hire a law firm to do something that it would be illegal for you to do? Somebody ask Harvey Weinstein.

The law-firm-cutout scheme was old hat for Hillary. In 1992, she hired notorious private eye Jack Palladino to squelch Bill's "bimbo eruptions," using a Denver law firm as the cutout. To avoid revealing that campaign funds were being used to silence the lengthy roster of Bill's sex partners, the campaign funneled $100,000 to Palladino through the law firm, and his services were billed as legal fees.[7]

Similarly, in the 2016 election, Hillary funneled millions of dollars in campaign money through a law firm to pay Russian government officials for incriminating information about Trump. Any bells going off? Something about "Russian collusion"?

The Washington Post's Fact Checker, by Glenn Kessler, gives "Four Pinocchios" to the claim that Hillary used a law firm cutout to collude with the Russians against Trump.[8] Kessler says, "For some, that may seem like a lot of smoke. But it's a huge leap to say Clinton colluded with Russians to do this. Instead, you have (a) the campaign hiring (b) a research firm that hired (c) a researcher who spoke (d) to Russian sources."

I'm guessing Kessler's not a lawyer. On his theory, it's illegal for Apple and Microsoft to get together and fix prices—but they could hire lawyers to meet and fix prices for them. And although I can't bribe a witness, I could hire a lawyer to bribe the witness for me. It would be a HUGE leap to hold me accountable for what I hire someone to do for me. What other crimes does Kessler imagine the concept of agency doesn't apply to? I think pimps are off the hook. Mexican drug lord El Chapo is, too. Definitely Charles Manson goes free, if he hadn't died in prison.

Don Jr. was accused of the blackest treason for agreeing to meet with a Russian lady who claimed to have negative information about Hillary. At almost the exact same moment, the FBI was drawing up an agreement to *pay* Christopher Steele to collect negative information about Trump from Russians. Showing consciousness of guilt, it was only when the dossier became public that the Bureau reneged on its agreement to pay Steele.

Does Director Wray know about this? The dossier got a lot of media attention.

In early 2018, there were reports that the independent counsel was investigating Don Jr.'s e-mailed response to *The New York Times* about his meeting with the Russian lady. His reply, reportedly dictated by his father, was:

> It was a short introductory meeting. I asked Jared and Paul to stop by. We primarily discussed a program about the adoption of Russian children that was active and popular with American families years ago and was since ended by the Russian government, but it was not a campaign issue at the time and there was no follow up. I was asked to attend the meeting by an acquaintance, but was not told the name of the person I would be meeting with beforehand.

That's a completely truthful statement. It just doesn't include the part about the British publicist telling him that the Russian lady had dirt on Hillary. It's not against the law to lie to the media and, in any event, Don Jr.'s statement wasn't a lie. He omitted other, truthful information. That's how the *Times* reports news. In fact, the *Times*' motto could be: *Omitting truthful information since 1851!* To cite one example of thousands, the newspaper never, ever, ever informs readers when child rapists and murderers are immigrants, even in long, gaseous thought pieces about their crimes. Here's the Times on a Hmong child rape ring in Fresno, California: "[it] could have happened anywhere, perhaps in a fraternity house or in a basement in a predominantly white suburb . . . "—never mentioning that it was Hmong immigrants doing the raping.

My fantasy *New York Times* Hitler obituary:

Chancellor of Germany Dies

Adolf Hitler, a decorated war hero and painter, died in an air raid shelter in Berlin on Tuesday . . .

What? I didn't say anything that was untrue. I had limited space and couldn't get to everything. Maybe I spent too much time on his paintings . . .

And yet the *Times* claimed that Don Jr.'s response to questions about the Trump Tower meeting—"one of the most consequential crises of the young administration"–had become a "focus" of the special counsel, with prosecutors asking how the statement was put together.[9] Can we get Mueller to investigate the *Times* for its habitual lying by omission? I have storage lockers full of examples.

True, Don Jr. probably shouldn't have said, "Opposition research happens on every campaign . . . I probably would have volunteered to go to Europe myself to try and verify if it would have helped get it out there before the election."

Oh, no—sorry. That's what Clinton spokesman Brian Fallon said about the Russia dossier paid for by the Democrats.[10]

The Clintons just don't think the same rules apply to them. Until November 8, 2016, they were right. Without a care in the world, the Clinton campaign and the DNC paid a British spy to collect Russian dirt on Hillary's opponent. The FBI didn't arrest her, or even investigate her campaign. Instead, the Bureau offered to pay the foreign spy itself, and then used his Russian-supplied dirt to initiate a massive federal investigation of the Trump campaign.

I think we have our Russian collusion, gentlemen.

CHAPTER SIXTEEN

October 24, 2017: It Was the Best of Dossiers, It Was the Worst of Dossiers

Why would the Resistance carry on about Russian collusion for most of Trump's first year in office, knowing that it was Hillary, the Democrats, and FBI agents who had aggressively colluded with Russia?

The answer is: they didn't know. No one knew who had paid for the Russia dossier until October 24, 2017, when a court finally ordered Fusion GPS to reveal who had financed it.[1] Now that we know the truth, it's easy to forget, but for ten months after *Buzz-Feed News* first published the dossier, *no one knew that the Clinton campaign and the DNC had funded it.*

In fact, of course, dozens of people knew—members of the Clinton campaign, the DNC, the law firm cutout and Fusion GPS, not to mention Christopher Steele and his friends and associates. Also, the FBI and the Department of Justice knew.

Incredibly, for ten months, our aggressive watchdog media—and what would we do without them?—were unable to discover who had paid for the dossier. You might even say the media deliberately lied about the dossier's sponsor. The day after *BuzzFeed* published the dossier, *The New York Times* falsely reported, "The story began in September 2015, when a wealthy Republican donor who strongly opposed Mr. Trump put up the money to hire a Washington research firm run by former journalists, Fusion GPS, to compile a dossier about the real estate magnate's past scandals."[2]

That's not at all how "the story began." The Republican donor had absolutely nothing to do with the dossier. As eventually became clear, this was a total red herring, inserted into stories about the dossier for the sole purpose of disguising the real client, Hillary Clinton.

In another article on the dossier, the *Times* intentionally misled readers with the following chronology:

- In September 2015, a Washington political research firm, Fusion GPS, paid by a wealthy Republican donor who did not like Mr. Trump, began to compile 'opposition research' on him. . . .
- Last June, after evidence of Russian hacking of Democratic targets surfaced, Fusion GPS hired a retired British intelligence officer, Christopher Steele, to investigate Mr. Trump's ties to Russia.
- After it became clear that Mr. Trump would be the Republican nominee, Democratic clients who supported Hillary Clinton began to pay Fusion GPS for this same opposition research.[3]

Any person reading that timeline would assume that the first two items came before the third: the dossier was compiled for a GOP donor, and then, later, a Democratic donor came in and said, *Hey, can we take this Russia dossier off your hands?* But the timeline is out of order. Obviously, no Republican was paying for research on Trump after May 3, when his last GOP rival dropped out.[4] Steele wasn't hired by Fusion GPS until *June*. Why, in the *Times'* list, does June come before May?

It's like saying:

1. Ivana divorced Donald Trump.
2. Donald Trump began dating Marla Maples.

What? Did I say anything that's untrue?
Or how about this:

1. Bush invaded Afghanistan.
2. Osama bin Laden was killed in a raid.
3. Obama became president.

The *Times'* sleazy, non-chronological ordering of events was a calculated attempt to create the false impression that a Republican had originally financed the dossier. Evidently, it was very important to keep the Democrats as far away from the dossier as possible. And it worked for ten joyful months.

In the halcyon days before the public knew that Steele was working for Hillary Clinton, the media cited the FBI's reliance on his dossier as proof of its bona fides. The dossier was like Kim Kardashian. Why is she famous? Because she's famous. Why was the dossier credible? Because the FBI believed it. The circularity of that argument became clear only when it turned out the "dossier" was nothing more than Hillary Clinton's opposition research.

Inasmuch as the Democrats and the media would soon be denouncing the idea that the FBI had ever taken the Russia dossier seriously, let's review their months of gloating over the FBI's absolute devotion to it. Only much later, when we found out that the dossier had been funded by the Democrats, did the FBI's faith in it became a vicious Republican lie.

In March 2017, Michael Isikoff of Yahoo News reported the "stunning" information that it was the dossier that had sparked the FBI's Trump investigation. The Bureau's investigation, he said, began "just a few weeks after Christopher Steele, the ex–British spy, who was the author of that dossier, first briefed FBI agents about the contents of his reports. So it appears more and more that he set the ball in motion, set the chain of events in motion, that led to this investigation."[5]

A few days later, NBC News' Ken Dilanian vouched for the dossier's allegations by noting that the FBI "was prepared to pay Christopher Steele to investigate for them . . . And, you know, I'm told that as many as 100 FBI agents are assigned to this investigation at three different field offices around the country."[6]

> CUT TO: Sound of gunfire at Marjory Stoneman Douglas High School, because the FBI was too busy spying on Trump to investigate Nikolas Cruz.

In April, CNN broke the news that the FBI had used the dossier to obtain a FISA warrant on Trump campaign adviser Carter Page. Well, now the dossier had to be true. You don't get a FISA warrant on uncorroborated gossip. *What do you say now, Trumpsters?*

CNN's Erin Burnett opened her show with the exciting news: "New details about an explosive dossier about Russian ties to Donald Trump's campaign. A CNN exclusive this hour." Evan Pérez came on to report, "Breaking news: the FBI used the now infamous dossier of allegations of Russian ties to Donald Trump's campaign to get a warrant to secretly monitor a Trump associate."

Former CIA operative Robert Baer told Burnett he was stunned. The fact that the dossier had been used for a FISA warrant, he said, "tells me that they had faith in the explosive dossier." He remarked that he "put a lot more credence in this dossier than I did initially, and the fact that they based the FISA partially on it, that's explosive in itself."[7]

The next morning on CNN's *New Day,* Chris Cuomo reported

that the FBI had used the dossier to "convince[] a secret U.S. court to allow surveillance on a top Donald Trump associate." That meant, he explained, that "the FBI saw in that dossier *articulable* facts that they could give to a judge as a basis of reasonable belief about Carter Page. And the judge bought it."[8]

Later that day, CNN's Kate Bolduan triumphantly cited the dossier's use in a FISA application to challenge former congressman Pete Hoekstra: "I remember pretty distinctly that you supported President Trump's criticism of this dossier . . . Do you want to dial back that criticism now?"[9]

CNN's report swept through MSNBC like wildfire. Chris Matthews said that the FBI's use of the dossier to get a FISA warrant "means investigators may have independently corroborated parts of the dossier. That's news."[10] Rachel Maddow said that the FISA warrant on Page proved that "parts of this dossier passed muster even in federal court." *Try calling the dossier "tainted" now, Republicans!*[11]

The dossier had to be true—it just had to be!

It wasn't as though it hadn't occurred to anyone to ask who had paid for the dossier until October 24, 2017. Republicans had been screaming from the rooftops that they wanted to know the name of the secret donor. The FBI and the Department of Justice remained silent.[12]

A week before the court forced Fusion GPS to reveal the client, Democrats were denouncing Republican congressman Devin Nunes for continuing to "meddle around the edges of the investigation," as *The New York Times* put it, "driving Republican inquires into who financed a dossier." Exasperated Democrat Adam Schiff said, "I view these things as obstacles that are in the way to overcome, and I am doing my best to overcome them almost daily."[13]

On October 21, 2017, just days before we found out that the dossier was Clinton-funded opposition research, Trump tweeted that the "FBI should immediately release who paid for it."

Then, finally, on October 24, 2017:

"Clinton Campaign, DNC Paid for Research that Led to Russia Dossier"
     —*THE WASHINGTON POST*

So how did Rachel Maddow break the bad news that the Russia dossier had been funded by the Clinton campaign?

"Well, tonight, after months of Republicans prying on this issue with a crowbar, tonight, *The Washington Post* was first to report that the Democratic donor who took over funding the dossier for the general election was a lawyer representing the Clinton campaign and the DNC, Marc Elias."[14]

Democratic donor Marc Elias! Maddow described Elias as "a donor who was in favor of Hillary Clinton's campaign." Yes, in the sense that he was general counsel to Hillary's campaign, as well as a partner at the law firm cutout hired by her campaign to pay for the Russia dossier.

PLEASE DISREGARD EVERYTHING WE'VE SAID FOR THE PAST TEN MONTHS ABOUT THE DOSSIER

After carrying on about the dossier all year, the Resistance did an immediate about-face, insisting the dossier was an irrelevant distraction. Frankly, they were baffled by Republicans' fixation on it.

Consider this exchange on *CNN Tonight,* with Don Lemon, one week after Hillary was exposed as the secret donor behind the Russia dossier:

Lemon: We just heard the president say in a radio interview . . . that he thinks the FBI used the dossier to order a FISA warrant. What's your reaction to that?

Chris Cillizza, CNN Politics Reporter: Well, I mean, he says a lot of things, most of which are either provably false or wind up being false.[15]

Flashback, April 18, 2017, CNN: "Breaking news: the FBI used the now infamous dossier of allegations of Russian ties to Donald Trump's campaign to get a warrant to secretly monitor a Trump associate."

I salute Don and Chris for not watching their own network. But I really admire CNN's Alisyn Camerota for ignoring her *New Day* cohost, Chris Cuomo:

Camerota, January 3, 2018: This is why I think this is so important, guys, because, as you know, there are all sorts of Republican lawmakers who have come on our show, namely Jim Jordan, to say that he has a hunch that it was the dossier that he believes was the trigger to go to the FISA court to get the warrant and then wiretap some people on the Trump campaign—Carter Page.[16]

Flashback, April 19, 2017, Chris Cuomo on CNN's New Day: *"The FBI saw in that dossier articulable facts that they could give to a judge as a basis of reasonable belief about Carter Page. And the judge bought it."*

On Erin Burnett's *OutFront*—the very show that had broken

the news that the dossier had been used for a FISA warrant against Page—CNN correspondent Jessica Schneider said that conservatives *"accused* the FBI of relying on the Steele dossier in its own investigations and they want to know how and if the FBI used the dossier to obtain FISA warrants on Trump associates."[17]

> *Flashback, Erin Burnett, CNN, April 18, 2017: "Sources: FBI Used Trump Dossier to Help Get Secret Wiretap Warrant on Associate in Russia Investigation."*
>
> *Flashback, Kate Bolduan, CNN, April 19, 2017: "Source: FBI Used British Dossier for Trump Associate FISA Warrant."*
>
> *Flashback, Anderson Cooper, CNN, April 19, 2017: "Sources: FBI Used Trump Dossier to Help Get Secret Wiretap Warrant on Associate in Russia Investigation."*
>
> *Flashback, Chris Cuomo, Alisyn Camerota, CNN, April 19, 2017: "Sources: FBI Used Trump Dossier to Help Get Secret Wiretap Warrant on Associate in Russia Investigation."*

The unfortunate discovery that the Clinton campaign and the DNC had paid Russians for dirt on Hillary's opponent didn't even put a dent in the Trump-colluded-with-Russia story. Oh, sure, they stopped citing the dossier as if it were the Rosetta Stone. But other than that, the accusations that Trump colluded with Russia continued without pause. They had a hole card: George Papadopoulos, recent college grad and model UN participant, who had been in a meeting with Trump once.

CHAPTER SEVENTEEN

George Papadopoulos, Headline Writer's Nightmare

The main point of the Russia collusion story is to create a patina of illegality around President Trump. The crime of which he is accused is meaningless, even if true, but his name must be made synonymous with "Russia collusion." On closer examination, the charges are incoherent jibes, conjoining different events, adding up to a totally contradictory account. But the media just keep moving fast—moving and moving and moving—playing games with words and facts to create the impression that they have a point.

One of the biggest fake-outs is the Hillary e-mails. There are two entirely different sets of e-mails. The FBI and the media confuse them to create a semi-plausible story to answer the genesis question: Why did the Bureau begin investigating the Trump campaign in the first place?

First it was the dossier that sparked the FBI investigation. Then we found out the dossier was a Hillary-funded opposition research project, so—no, it wasn't the dossier at all! Then it was international man of mystery Carter Page, a man so dangerous that our own government took out a FISA warrant on him! Then we found out that the principal evidence against him was the notorious dossier. Next we saw the first batch of texts Peter Strzok had sent to his FBI mistress and it seemed that the lead investigator on the FBI's Russia investigation was an anti-Trump zealot. At that point, the entire weight of the Russia investigation came down to twenty-eight-year-old Trump aide George Papadopoulos and his drunken confession to an Australian diplomat about Hillary's "e-mails."

The diplomat, Australian high commissioner to the United Kingdom Alexander Downer, contacted the FBI in the summer of 2016, claiming that Papadopoulos had known that WikiLeaks was going to start posting the DNC's e-mails *two months before* Julian Assange began posting them.

This was HUGE. Ezra Klein tweeted:

> @ezraklein–30 Dec 2017
> It is difficult to believe that Papadopoulos told an Australian diplomat that Russia had dirt on Clinton but didn't mention anything to the campaign he was part of. Very difficult. Virtually impossible.[1]

This tweet was considered so insightful that it made *The Washington Post.*[2] *There's your smoking gun, Trumpsters!*

The New York Times claimed it was the FBI's breathtaking discovery that Papadopoulos may have had "inside information" about the Russian "hacking" of the DNC that was a "driving factor" in the Bureau's opening of the Russia-Trump conspiracy investigation.[3]

First of all, so what? Papadopoulos heard the Russians had e-mails embarrassing to Hillary. What was he supposed to do? Unhear it?

But, second, the FBI is playing a word game with the Papadopoulos deep throat intel. When Papadopoulos met Lewandowski and—sorry, we're out of room. Sometimes you need to go back and

reconstruct events. It turns out that when Papadopoulos was blab-
bing to the Australian about the Russians having embarrassing Hillary e-mails, *everyone* was talking about the Russians having
embarrassing Hillary e-mails.

As is often the case with Clinton scandals, it's easy to confuse them, but Hillary had two completely different e-mail scandals.
Both sets of e-mails were embarrassing to Hillary. Both were alleged
to be in the possession of the Russians—with either the Democrats
or the Republicans doing most of the alleging.

First, there were the "damn e-mails" that Bernie Sanders
was sick of hearing about—the ones our Machiavellian secretary
of state kept on her private server, to shield them from a Freedom
of Information Act request. Hillary's team successfully scrubbed
about thirty thousand of her official government e-mails before
the FBI got its hands on her server. None of those e-mails ever
showed up on WikiLeaks. They'll probably turn up two years from
now in the upstairs library of the White House, just like Hillary's
Whitewater billing records.

Second, totally separately, there were the DNC e-mails that
appeared on WikiLeaks in June 2016, revealing that party officials had schemed against Bernie Sanders, Hillary's opponent. In
a desperate attempt at damage control, in July 2016, the Democrats began claiming that Russia had hacked those e-mails.

The FBI confuses the media—not hard—by weaving in and out
of the two sets of e-mails—*Hillary's* e-mails as secretary of state,
which were deleted from her private server, and the *DNC's* e-mails,
which were posted on WikiLeaks. According to the FBI's frantic
leaking to *The New York Times,* George Papadopoulos told Downer,
in May 2016, that the Russians "had thousands of emails that would
embarrass Mrs. Clinton, apparently stolen in an effort to try to damage her campaign."[4] When WikiLeaks began publishing the DNC's
e-mails a few months later, Downer said *Eureka! These must be the*

precise e-mails Papadopoulos was talking about. FBI agents promptly flew to London to meet him. How could Papadopoulos have known about the WikiLeaks e-mails in advance unless the Trump campaign was colluding with Russia?

For news readers, there's a much, much, much more likely explanation. It was an explanation that would be well known to the FBI, if not to imbibing Australian diplomats.

"Hillary's e-mails" had dominated the news for more than a year before Papadopoulos's May 2016 revelry with Alexander Downer. From the moment we found out, in March 2015, that Secretary Clinton had installed a private server in her home for government business, speculation ran wild that the Russians were in possession of Hillary's e-mails.

To take you back in time, here are a few other places where someone might have gotten the idea that the Russians were in possession of thousands of e-mails that would be embarrassing to Hillary.

In March 2015, CNN warned that the Russians had probably gained access to Hillary's private server.[5] The *Washington Examiner* editorialized that, "short of asking the Russian or Chinese intelligence services, who likely have everything by now, there is no way for the people of this country ever to know whether their government has a complete record of Clinton's official work product at the State Department."[6]

In April 2015, the left-wing *Guardian* said that cybersecurity experts were "increasingly concerned" that Russians or other foreign hackers had penetrated Hillary's "'home brew' system."[7]

In July 2015, the Associated Press reported that "current and former U.S. intelligence officials say they assume that all of the email that transited Clinton's home server is in the possession of Russian or Chinese intelligence services."[8]

In August 2015, *The New York Times* reported that the FBI was "trying to determine whether foreign powers, especially China or Russia, had gained access to Mrs. Clinton's private server."[9]

In September 2015, NPR's Aarti Shahani observed that "hackers from Russia or China could have targeted Clinton, sent her innocent-looking e-mails with malicious software attached to break in."[10]

A few weeks later, it was revealed that Russian hackers had, in fact, targeted Hillary's private e-mail server at least five times.[11] This was huge news, covered everywhere, even on *The View.*[12]

In January 2016, former secretary of defense and CIA director Robert Gates said, "The odds are pretty high" that Russia, China, and Iran had hacked Hillary's e-mails.[13]

I haven't even mentioned Fox News, where the likelihood of Hillary's private server having been hacked by a foreign power was mentioned approximately every six minutes from March 2, 2015, to November 7, 2016.

In March 2016, *The New York Times* rushed out with this exciting news: "Security Logs of Clinton's Email Server Are Said to Show No Evidence of Hacking." She had received spam e-mails with malicious links from Russia, "but it was not clear from the emails alone whether anyone clicked on those links or whether the security was compromised."[14] Yay, Hillary!

In a column *defending* Hillary's honesty, in April 2016, the *Times*' Nicholas Kristof wrote that her e-mail server "may have been penetrated by the Russians, though we don't know that."[15] I've left out about 300,000 other mentions of the Russians hacking Hillary's government e-mails, but the point is: The possibility that the Russians had e-mails damaging to Hillary was a story that, for the previous year, was never *not* in the news.

A few weeks later, Papadopoulos shared the amazing, stunning, never-heard-before rumor that *the Russians were in possession of e-mails damaging to Hillary*! Maybe Papadopoulos's source knew about Hillary's e-mails from reading *The New York Times*. Maybe the Russians got it from the *Times,* just like in *Dr. Strangelove.*

The covert intelligence Papadopoulos spilled to the Australian diplomat was something that everyone who speaks English knew. But, according to the FBI, the Trump aide's drunken "admission" was the smoking gun that so horrified agents that they decided to open an investigation into the presidential campaign of Donald J. Trump four months before the election. Again, Downer may have been completely oblivious to the major international news about Hillary's private server. I don't know him. Perhaps he spends a little too much time drinking with twenty-eight-year-olds.

But no one at the FBI was oblivious: At that precise moment, the Bureau was concluding its year-long "investigation" of Hillary's private server. If the excited utterances of a clueless foreign diplomat were really the grounds for the FBI to pursue a contrived Russian conspiracy theory against Trump, we might want to put the Washington Bureau on something simpler, like parking tickets and jaywalking.

CHAPTER EIGHTEEN

Mueller Exposes the Blogging Gap

The standard response to the claim that Mueller is on a witch hunt is *Oh, yeah? Well, he's caught nineteen real witches!*

MSNBC's Chris Hayes: The Special Counsel Russia investigation decried by the president as a hoax and a witch hunt has now charged nineteen people with federal crimes. And as of tonight, four of those people have already pleaded guilty.[1]

Senate Minority Leader Chuck Schumer (D-NY): It's not a witch hunt when seventeen Russians have been indicted. It's not a witch hunt when some of the most senior members of the Trump campaign have been indicted.[2]

CNN's Anderson Cooper: But it's only a witch hunt if you don't find any witches, and they have here. In just a year, the special counsel charged nineteen people, and three companies, including a former White House adviser.[3]

Nineteen! Not ten, not twelve, but *nineteen*! The Resistance isn't avoiding details because the details aren't important. They're avoiding details because the details don't help them. The specifics are: Mueller has won a slew of indictments against Trump's short-lived campaign manager Paul Manafort for crimes having nothing to do with Trump or the 2016 campaign. He's gotten a few other Trump associates to plead guilty to process crimes like "lying to investigators." And he got up to nineteen with his monster indictment of thirteen Russian companies and individuals, on charges he never thought would go beyond the indictment stage.[4] That is not going to strike most people as proof that Trump colluded with Russia.

Mueller's indictment of the thirteen Russians on February 16, 2018, was pure political theater. He assumed that there was not the remotest possibility that the accused would show up in any American court to defend themselves, so he could say anything. The sole purpose of the indictment was to put "indictment" in the same sentence with "Russians."

Only by perseverating—*coconspirators, illegal, illegal, Russian, Russian collusion collusion*—can Mueller and his fanboys in the media make a social media marketing plan sound criminal.

The grand thesis of the Russian indictments is that computer bots tricked voters into supporting Trump. Yes, Americans would never have realized that Hillary was a screeching harridan if the Russians hadn't told them so. If the Russians really wanted to help Trump win, they would have arranged more TV time for Hillary.

There has never been any evidence that simply reading something magically causes people to believe it. Ask Meg Whitman if $140 million made her governor of California. Or come with me to visit the presidential libraries of Jeb! Bush, Hillary Clinton, Howard Dean, Phil Gramm, John Connolly, and Henry M. "Scoop" Jackson. All of them entered presidential election years with more money than any other candidate.[5] When has spending on campaign ads ever worked?

But we're supposed to believe that Trump heard about the Russians' social media plan and said, *If you guys are serious about sinking $100,000 into Facebook ads, there's nothing I wouldn't give you. You purchase those ads, damn straight I'll give you the nuclear codes. Can you get something on MySpace, too?* Trump isn't an idiot.

The idea that Russian social media postings influenced the electorate merely illustrates the utter contempt liberals have for Trump voters. Of course, educated elites wouldn't have fallen for Russian bots and Facebook ads—but idiot Trump voters would! As Evan Osnos of *The New Yorker* puts it, "At the heart of the Russian fraud is an essential, embarrassing insight into American life: large numbers of Americans are ill-equipped to assess the credibility of the things they read."[6]

Even accepting the snooty liberal belief that red-state Americans are uniquely suggestible, we had a mainstream media that also kind of had its thumb on the scale during the election. The message from the media could not have been clearer: YOU ARE NOT TO VOTE FOR TRUMP. IF YOU DO, YOU ARE A RACIST, SEXIST, XENOPHOBIC MORON.

Trump voters, quite clearly, were not listening to *any* media.

MAD RUSSIANS WANT MORE PAGE VIEWS!

To be sure, the details of the Mueller indictment are shocking. The shock is: the Office of the Independent Counsel knows less about social media than the senators who questioned Mark Zuckerberg.

Actual paragraph from the indictment:

To measure the impact of their online social media operations, Defendants and their co-conspirators tracked the performance of content they posted over social media. They tracked the size of the online U.S. audiences reached through posts, different types of engagement with the posts (such as likes, comments, and reposts), changes in audience size, and other metrics. Defendants and their co-conspirators received and maintained metrics reports on certain group pages and individualized posts.

Is this a criminal conspiracy or the business plan of *HuffPo*? No one in Mueller's office seems to realize: this is what people do on the Internet. They do it for fun, to troll, maybe eventually to make money. The vast majority of bloggers make less than $100 a month. Amazon is the fourth-largest public company in the United States, and in twenty years it has posted profits in only a handful of quarters.[7] Billionaires in the U.S. have paid more for less impressive Internet projects. Mueller's evidence that the Russians were trying to swing the election is indistinguishable from evidence that they were trying to generate Web traffic.

The indictment reads like Monty Python's "Non-Illegal Robbery" sketch, in which gangsters huddle over a map, meticulously planning a perfectly legal transaction:

> At 10:51, I shall enter the British Jewellery Centre, where you, Vic, disguised as a customer, will meet me and hand me £5.18. At 10:52, I shall approach the counter and purchase a watch costing £5.18 . . .

The stated charge is that the Russians committed "fraud and deceit" to "obstruct the lawful functions of the United States government."

That's kind of vague. The precise claim is that, using Facebook ads, tweets, and Instagram posts, a dozen Russians managed to overwhelm the entire U.S. media and the Clinton machine. As the *Los Angeles Times* breathlessly described the Russian scheme outlined in the indictment: "Thousands of dollars were spent each month buying targeted social media ads with messages such as, 'Hillary Clinton Doesn't Deserve the Black Vote' and 'Hillary is a satan, and her crimes and lies had proved how evil she is.'"[8]

Not hundreds of dollars, but *thousands!*

Total campaign spending on the 2016 presidential contest was $2.4 *billion.*[9] If the Russians can flip an American election with 0.83 percent of total campaign spending, I hope they are running our country. It would run very smoothly.

The Russians think we're nuts. As the indictment admitted, one of the indicted Russians e-mailed her mother, in September 2017, saying, "We had a slight crisis here at work. The FBI busted our activity. Not a joke."

To cover for the lunacy of Mueller's indictment, the media supplied the outrage, making Facebook ads sound like the work of Julius and Ethel Rosenberg. Here's how Brian Williams opened his MSNBC show, *The 11th Hour,* the night of the indictment:

> The breaking news tonight, the stunning evidence of how far Russia reached into our lives, our media, and our presidential election. Robert Mueller's bombshell indictments alleging the Russians arrived in this country to turn Americans against one another, psychological and information warfare, that didn't stop with the election.[10]

The alleged psychological warfare, turning one American against another, consisted of: Russians posting election-related content on the Internet. Wake me up when you have them changing vote totals. It would be one thing if California or New York had flipped to Trump. But Trump's victory followed the precise path anyone could have predicted it would. Large industrial states in the Midwest went for the guy who said he'd deport illegals and tear up NAFTA.

The media gave quite a different picture of the indictment:

"a grand conspiracy of Russian election sabotage"

"a highly sophisticated well-funded and vertically integrated enterprise intended to influence voters. Effectively a third campaign"[11]

"a much more far-sweeping conspiracy to violate U.S. election laws than we really knew"

"really well financed, well researched, well-executed conspiracy"[12]

"dark Facebook ads . . . referring to conspiracy theories"[13]

"a huge but hidden social media trolling campaign"

"bogus social media postings"

"ads falsely purchased . . ."

"Russians manipulated social media sites"

"deceptive and malevolent activity"

"an elaborate plot to interfere in the 2016 U.S. presidential election"[14]

The left is fantastic at producing accusatory government documents against the Trump administration, but things always fall apart at the evidence stage.

CNN anchor George Howell called the indictment a "game changer," that laid out the evidence of Russian collusion in "black and white . . . in granular specificity."[15] CNN's Brianna Keilar said, "You are looking here at *proof* of a systematic effort to meddle in the U.S. election by Russian operatives." CNN's Shimon Prokupecz responded, "Yes, it's quite systemic, Brianna. *I mean, you're talking about Facebook*."[16]

On MSNBC's *The Last Word with Lawrence O'Donnell*, Neera Tanden, of the Center for American Progress, said the indictment "really proves what the intelligence agencies said over a year ago. It proves what the intelligence agencies said and what Donald Trump has been denying on an almost weekly basis."[17]

Game over. The evidence was in. Case closed. The only question the Resistance wanted answered was: What was Trump going to do about it?

Commentators demanded that Trump come out guns blazing in response to the indictment and take action against Russia. As John Dean said on CNN, a "normal" president would react "both proactively and retroactively" to such an indictment.[18]

It's an indictment. Fifty years ago, President Nixon was pilloried for saying Charles Manson was guilty when he was still on trial. Days later, Manson showed the jury the *Los Angeles Times*' two-inch headline: "MANSON GUILTY, NIXON DECLARES." His lawyers promptly moved for a mistrial. With the same confidence of commentators today, journalists hooted about idiot Nixon "freeing Manson."[19] (No mistrial was declared.)

Nixon made his off-the-cuff remarks a few weeks into Manson's trial, well past the indictment phase. And, of course, Manson was guilty (except according to *The Washington Post*'s fact-checker,

Glenn Kessler, who doesn't believe the concept of agency applies to criminal law—see chapter 15). But today the Resistance is appalled that Trump refuses to presume the guilt of the accused based on an indictment that (1) is obviously political and (2) the prosecutor never expected to have to defend in court.

THEY'RE . . . THEY'RE . . . BLOGGING!

The more commentators talked about Mueller's indictment, the more it became clear that no one in the media had actually read it. They just rushed to a thesaurus to find synonyms for "malevolent," "conspiracy," and "sabotage." (What *is* a "dark Facebook ad"—as a *New York Times* op-ed called the Russians' social media postings?)

Here's the biggest smoking gun from the indictment: "Specialists were instructed to post content that focused on 'politics in the USA' and to 'use any opportunity to criticize Hillary and the rest (except Sanders and Trump—we support them).'"

If you were only trying to attract clicks, which candidates would you support? That's right: Sanders and Trump. And whom would you bash? According to a quarter-century of conservative direct mail: Hillary Clinton. Ever since Hillary first entered the national consciousness, in 1992, she has been a fund-raising magnet for conservatives. Mail a $20 check to the Heritage Foundation and, every week for the rest of your life, you'll get sixteen mailings promising to *Stop Hillary*. The father of direct mail, Richard Viguerie, told *The New York Times* in 2007 that his Hillary Clinton mailings were the most successful he'd had in forty years of fund-raising.[20]

If the Russians were trying to swing the election to Trump, their message was a little confused. They sponsored groups supporting Ted Cruz, Marco Rubio, Jill Stein, Black Lives Matter,

Muslims, Christians, and "Heart of Texas," among others. Some were even supportive of Hillary. Again, this is according to Mueller's own indictment. Is he holding the good stuff back?

Especially tricky to explain is the fact that, right after the election, the Russian troll farm leapt on the Resistance bandwagon. Again—according to the Mueller indictment—these same Russians who were desperate to elect Trump sponsored a "Trump is NOT My President" rally in New York and a "Charlotte Against Trump" rally in North Carolina a few weeks after the election.[21]

To explain why some Russian social media groups supported Hillary and some even promoted the Resistance, the "Russian Conspiracy to Elect Trump" simply transformed into the "Russian Conspiracy to Sow Discord." According to deputy attorney general Rod Rosenstein, Mueller's indictment revealed the Russians' plan "to promote discord in the United States and undermine public confidence in democracy." If the Russians were trying to sow discord and undermine confidence in our democracy, then the guy they probably colluded with was Robert Mueller.

After the fact, a conspiracy can be imposed on any set of facts. The Resistance should have a game show where contestants compete to see who can turn ordinary events into a Russian conspiracy the fastest.

A few years ago, I discovered a guy, Greg Packer, who is quoted in nearly every "man on the street" interview in the New York media. He was quoted buying Hillary's "Living History"; on his reaction to military strikes against Iraq; at the St. Patrick's Day Parade, the Thanksgiving Day Parade, and the Veterans Day Parade. He was quoted at not one but two New Year's Eve celebrations in Times Square. He was quoted at the opening of a new *Star Wars* movie, an H&M clothing store on Fifth Avenue, and the viewing stand at Ground Zero. He was quoted at Yankees games, Mets games, Jets games—even getting tickets for the Brooklyn Cyclones.[22] Last year, he was quoted on Cardinal Dolan's flu keeping him from Christmas mass at Saint Patrick's Cathedral in New York. After I wrote a column mentioning Packer's ubiquity as the media's man on the street, he showed up at one of my book signings to shout insults at me. Days later, he was at another one of my events, shouting marriage proposals.

If they thought hard enough, I'm sure Mueller's top-flight attorneys could come up with a conspiracy to explain Packer's behavior. But Occam's razor says: He likes to read his name in the newspaper. And Occam's razor also says: The Russians were sponsoring different social media groups to attract followers.

The Russian conspiracy is like global warming: no matter what the facts are, it proves the existence of global warming. So, too, no matter what the evidence is, Russia was screwing with our election. When attacking Trump, we have a new scientific method: the conclusion comes first, *then* data is arranged to support it.

The day the indictment was released, Facebook's vice president for ads, Rob Goldman, tweeted, "I have seen all of the Russian ads and I can say very definitively that swaying the election was *NOT* the main goal." He added: "The majority of the Russian ad spend happened AFTER the election."[23] Nazi block watchers in the press quickly pounced on Goldman, announcing that it was *against company policy* for a Facebook executive to talk to the media. Journalists were aghast that a rogue insider, speaking on a matter of public importance, had violated corporate policy!

The New York Times claimed that Goldman "eventually walked back" his tweets.[24] In fact, all he did was clarify the painfully obvious point that his tweets had nothing to do with Russia hacking the DNC's e-mails. Yes, and his tweets also had nothing to do with Stormy Daniels, Benghazi, or Hope Hicks's boyfriend beating his wives. Not much of a walk-back, *New York Times*.

In one case mentioned in the indictment, a Russian-based Facebook group, "United Muslims of America," sponsored a rally called "Support Hillary. Save American Muslims." The Russians produced participants on both sides of the rally, persuading one "U.S. person" to show up holding a sign that read, "I think Sharia Law will be a powerful new direction of freedom," attributing the quote to Hillary.

Head Russian: How is this supposed to work again?

Assistant Russian: When Americans find out Muslims support Hillary, she is DEAD!

> *Cut to:* Khizr Khan, standing with his hijab-wearing wife, denouncing Trump in a thick Pakistani accent at the Democratic National Convention.

The special counsel's most hilarious accusation was that the Russians' social media posts had suppressed the black vote for Hillary. *What else could possibly explain how Hillary got less of the black vote than Obama?* Keep thinking that, liberals.

Paragraph 46(a) of Mueller's indictment states:

> On or about October 16, 2016, Defendants and their co-conspirators used the ORGANIZATION-controlled Instagram account "Woke Blacks" to post the following message: "[A] particular hype and hatred for Trump is misleading the people and forcing Blacks to vote Killary. We cannot resort to the lesser of two devils. Then we'd surely be better off without voting AT ALL."

Reporters were blown away. *Do we need to draw you a picture?*

"The fact is," CNN political analyst Jonathan Martin said, "reading this indictment, the Russians tried to suppress Hillary Clinton's vote, especially with black voters."[25]

We've thought and we've thought and we've thought, but nothing else explains why the black turnout would be smaller for Hillary than for the first black president.

Speaking as a black man, *New York Times* op-ed contributor Noam Cohen took the Russians' suppression of the black vote personally. As Cohen explained, "dark Facebook ads, bought by suspected Russian fronts," were designed to "depress black support for Hillary Clinton." The 2016 election, Cohen triumphantly announced, saw a seven-percentage-point decrease in African American turnout from 2012.[26] *Idiots! What could explain that, except a Russian plot?*

MSNBC's Chris Matthews said the Russians "know what they're doing." African American voters who didn't vote would "probably be for Hillary. That's a reasonable assumption. Get them not to vote."[27] Google "This is the last time we vote for an all-white ticket" to see if there might be another explanation for the lower black turnout for Hillary.

Two months before the Russians mesmerized black voters with an Instagram post from "Woke Blacks," Quanell X, leader of the People's New Black Panther Party, in Houston, said on local TV:

"I ask us to truly examine what [Trump] said, because it is a fact that for fifty-four years, we have been voting for the Democratic party like no other race in America . . . We are being pimped like prostitutes, and they're the big pimps pimping us politically, promising us everything and we get nothing in return."[28]

The media knew damn well that African Americans were not head over heels about Hillary. The fact that Trump was out there asking black people for their vote enraged them. (*HuffPo:* "Milwaukee's African-American Leaders Pan Trump's Speech on Race and Policing.")

In September 2016, days after Quanell X's derogatory remarks about the Democrats, Trump appeared at the Great Faith Ministries International church, in Detroit, and got a standing ovation from the congregation. As Trump was being blessed by the black minister, a Reuters cameraman can be heard on video refusing to stop filming—as his supervisor was evidently demanding. "I'm not leaving," he said. "I'm shooting this. I don't care what . . . I'll take a demotion for this."[29]

But it was probably the Russians' October 16 Instagram post seen by seventeen people that depressed Hillary's black vote.

"HAPPY BIRTHDAY" IS CODE FOR "OUR PRECIOUS BODILY FLUIDS"

Another Russian trick to flip the election to Trump—important enough to be cited in Mueller's indictment—involved the Russkies persuading some random American to take a picture of himself standing in front of the White House with a sign that read, "Happy 55th Birthday Dear Boss" the day before the fifty-fifth birthday of the Russian oligarch funding them.

The indictment doesn't clarify what percentage of the Russian firm's social media posts were nonpartisan pranks, like birthday messages for their bosses. Our media's pranks were never nonpartisan.

Leaving aside the $1.2 billion spent by the Democrats to get Hillary elected, from the moment Trump announced, the entire mainstream media turned their newsrooms over to a 24/7 *Stop Trump* operation, amounting to approximately a kazillion dollars of in-kind donations to the Clinton campaign. The Resistance's argument is that the left's total, 100 percent domination of the American media was no match for thirteen Russians.

The sole purpose of Mueller's indictment of the Russians was, as *The New York Times* admitted, "to name and shame" the alleged "operatives." Everyone assumed that none of the accused Russians would ever show up to defend themselves. The indictment was "clearly a message document," Robert S. Litt, former national intelligence lawyer, told *The New York Times*. "Mueller wants to end the debate."[30]

Harvard professor Jack Goldsmith called the indictment "a remarkable rebuke" of the president. Which was the only point. As with the evidence-free "report" by American intelligence agencies, the indictment served merely to "[educate] the American public" about the Russian conspiracy. It was so cool, so great, such a diss of Trump—right up until the charges had to be tested in court.[31]

Then, Mueller's prosecutors lost their mojo. When one of the indicted Russian corporations sent lawyers to the arraignment, suddenly the independent counsel's evidence was not so watertight. As *BuzzFeed News* put it: "Everyone Thought the Russians Wouldn't Bother to Defend Themselves Against Mueller's Charges. Then This Happened."[32]

Mueller's attorneys rushed to court to request a delay and began furiously raising technical objections. Meanwhile, the Russian corporation asserted its right to a speedy trial.[33] Although the special counsel's office wasn't ready to prosecute even one Russian defendant, prosecutor (and Hillary donor) Jeannie Rhee claimed the office would be "thrilled" if all the defendants showed up.[34]

I bet.

It would be one thing if all this conspiracy-mongering were to prove Russian perfidy—and it were 1970. But there's no Soviet Union anymore. It was you guys, *New York Times*, who struggled mightily to tell us to calm down about mass-murdering Soviet Communists. *Hello? Strobe Talbott?* Now we're supposed to be flipped out over the Red Menace? Yes, we are! And the evidence of their depravity is a few million dollars in Facebook ads.

The Resistance needs to get a new hobby.

CHAPTER NINETEEN

Michael Cohen: Liberals Discover the Bright Side of Bullying!

The gleeful destruction of Trump's personal lawyer, Michael Cohen, suggests that liberals may not be quite so serious as they claim to be about protecting a suspect's legal rights. And their beatification of porn star Stormy Daniels is a little hard to square with their indignation over the *Access Hollywood* tape.

Stormy Daniels's lawsuit against Trump led to religious ecstasies in the press. The gravamen of her complaint is that she never imagined Trump would become *president,* and if she had, she certainly would not have agreed to take so little money in exchange for her silence about her alleged affair with him. So she sued to be released from the nondisclosure agreement. Apart from the fact that making a bad business deal does not state a cause of action, Daniels didn't exactly seem encumbered by her vow of silence.

The press indignantly accused Cohen and Trump of lying about the payment to Daniels. Journalists think they are at the point where tectonic plates meet in the center of history when they catch Trump's personal lawyer sending an e-mail to a porn star's lawyer from a "Trump Organization" address.

ABC's *World News Tonight with David Muir*, March 9, 2018: There is word tonight that Trump's personal lawyer used his Trump organization e-mail to arrange payment . . .

CNN Tonight, March 9, 2018:

Michael Avenatti, Stormy Daniels's Attorney: If you look at the e-mail, the top—the last e-mail in the string, it talks about how the office is closed for Yom Kippur.

Anderson Cooper, Host: The Trump organization offices?

Avenatti: That is correct and Anderson, if I could set the stage relating to this e-mail . . .

MSNBC's *The Beat with Ari Melber*, March 9, 2018: There's also a new report here that Trump's personal lawyer Michael Cohen used his Trump e-mail address to arrange the details of this transfer.

Boring facts can be used to prove big crimes, but in the case of Cohen's payment to a porn star, what we have is a boring fact being used to prove a boring crime: an alleged violation of the campaign finance laws zzzzzzzzzzzzzzzzzzzzzzz . . . Worse: They're trying to prove a reporting violation. If Trump paid the $130,000 himself, solely to help his campaign, and he wouldn't have minded at all having a porn star telling the tabloids she'd had sex with him except for the fact that he was running for president, it would be a reporting violation and OH MY GOSH—HE'D HAVE TO PAY A FINE!

Their argument is *what if he didn't pay it himself?!* That's why they're obsessed with when and how Cohen e-mailed the lawyer, trying to find bread crumbs that someone else paid Stormy in order to claim it was an illegal campaign contribution—again requiring that the payment be motivated solely by the fact that Trump was running for office. This is how they lure you into arguing about something that doesn't matter.

In the 1990s, Chinese nationals were literally dragging duffel bags of money into the DNC[1] as President Clinton allowed sensitive ballistic-missile guidance technology to be transferred to the Chinese government.[2]

No charges. No independent counsel.[3]

Clinton held illegal campaign fund-raisers at the White House, where Chinese citizens handed checks directly to White House staff.[4]

Still no charges and no independent counsel.

Videotapes of the White House fund-raisers surfaced, featuring the president and vice president glad-handing campaign donors on federal property.[5]

And again, no charges, no independent counsel.

The New York Times' response to attorney general Janet Reno's refusal to assign an independent counsel to these textbook campaign finance violations was a forceful editorial lightly ribbing Reno for her "blunders."[6]

Saturday Night Live was tougher on the attorney general.

"Weekend Update with Norm Macdonald," November 8, 1997:
With the release of over one hundred hours of videotape of President Clinton at campaign fund-raisers, the pressure continues to mount on Attorney General Janet Reno to name an independent counsel to investigate the president. In addition, some senators are said to be furious that, instead of watching the videotapes, Reno has been taping over them with episodes of *Xena: Warrior Princess*.[7]

But now we're supposed to care that Trump's personal lawyer lied about a legal payment to, depending on your point of view, a mistress or an opportunistic grifter—AND HE USED A TRUMP ORGANIZATION E-MAIL ADDRESS.

DID YOU HEAR THE ONE
ABOUT JOHN EDWARDS?

Lying to the press isn't a crime, and paying money to cover up an affair isn't a crime, either, even if you're running for president. If these were crimes, John Edwards would be on death row.

As a presidential candidate in 2008, Edwards lied up a storm about getting his mistress pregnant as his wife was dying of cancer. Only through the generous support of his well-heeled donors was he able to hide his mistress from the public. This donor-funded scam went on for months, until the *National Enquirer* finally caught Edwards visiting his mistress and newborn baby in the Beverly Hilton hotel.[8] Edwards was later charged with campaign finance violations for using campaign funds to hide an affair. The prosecution was widely ridiculed, and the jury returned a verdict of not guilty.

If that's not a violation of the campaign finance laws, then Trump's $130,000 payment to Daniels sure isn't.

THE TRUMP EXCEPTION TO
THE FOURTH AMENDMENT

Soon after Cohen came under investigation, on a referral from the independent counsel, his law office was raided. We were assured by eminent legal scholars that a raid on a lawyer's office would not be undertaken without good cause. The prosecutors must have had some serious evidence against Cohen, because the raid would require approval from a judge and top Justice Department officials. Why, deputy attorney general Rod Rosenstein had signed off on it!

The last time we heard that exact excuse, it was about the FISA warrant on Carter Page. *A judge approved it! Rod Rosenstein signed off on it!* Only later did we find out the warrant had been corruptly obtained with Hillary Clinton's Russia dossier. "Rosenstein signed off on it" is no longer your best argument, liberals.

Almost immediately after the raid, Cohen's private information began pouring out to the press. First, a private hush-money deal Cohen had negotiated for a wealthy Republican fund-raiser was leaked to the media. It is not a crime to pay money to avoid embarrassment. In fact, I believe the whole point of paying a Playboy Bunny $1.6 million was to *avoid* having it lead the news for days on end.

No one in the press cared about this stunning breach of privacy. They were too busy leering over the details of the hush-money arrangement. The Resistance's position was: The Republican donor was friends with Trump. He deserved it.

A few weeks after the raid, Cohen's personal banking transactions were plastered all over the news. For obvious reasons, it's a very serious crime to leak private financial records. But the press didn't mind the government illegally flinging a citizen's personal information into the public square. They were too busy gawking at the disclosures. Cohen was trading on his relationship with Trump! If influence peddling were a crime, half of Washington would be in prison. (Which isn't a bad idea—let's start with former representative Eric Cantor.)

The leaker of Cohen's banking records, an anonymous "law-enforcement official," called *The New Yorker*'s Ronan Farrow to justify his actions. He claimed he had illegally leaked Cohen's financial statements to prevent the Trump administration from stealing them!

"I find that laughable," a JPMorgan Chase banker told *The Washington Post*.[9] There is no American institution above breaking the law in the service of smearing Trump and anyone associated with him.[10] The records humiliated Cohen. The raid was a stunning success!

Perhaps there is some infamous crime lurking in Cohen's files. But the Niagara Falls–like leaks following the raid of his office reveal transactions that are embarrassing, not criminal. If, instead of being "Michael Cohen, personal lawyer to Donald Trump," he had been "Mohammed Kahani, personal lawyer to Osama bin Laden," liberals would be having die-ins across the country to protest the raid.

The Resistance has postulated other possible scandals associated with Cohen, such as that the Republican fund-raiser's pregnant Playboy Bunny was actually Trump's mistress—and maybe Trump was receiving kickbacks from Cohen's influence peddling! In light of the left's other speculations that disappeared like footprints in the sand, it's probably best to wait for evidence.

COALITION OF THE BULLYING

The media, usually heroic opponents of bullying, were overjoyed at the total destruction of Michael Cohen. MSNBC's Lawrence O'Donnell couldn't contain his happiness over Cohen's unfathomable legal expenses, cackling with glee about his likely bankruptcy:

"In Michael Cohen's lifetime he has *never* been hit with a bill as big as he is going to face, having 15 lawyers working around the clock for several hundreds of dollars an hour for each one of them— these are high-priced New York City lawyers. If Michael Cohen had to reportedly take out a home equity loan to get the $130,000 to pay off Stormy Daniels for her silence, Michael Cohen is going to have to sell everything he's got, to pay for those 15 lawyers working around the clock."[11]

O'Donnell couldn't have been giddier if his daughter had just won five Olympic gold medals. Liberals would laugh if Cohen committed suicide. It may be time for Obama and Hillary to cut another "It Gets Better" anti-bullying video.

The Resistance believes that because they are literally shaking and Trump is literally Hitler, an independent counsel should be allowed to use the full power of the federal government to humiliate Trump and everyone around him. If Rosenstein were honest, his letter appointing Mueller would have read: *This guy's a sleaze, there must be something there.* That's true about a lot of people. I would like George Soros and Terry McAuliffe investigated. I would like the Clinton Foundation investigated. Can we do that?

CHAPTER TWENTY

Liberals Now Love the Police State!

As each seedy element of the FBI's investigation of the Trump campaign came out, the Bureau's response was hot indignation. *How dare you ask about tradecraft undertaken to protect national security!* The media had a striking change of heart about the government spying on its citizens. On second thought, civil liberties aren't that important.

In May 2018, the news broke that the FBI had been paying a Cambridge professor to spy on Trump "advisers" during the campaign. The FBI's response was innocent bewilderment. *The Bureau was just trying to protect the Trump campaign!*

Non-joke headline in *The Washington Post*: "The FBI Didn't Use an Informant to Go After Trump. They Used One to Protect Him—What the president doesn't get about counterintelligence." The author, Asha Rangappa, a former FBI special agent who currently is admissions director at Yale University's Jackson Institute for Global Affairs,* claimed that sending an informant after Trump's campaign aides was the least "intrusive" means of protecting the

---

*Note to black Americans: You're losing all the good diversity jobs to immigrants who did not come here on slave ships.

campaign from Russian spies. A more overt approach, Rangappa said, would have invited "speculation" that the campaign was under investigation.[1]

And if there's one thing the FBI wanted to be sure of, it was that the investigation of Trump's campaign be kept out of the news! Actually, I think the cat was out of the bag on that one.

The New York Times, October 31, 2016, opening paragraph:

> For much of the summer, the F.B.I. . . . . scrutinized advisers close to Donald J. Trump, looked for financial connections with Russian financial figures, . . . and even chased a lead . . . about a possible secret channel of email communication from the Trump Organization to a Russian bank.[2]

If the FBI was protecting Trump's campaign from unscrupulous international operatives, worried that the poor devils might have been tricked already, who did the Bureau assign to "protect" the Clinton campaign? We're supposed to believe that, in her case, the FBI said, *We don't care about Hillary—screw her! We've got to protect Trump!*

TRUMP ONLY WISHES HE WERE SPIED ON LIKE MARTIN LUTHER KING

Historically, the left has not cottoned to arguments that the government is protecting Americans by spying on them—even when it's true.

President John F. Kennedy and his brother Bobby, the attorney general, authorized the bugging of Martin Luther King's hotel rooms, and they really did do that to protect him. In that case, the danger was real and the infiltration was real.

Thurgood Marshall, the great civil rights lawyer, was well

aware that Communist agitators were trying to penetrate the movement and worked hand in hand with the FBI to rid the NAACP of
saboteurs. As historian Denton L. Watson writes, Marshall knew
that their real goal was "to organize blacks as a fifth column in the
international struggle to undermine capitalism and to get the West
to disarm." In 1949, NAACP delegates adopted a resolution calling
on the board of directors "to take the necessary action to eradicate"
Communists from the organization, in response to "the grave harm
done by Communists to the legitimate struggle of the Negro for civil
rights."[3]

Meanwhile, as has been well documented by David Garrow,
Martin Luther King surrounded himself with Communists—
including his most trusted adviser, Stanley Levison, and Jack
O'Dell, another top Communist Party leader.[4]

The Kennedy brothers repeatedly warned King about Levison and O'Dell. "They're Communists," the president told King.
"You've got to get rid of them."[5] But King refused. Only then did
the Kennedys authorize the wiretaps, "in order to protect King, to
protect the civil rights bill, to protect themselves," in the words of
Kennedy historian Arthur M. Schlesinger.[6]

By contrast, the Trump campaign was never given any warnings. Instead, informers sidled up to low-level Trump advisers, hoping they would blurt out something idiotic that could be reported
back to headquarters. It was only when the FBI's spying was found
out that the Bureau claimed it was trying to "protect" the campaign.

Unlike Trump, whose position on Russia never changed during
the campaign, under Levison's influence, King would soon dra-
matically change his message. Instead of inspirational civil rights
speeches, he began spouting pure Communist agitprop, calling
America "the greatest purveyor of violence in the world today" and
comparing this country to Nazi Germany—for trying to protect
South Vietnam from a Communist takeover. "Just as the Germans

tested out new medicines and new tortures in the concentration camps of Europe," King said, so Americans were testing new weapons in Vietnam.[7]

President Lyndon Johnson picked up where the Kennedys left off, ordering "an unprecedented program of illegal political espionage" against King, as Garrow says, including sending in agents posing as reporters.[8]

Everything the FBI earnestly claims about the black ops against Trump was true in the case of King: Russia actually was inserting moles into a great movement in order to sow discord and undermine our democracy. In King's day, Russia was a totalitarian regime bent on world domination, and the spies weren't imaginary. A powerful populist leader had come under Soviet control.

But, curiously, the FBI's surveillance of King is not enthusiastically defended by the left. To the contrary, Garrow says the authorization of wiretaps on King "is widely viewed as one of the most ignominious acts in modern American history." He calls the King wiretaps "notorious," leaving "stains on the reputations of everyone involved."[9]

The FBI's spying on King is considered so indefensible that historians have taken the precaution of blaming J. Edgar Hoover for somehow hypnotizing two powerful presidents into authorizing the wiretaps.[10] Hoover's powers were so great, he even lured LBJ's helpless assistant, Bill Moyers, into widely distributing salacious tapes of King's hotel room orgies to members of the press.[11]

J. EDGAR HOOVER IS JEALOUS

Hoover could only dream of the widespread media support enjoyed by the Bureau today. Trump demanded an investigation into the FBI's attempt to entrap his campaign aides. The Bureau haughtily refused. What ever happened to "No one is above the law"? Our law enforcement agencies seem to think they are. The media fully agreed, and denounced Trump.

Director Christopher Wray proclaimed, "The day that we can't protect human sources is the day the American people start becoming less safe."[12] The press wept in sympathy with the FBI's precious human resource, Stefan Halper. When his spying on Trump aides was exposed, he was at serious risk of being chosen *Time* magazine's Man of the Year!

The left has a tendency to go in about ten seconds from a political disagreement to PEOPLE WILL DIE! This is true even when they're the ones in favor of what is, technically, the killing. Their argument in favor of legal abortion is: WOMEN WILL DIE IN BACK-ALLEY ABORTIONS! (How about: *If we don't legalize wife beating, we'll be forcing men to kill their wives and bury their bodies*? The logic is the same.)

Here are some more Trump-era PEOPLE WILL DIE arguments:

—Trump criticizes the media in a speech at CIA headquarters . . .

CIA AGENTS DIED SERVING THEIR COUNTRY!

—Trump criticizes CNN . . .

CHRISTIANE AMANPOUR'S AFGHAN TRANSLATOR DIED HELPING REPORT THE NEWS!

—Trump wants information about an FBI informant who was spying on his campaign staff during the election . . .

THE FBI'S HUMAN SOURCES WILL DIE!

Oh, give me a break. We're not talking about a daring spy risking his life behind the Iron Curtain. Halper is a Cambridge professor with a horse farm in Virginia. He was paid astronomically well by our government for engaging in comical espionage against tertiary Trump aides. Upon being outed as a spy against Trump, he was hailed as a hero nearly as brave as Stormy Daniels.

In 1976, a left-wing magazine, *CounterSpy,* gleefully printed the names of hundreds of CIA agents. Six months later, one of the outed agents, Richard Welch, was gunned down by masked assassins in Athens. Courageous *New York Times* types dismissed Welch's murder as a distraction from "legitimate criticism" of our intelligence agencies. (That would be Anthony Lewis.)[13]

But that was then, this is now.

At *The New York Times,* Trump's call for an investigation of the FBI's spying on his campaign had echoes of—guess what? That's right: Watergate. By "ordering" the Justice Department to investigate, the *Times* reported, Trump had "crossed over into applying overt presidential pressure on the Justice Department to do his bidding, an extraordinary realm where past presidents have hesitated to tread." The *Times'* go-to expert was professor Stephen Vladeck, at the University of Texas School of Law, who said, "We're heading for another Saturday Night Massacre."[14]

Citing "legal experts," resident hysteric David Leonhardt said that "such a presidential intervention had little precedent, and could force a clash between the sitting president and his Justice Department that would be reminiscent of the one surrounding Richard M. Nixon during Watergate."

Leonhardt concluded: "Other presidents did nothing like this."[15]

December 9, 2016
"Obama Orders Investigation into Cyberattacks
During Election Campaign."[16]

January 22, 2009
"President Barack Obama Ordered the Justice Department on Thursday to Review the Case of Qatar Native Ali al-Marri."[17]

May 26, 2006
"Bush Orders Documents Seized by FBI Sealed for 45 Days."[18]

April 21, 1993
"Clinton Orders Investigation into Waco Tragedy."[19]

On further reflection, presidents issue orders to the Justice Department *all the time,* especially when the government is suspected of wrongdoing—as was the case in l'affaire Drumpf.

It doesn't help to complain that Trump was ordering an investigation "for political purposes." The FBI's surveillance of Trump's campaign was undertaken for political purposes, too.

Moreover, Democratic presidents have happily issued orders to the Justice Department in pursuit of purely political ends. President Obama ordered his DOJ to ignore large parts of federal immigration law. President Clinton ordered the Justice Department to investigate "racial profiling" in New York City's police force—coincidentally, just as his wife was gearing up for a Senate race against—it was assumed—that city's mayor, Rudy Giuliani.[20]

No one had a problem with that.

Nixon was forced to resign because of dirty tricks during a presidential campaign done by his reelection committee. Today, the Democrats run their dirty tricks straight out of the FBI, then scream bloody murder when anyone asks questions. Imagine what G. Gordon Liddy could have done working from the inside of the FBI, with FISA warrants and government-paid spies!

The left is against everything the FBI does, except when it runs a counterintelligence operation against Trump. In that case, the G-men will have no greater defenders. *The FBI can't answer questions! Professor Halper might get upset and suffer a paper cut!*

THAT'S NOT A CIVIL LIBERTIES CRISIS.
THIS IS A CIVIL LIBERTIES CRISIS.

In the late 1970s, the FBI captured a dozen politicians, including seven members of Congress, on videotape, stuffing fat envelopes of cash in their pockets from men they believed were Arab sheiks bribing them for visas and building permits. (Incidentally, that's what most people have in mind when they hear about politicians colluding with a foreign government.) In fact, the "sheiks" were undercover FBI agents running a sting known as Abscam.

All of the bribed politicians were Democrats, except one. Their guilt could not have been clearer. One of the corrupt Democrats, Representative John Jenrette, took the bribe, saying, "I've got larceny in my blood. I'd take it in a goddamn minute."

The Democrats were outraged—not at the rampant criminality in their midst, but that the FBI would dare investigate hardworking public servants. Hearings were convened, and the FBI was raked over the coals for "entrapping" these poor, blameless politicians—although I notice that several officials summoned the strength to refuse the bribes. The Senate committee's report on Abscam complained that such cases raise "serious risks to citizens' property, privacy and civil liberties."[21]

It's a civil liberties crisis when an FBI investigation captures Democrats on tape, pocketing bribes from Arab sheiks. But if the FBI is used to spy on the Trump campaign at the behest of Hillary Clinton's campaign—well, that's none of your business.

CHAPTER TWENTY-ONE

Foreign Policy: We'll Have More Flexibility After Trump Is Re-elected

In order to bash Trump, the conspiracy-mongers are doing real damage to American foreign policy. Trump ran on having better relations with Russia, a nuclear-armed power that's gone from mass murder and gulags—among other things—to a normally corrupt country. If we can have better relations with Russia, why not?

As Anders Corr, a former government analyst, summarized the candidates' foreign policy views on Bloomberg Radio during the campaign:

> Bernie Sanders is very, very soft on Russia and China.
>
> Hillary Clinton will be similar on Russia and China to what Obama did. Maybe she'll have a bit more of a chip on her shoulder and she'll have to prove herself a bit more so she might be marginally tougher.
>
> Trump will be tough on China, and soft on Russia.[1]

We knew what we were voting for. And that's what we got, but even more so—as indicated by these reports in *The New York Times*:

"After relations with the United States curdled in the final years of President Barack Obama's tenure, many people [in Russia] were relieved by Mr. Trump's election."[2]

"Secretary of State Rex W. Tillerson pledged Saturday that the United States would soon lift cold-war-era trade sanctions on Russia."[3]

"Mr. Trump's administration said Wednesday that it would not expel Russian diplomats and it expressed no indignation that its putative partner was spying on it."[4]

"Mr. Trump [pressed congressional leaders] to strengthen the relationship with Russia."[5]

"Russia's leaders this week could not say enough good things about President Trump."[6]

Except, oops! None of that was about Trump. It was all Obama.

At the time, *The New York Times* editorialized, "We are relieved that Washington and Moscow are talking about cooperation."[7] One *Times* op-ed writer expressed delight that "the cold war really is over."[8] Another said that "Putin's Russia, though obnoxious enough, scarcely represents a strategic threat."[9]

Indeed, throughout Obama's "reset" of the relationship with Russia—which had "deteriorated alarmingly" under President Bush, according to the *Times*[10]—any number of foreign policy experts were thrilled by the thawing of tensions between the two countries. Even when Obama's Justice Department brought charges against Russian spies captured on U.S. soil, Obama refused to impose sanctions on Russia. As the *Times* put it, "Mr. Obama has resolved not to let the ghosts of the 20th century get in the way of his goals in the 21st."[11]

During the 2012 presidential campaign, Putin made absolutely clear that he preferred Obama to Mitt Romney. The exact same people who are ready to launch a thermonuclear war to prevent Russia from annexing Crimea—despite the people of Crimea voting by a substantial majority to join Russia—laughed themselves silly over Mitt Romney calling Russia our "Number 1 geopolitical foe" in 2012—a remark even he soon retracted.

The *Times* ridiculed Romney in an editorial titled "The Never-Ending Cold War," which said that he revealed "either a shocking lack of knowledge about international affairs or just craven politics."[12]

The BBC cited "experts" who said Romney's statements on Russia reflected "his lack of experience in foreign policy."

MSNBC's Lawrence O'Donnell proved Romney was wrong with a video clip of Andrea Mitchell stating, "Russia is not the greatest foreign policy challenge." Enough said!

MSNBC's Rachel Maddow couldn't contain her hilarity over the Republican National Convention's offering "an extra bonus of threatening Russia." (Top story *on The Rachel Maddow Show* tonight: Russia—Threat or Menace?)

At a 2012 presidential debate, Obama memorably said to Romney, "The 1980s are now calling to ask for their foreign policy back." To hoots of laughter at the Democratic National Convention, the president accused Romney of being "stuck in a Cold War mind warp." Then-Senator John Kerry joked, "Folks, Sarah Palin said she could see Russia from Alaska. Mitt Romney talks like he's only seen Russia by watching *Rocky IV*."

Then Trump came along and suddenly Russia became a regime of unimaginable evil. Are we talking about the same country?

This is what Trump has done to the left. Their position changes from moment to moment, they can't think rationally, and they don't mind looking ridiculous.

DIANA DENMAN, THE ROSA PARKS
OF THE RUSSIA CONSPIRACY

It's the story that won't go away. The Trump campaign changed the Republican platform on Ukraine to please Putin!

The truth about the platform has been told in laborious detail by Byron York of the *Washington Examiner* at least twice—in March 2017[13] and again in November 2017.[14] He's tweeted it. His articles have been reprinted and quoted everywhere. We think liberals have finally moved on—and they roll it back out again.

This platform-change story was launched by Josh Rogin in a *Washington Post* article titled "Trump Campaign Guts GOP's Anti-Russia Stance on Ukraine." Rogin noted ominously that after intervention by Trump campaign officials, "the official Republican party position on arms for Ukraine will be at odds with almost all the party's national security leaders." By "the party's national security leaders," Rogin meant the GOP's leading warmongers and Russia hysterics, John McCain and Lindsey Graham.

Foolishly relying on its own news section, the *Post* editorialized on the "pro-Kremlin tilt" of Trump's Republican Party:

> One of the few changes in the GOP platform pushed by the Trump campaign was the weakening of language calling for support for Ukraine's current democratic government, which replaced the man Mr. Manafort represented—and which Mr. Putin is attempting to destroy.[15]

It would have been just another false story in the *Post* that no one noticed, except Trump won, sending all the conspiracy buffs to scour the record and figure out how he had cheated. In Rachel Maddow's telling, the Trump campaign had demanded "that that plank only, *that* one, had to be taken out, that language could not stand."[16]

The platform change story is now a crucial part of Russian collusion folklore, not hurt at all by the fact that it is not remotely true.

As York has patiently explained, Republican delegates actually made the original platform more bellicose toward Russia, despite Trump's stated preference for not restarting the Cold War. The platform already droned on and on about how beastly Russia was to Ukraine, presumably because the only people who care about Ukraine are dying for the United States to intervene so they can go on TV and bore us with their useless knowledge of the place.

Nonetheless, the platform committee increased the saber rattling, adding a paragraph about imposing sanctions on Russia "unless and until Ukraine's sovereignty and territorial integrity are fully restored."

As York established, any "softening" was done not to the platform, but to a proposed amendment from Texas delegate Diana Denman. She had visited Ukraine as an international observer in 1998 and, based on that experience, showed up at the GOP Convention twenty years later with a whopper of an amendment. Had it been adopted in full, York notes, Ukraine would have occupied "an outsized presence in the platform." This would be odd, inasmuch as, in the ranking of America's national interests, Ukraine is number 1,783,749,393.

Still, the congenial committee accepted Denman's amendment, trimming only the duplicative parts—as well as her proposal to give the Ukrainians *"lethal defensive weapons."*

I'm sure Denman is a lovely lady, but this is insane. Ukraine has historically been a part of Russia and is not the slightest national security concern of ours. It would be like Russia vowing to give San

Diego "lethal defensive weapons" to defend itself against California. (Which isn't a bad idea.) In a bow to common sense, Denman's "lethal" weapons language was replaced with the phrase "appropriate assistance to the armed forces of Ukraine."

Whether it was a good idea or a bad idea to cut the Strangelovian aggression from Denman's amendment (good idea!), it was "a delegate's amendment," not "the platform," that was softened. York spoke to Denman, he spoke with delegates, he read the original platform and compared it to the final. It is an implacable fact that the platform committee made the Ukrainian section *tougher* on Russia.

York's exhaustive explanation about the "platform" change never made it to the media, or, apparently, to the independent counsel's office. As with all the other "proof" of the Trump campaign's Russian collusion, the story was a bust, so the Resistance pretended to have overslept that day.

By 2018, the inanity reached comedic heights with reports that the independent counsel's office was looking into changes made to Denman's amendment.[18] Even if the platform itself had been changed, on what legal theory is a federal prosecutor reviewing how a policy matter is decided by a legal political party in the United States?

Rachel Maddow chirpily reported that the special counsel was asking witnesses "how and why Republican Party platform language hostile to Russia was deleted from a section of the party platform," describing it as "a murky incident that took place at the Republican National Convention in 2016." To this day, she said, "nobody really admits who exactly insisted that the Republican Party's *national platform needed to be changed to go softer on Russia*" [emphasis added].[19]

Boy, these guys miss Stalin.

Curiously, *The New York Times* never put the changed-platform story in its news pages. The *Times* puts the really embarrassing stuff in the letters section and guest editorials:

To the Editor:

> ... What did the reported millions paid to Paul Manafort buy for the pro-Russia interests? We might start with the changes in the 2016 Republican platform, made at the behest of Donald Trump's representatives, that softened calls for giving weapons to aid Ukrainian resistance to Russia.
>
> The hijacking of part of the platform of one of our major parties by a foreign power should give all of us pause, especially the members of that party.

RAPHAEL CRYSTAL
TUSCALOOSA, ALA.[20]

MSNBC's Chris Matthews was baffled by the "weirdness" of Trump ignoring the neocon "hawks" and "carrying water for the Russians." Why wouldn't he support sending "lethal" weapons to Ukraine? Former U.S. attorney Joyce Vance agreed, saying, "It's completely inexplicable."[21]

[*Frantically raising my hand*] Because it would be demented?

You know who else didn't want to send lethal weapons to Ukraine? Obama. German chancellor Angela Merkel.[22] Leslie Gelb, president emeritus of the Council on Foreign Relations. Professor Graham Allison of Harvard, national defense expert.[23]

As Matthew Rojansky, director of the Kennan Institute, explained to *The New York Times* in 2015, sending lethal weapons to Ukraine would make the United States "a belligerent party in a proxy war with Russia, the only country on earth that can destroy the United States. That's why this is a big deal." This was "the view of many experts," the *Times* added.[24]

On the other side, we have Diana Denman, GOP delegate, who visited Ukraine in 1998.

OCEANIA HAS ALWAYS BEEN
AT WAR WITH EASTASIA

What's stunning about the platform-change hoo-ha is not only that it's false. I'll never finish this book if I have to tabulate everything false that's been said about Trump. It's that absolutely no one cares about the underlying policy. The only question for the Resistance is: *What position do I need to take to hurt Trump today?*

During the campaign, Trump asked, quite reasonably, *What's wrong with having better relations with Russia?* Russians may have a criminal nature, especially after half a century of Communism, but that should be of more interest to our immigration authorities and men seeking Russian brides than the commander in chief.

The Cold War is over. We won! Opposing Russia has nothing to do with the threat of Communist world domination—which the left supported at the time. But idiot Republicans think it's Reaganesque to say that when they look into Putin's eyes, they see "KGB." Really. When they look into Merkel's eyes, do they see "East German Stasi"? Even if our number-one foreign policy concern were still the Communist threat, German chancellor Angela Merkel is a bigger problem than Putin.

Putin was born in the atheistic Soviet Union. He had no choice about that. And yet he was baptized in the Russian Orthodox Church as a child.

Merkel was born in free West Germany, but her parents *voluntarily* moved to the Communist East. She joined a Communist youth group and learned to speak Russian. Even after Gorbachev's perestroika, Merkel was a dedicated Communist, in charge of "agitation and propaganda" at her graduate school. Today, she's actively destroying Western Europe with the importation of millions of Muslims.[25] (I hear they're doing wonderful things over there.)

True, Putin is a bad guy who kills journalists. As I recall, the left didn't mind the USSR's systematic murder of journalists—also scientists, Christians, writers, kulaks, and Ukrainians—for most of the twentieth century. When that was happening, the beloved Democratic president, Franklin Roosevelt, affectionately referred to Stalin as "Uncle Joe." *The New York Times'* Walter Duranty was writing fanboy news reports about the misunderstood despot.

Now liberals are interested in a Russian leader's flaws? For those of us who remember what happened yesterday, this is a jaw-dropping development. We really could have used some of this fighting spirit about fifty years ago.

What is the point of signing up every single Western European country to NATO? Currently, American troops are committed to fighting with NATO if Putin touches one hair on the head of precious little microstate Estonia. That's a Bush family commitment.

What if Russia got in a war with the reptile Recep Tayyip Erdoğan in Turkey? It looked like they might come to blows in 2015, when their planes were shooting at one another in Syrian airspace. Do we really want to fight on the side of the Muslims—our NATO "partner"—against the civilization that produced Pushkin, Turgenev, Tolstoy, and Nabokov?

In 1956, the Russian army—of the Communist Soviet Union—conquered Hungary. You know who didn't want to start World War III over it? President Eisenhower.

If Russia takes over Ukraine, does that mean they're going to take Paris? The only way Putin is moving on France would be as the new Charles Martel to stop the Islamic invasion.

Trump is right. NATO is absurd.

Russia is no longer threatening us with thermonuclear war.

It is no longer godless. In fact, Putin has promoted the Russian Orthodox Church, seeing it as part of the country's history and identity. He's practically bribing his citizens to have kids. Russia has a good education system, probably better than ours—but then, so does Burkina Faso. Putin is fighting ISIS and refuses to accept the Muslim "migrants" swarming through Western Europe.

The number-one enemy of Western civilization today isn't Russia. It's Islam.

And who is a key ally in that fight? Russia has been dealing with these troublesome creatures for centuries. Russia is fighting ISIS in Syria. It was Russian officials who tried—in vain—to warn our incompetent leaders about the Boston Marathon bombers.

On the primary threat of our time, Islamofascism, Russia is a lot more sensible than the rest of the West. In the Netherlands, Finland, Denmark, and many other Western European countries, citizens are being criminally prosecuted for criticizing Muslims.[26] The way things are going, in fifty years, Russia may be one of the few recognizably Christian countries left on the continent.

Instead of arming the soon-to-be-Muslim nations of Western Europe against Russia, we might think about arming the Russians against them.

But unfortunately, Republicans are gutless cowards. After six months of the Resistance's hysterics about Russia, in August 2017, the Republican Congress voted overwhelmingly to impose *new* sanctions on Russia and also to block the president from rolling them back without congressional approval. The sanctions will tie the president's hands on Russia "probably for years to come," the *New York Times* reported.[27] But Congress felt it had to act after a careful weighing of America's national security interests—just kidding! Their calculus was: *The media will be hysterical with us if we don't do this.* Because that's how the framers of the Constitution envisioned the distribution of powers: foreign affairs run by committee! Except our foreign policy isn't even being run by Congress. It's being run by Samantha Bee.

The vote in the Senate was 98–2, and in the House, 419–3. In the Senate, only Rand Paul and Bernie Sanders opposed the contrived bill. The same day, Vice President Mike Pence was in *Montenegro,* pledging the full commitment of the armed forces of the United States if Putin were to invade the small Balkan country, our precious NATO ally.

The hawks aren't even consistent. It might make a certain kind of mad logic if they were in appeasement mode on everything. But when it comes to a trade war with China, they say, *Don't make them stop cheating us—they'll be mad!* Only the Russians must be blocked at every turn. Either it's a bad idea to go around picking fights with everyone, or we're imposing tariffs on Chinese goods. Pick one.

In December, the White House approved the sale of—guess what?—lethal weapons to Ukraine. Trump got zero credit from the Resistance, but conservatives cheered.[28] *See? Trump isn't controlled by Putin! What do you say now, Resistance?* Fantastic. So, to disprove a totally bonkers conspiracy theory dreamed up by Hillary Clinton and Nancy Pelosi, the sole driving objective of our foreign policy is proving that Trump does not like Putin.

When the dossier was first published, in January 2017, the men who had created it, Glenn Simpson and Christopher Steele, claimed they had done it because of their "dark views" of Putin, as the *Times* put it.[29] Oddly, their "dark views" of Russia didn't compel them to put together a scandal sheet on Obama when he was pursuing warmer relations with Russia. The 2012 presidential campaign would have been a terrific time to undermine Obama and help Romney if they were really worried about Russia.

In any event, America's foreign policy is not for Simpson and Steele to decide. It's not for Hillary Clinton or John McCain to decide. The American people decided. They chose Trump. Evidently, the *Times'* foreign policy reporters weren't the only ones "relieved" about Washington and Moscow cooperating. So were the Americans who made Trump president.

There were plenty of Republicans proposing to take a bellicose position toward Russia during the primaries. Former New York governor George Pataki, for example, said at the December 15, 2015, GOP debate, "I would give the Ukrainians lethal weapons so they could defend themselves."[30] You might have missed that because Pataki was out of the race two weeks later.

By contrast, Trump said repeatedly, unequivocally, throughout the campaign that he wanted to get along with Putin. His position on Ukraine was that it's not our problem. "Why are we always doing the work?" Ukraine's neighbors, he said, "aren't doing anything. They say, 'Keep going, keep going, you dummies, keep going. Protect us . . .'"[31]

That's the guy who won the debates, the nomination, and then the general election.

John McCain, Lindsey Graham, and George Pataki may be "the party's national security leaders" in the eyes of the media, but not according to the voters.

For Democracy to Live,
We Must Kill the Media

As is evident from the previous 216 pages, for any progress to be made in this country, the media has to be destroyed. A vital part of immigration reform, health care reform, federal court reform—even Trump reform—is cutting out the cancer of the mainstream media.

Don't feel sorry for them. They had plenty of opportunities to do the right thing. They chose not to. The press no longer provides news. The media have become something people go to for confirmation, not information. Once venerated outposts of journalism have imploded under Trump, reducing their value to zero. *The New York Times* treats the rules of journalism like a speed limit sign on a back road in New Hampshire: rules that exist only for our amusement. Reporters say, *you'll be sorry when you can't get the truth!* They seem not to realize that we don't feel like we're getting it now.

Polls show that a majority of Americans of all political stripes think the media publishes fake news.[1] Henceforth, when the MSM reports anything, it should be prefaced with, "Perhaps you should look into this. We know you don't trust us." We have to be ruthlessly unsentimental. There will be a rash of reporter suicides and vows to do better. We will accept no promises of future good behavior. There's no fixing this problem. They all have to go.

For many of us, this is old news. The press is like a mob hit man who has been hiding out in Indiana for thirty-two years, then suddenly decides, *Oh, screw it. I'm going to run for Congress using my own name* . . . BAM! Dead. That's what's happening with the press. They decided, *Yes, we'll look like scum, but it's all hands on deck to stop Trump.* Driven absolutely crazy by Trump's election, journalists' number-one job is destroying him. Now everyone knows what they are.

Hilariously, the media blame opposition to "free speech"—as they call what they do—on Trump. Yes, that's the problem. No one had any reason to criticize the media until Trump came along. Heard of Reed Irvine and Brent Bozell? Heard of Ann Coulter? Irvine founded the watchdog group Accuracy in Media in 1969 to document the media's gigantic left-wing bias. Brent Bozell has made a booming career out of exposing the media since 1987, when he founded the Media Research Center. The fourth estate has actually shocked us by getting slightly worse under Trump.

Media: TRUMP TRIED TO HIDE WHITE HOUSE NEWS BY DROPPING PARDON AND TRANSGENDER BAN IN THE MIDDLE OF A HURRICANE!

"White House Buries Controversial News Under Hurricane Harvey Watch"
　　—*TIME*, AUGUST 26, 2017[2]

"3 headlines the White House hopes you'll miss as Hurricane Harvey hits"
　　—CNN, AUGUST 26, 2017[3]

"Trump gives new meaning to the Friday night news dump, enraging his critics"
— *THE WASHINGTON POST*, AUGUST 26, 2017[4]

Trump: Aren't TV ratings higher than usual in the middle of a hurricane?

Media: TRUMP BASED DECISION TO RELEASE NEWS ON TV RATINGS!

"Bash: Trump's ratings comment was abhorrent"
— CNN, AUGUST 28, 2017[5]

"Trump Eyed 'Far Higher' Ratings in Pardoning Joe Arpaio as Hurricane Hit"
— *THE NEW YORK TIMES*, AUG. 28, 2017[6]

"Trump really is the pure spirit of Television Past: cares ONLY about ratings and votes, conflates them entirely with value, dead to meaning."[7]
— EMILY NUSSBAUM OF *THE NEW YORKER* ON TWITTER

You can't win.

Thomas Friedman, noted admirer of lefty authoritarianism, wrote, "I don't know whether Russian oligarchs own him financially or whether Russian spies own him personally because of alleged indiscreet behavior during his trips to Moscow."[8]

Are those our only options? *I don't know whether Thomas Friedman was dropped on his head as a child or the umbilical cord cut off oxygen to his brain . . .*

The day of the shooting at YouTube headquarters, on April 3,

2018, MSNBC's disgraced fabulist Brian Williams took to the anchor desk for a live report. He rucfully remarked that *not only* would the FBI have to investigate this horrible attack, but agents would have to do it while under relentless attack by Trump! His knee-jerk response to a workplace shooting is *I don't know how the FBI is going to solve any crimes with Trump denigrating them!* Some things have nothing to do with Trump, MSNBC. The YouTube shooting doesn't go in the "Trump" file.

The media treated former FBI director James Comey's low opinion of the man who fired him as if it were a fact in an encyclopedia. Responding to his meaningless claim that, in his opinion, Trump might have been compromised by the Russians—"I don't know, and the honest answer is it's possible"—ABC's George Stephanopoulos replied, "That's stunning."

It's not "stunning." It's "an opinion." *But it's right there in black and white! James Comey says he thinks it's "possible."* It's also "possible" that Trump is a secret taxidermist. In what sense is Comey's opinion probative? He appears to enjoy a low opinion of the man who fired him. Saddam Hussein probably had a very negative opinion of President Bush.

Testifying before the Senate Intelligence Committee on June 8, 2017, the bitter, recently fired former FBI director accused both Donald Trump and *The New York Times* of falsehoods.

Trump had said that, under Comey, the FBI was "in disarray," was "poorly led," and "had lost confidence in its leader." In a surprise development, Comey strongly disagreed. He called Trump's assessment of his leadership "lies, plain and simple."[9] That's kind of subjective. Did Comey poll all 35,000 employees to determine whether they had confidence in him? Or did he go with a quick show of hands? Did he have any sort of vested interest in the answer?

Comey also described a *New York Times* story as "entirely wrong."

Senator Tom Cotton: On February 14th, *The New York Times* published a story, the headline of which was, 'Trump Campaign Aides Had Repeated Contacts With Russian Intelligence.' You were asked earlier if that was an inaccurate story, and you said, in the main. Would it be fair to characterize that story as almost entirely wrong?

Comey: Yes.[10]

That's a little more specific than arguing about the general esprit de corps of an enormous organization. The *Times* article said Trump aides had repeated contacts with Russian intelligence. Either they did or they didn't. Comey's verdict was: "almost entirely wrong."

Here are the *Times*' headlines on the two falsehoods identified by the former director at the same hearing:

"Comey Bluntly Raises Possibility of Trump Obstruction and Condemns His 'Lies'"[11]

"Disputing Times Article About Inquiry into Russia"[12]

If Trump kills someone, it's "murder"; if the *Times* does it, it's "assisted suicide." Someone should take this to the *Times*' public editor—oh, we can't. They fired her and abolished the position a few months into the Trump administration. Their reporting is *fine.*

It would be different if the *Times* called itself "The George Soros Newsletter." But it doesn't do that.

Trump was elected president, which means—hold on to your hat!—some people voted for him. Not only that, but he got the nomination by winning more votes than any Republican in history. It might be nice to have someone writing at your newspaper who voted for him.

As far as the media are concerned, rousing political debate, with a testing of both sides, means pitting left-wing Democrats against NeverTrump Republicans. Asking NeverTrumpers about the Trump administration is like interviewing Neville Chamberlain on the D-Day Invasion:

Katy Tur: Mr. Chamberlain, why a second world war at all?

Chamberlain: Well, that's precisely the point! This is a failure of diplomacy. As I said when I returned from Munich...

DON'T INTERRUPT US—WE'RE PROJECTING!

Consider the fact that Russia—the most evil regime in the world—is accused of doing to the Democrats what the media do to Republicans every election cycle. The claim is that the Kremlin meddled in our election by (1) putting information into the public sphere during an election that the Democrats didn't want the public to know and (2) pushing deceptive memes on social media designed to help Trump and hurt Hillary.

The media has been releasing negative information about Republicans forever. On the upside, that's why there are never any bombshells about our presidential candidates. Any Republican who's been around long enough to run for president has had his entire life unearthed. By contrast, there are almost always exciting surprises with the Democrats' candidates. Until Michael Dukakis ran for president, it was not generally known that he had defiantly paroled a depraved murderer who then went on to torture and rape an innocent couple in Maryland. No media outlet had ever checked to see if John Kerry had been lying about being Irish his entire life, and was actually Jewish. Only when he was running for president did we begin to hear of Bill Clinton's spectacular sexual assault record.

Among the scandals the media have launched against Republicans in a campaign year are: the repeatedly investigated charge that the first President Bush had had an affair years earlier; allegations that Senate candidate Jack Ryan had taken his ex-wife to sex clubs; and CBS's claim that the second President Bush had shirked his National Guard duty, based on a source who was literally foaming at the mouth.[13] (Not Dan Rather—I mean the other guy.)

At least what WikiLeaks published was true. Those were real e-mails. The source wasn't a mentally disturbed man or an ex-wife's accusations in a custody dispute. The source was the DNC's computer hard drive. Naturally, the Democrats didn't want anyone to see their private e-mails. Jack and Jeri Ryan didn't want anyone to see their divorce records, which is why they filed them under seal. Donald Trump didn't want his secretly recorded remarks on an *Access Hollywood* tape being blasted around the globe one month before the election. The media did all that.

Instead of reporting news when they get it, the media act like an opposition party, releasing negative information tactically. Ryan's sealed divorce records came out years after his divorce, but immediately after he became the GOP Senate nominee against Barack Obama. ABC News broke the story of Representative Mark Foley's sexually suggestive texts to underage male pages—sent between 1995 and 2005—on September 29, 2006, the day Foley's name could no longer be removed from the ballot.[14] And by the way, Foley didn't want the public reading his texts, either. NBC held on to that *Access Hollywood* tape until one month before the election. That must have taken incredible self-discipline, like keeping a chocolate bar in the freezer until you've done something to deserve it.

Thanks to WikiLeaks, now the Democrats know what it's like to have negative information strategically leaked against them in an election year.

As for the Russians' deceptive social media posts, how about comparing the effect of Russia's "Woke Blacks" Instagram account to the media's "HANDS UP, DON'T SHOOT" hoax? For nearly four months, our entire North American press corps retailed a ghastly narrative about a white policeman in Ferguson, Missouri, gunning down an innocent black man, Michael "Big Mike" Brown, as he begged for his life. Eventually, we learned the truth. It turned out the media's account was a complete fabrication.

Was that false story helpful to Hillary? She sure thought so. At her invitation, Brown's mother appeared onstage at the Democratic National Convention as an honored guest. How many votes did Hillary get from the cooked-up media campaign about a racist cop?

How many voters were influenced by the Russians' "United Muslims of America" Facebook group, as compared with the *Access Hollywood* tape of Trump that played around the clock on every network for weeks before the election? The Republican Party thought that tape had ended Trump's candidacy. According to news reports, the day after its release, RNC chairman Reince Priebus begged Trump to withdraw from the race, saying he faced certain and humiliating defeat.

NBC's leaking of that tape was every bit as disreputable as WikiLeaks' publication of the Democrats' e-mails. Why is one illegally leaked conversation (the DNC e-mails) an attack on our democracy when the Russians do it, but the finest of American journalism (the *Access Hollywood* tape) when the media do it? What else can the media do that would be an act of war if done by foreigners? Can *The Washington Post* bomb Pearl Harbor?

We have the Department of Justice, the CIA, the FBI, the NSA, and the independent counsel hot on the trail of a claimed Russian plot to interfere with our election by hacking the DNC's e-mails. Can they spare a few agents to find out who illegally leaked the *Access Hollywood* tape?

The media's position is that *they're* allowed to engage in lies, deception, and even illegal acts to swing an election. But if foreigners do it, it constitutes:

> *"the political equivalent of 9/11."*
> —FORMER ACTING DIRECTOR OF THE CIA MIKE
> MORELL[15]

> *"an act of war."*
> —REPUBLICAN SENATOR JOHN MCCAIN[16] (AND CLAIRE
> MCCASKILL)

> *"subversion of an election by a foreign power."*
> —*THE NEW YORK TIMES* COLUMNIST PAUL KRUGMAN[17]

> *"a well-planned, well-coordinated, multifaceted attack on our election process and democracy."*
> —BILL PRIESTAP, ASSISTANT DIRECTOR OF THE FBI'S
> COUNTERINTELLIGENCE DIVISION (AND INSTIGATOR
> OF THE FBI'S RUSSIAN INVESTIGATION)[18]

> an *"assault on American democracy."*
> —REPUBLICAN EVAN MCMULLIN[19]

"something that should scare all of us as Americans."
—DEMOCRATIC CONGRESSMAN ELIOT ENGEL[20]

Media: Oh no! You don't have to say anything original! The more repetitive, uninteresting, and pointless, the better! It shows you're well grounded.

DRILLING DOWN INTO VACUITY

Forget left and right. What do the media consider priorities? Precious resources are wasted "drilling down" on the most idiotic issues, in hopes of producing a small nugget of bad news for Trump. How about this fascinating segment on a February 2018 *Meet the Press* with host Chuck Todd "drilling down" on *rumors* that the White House chief of staff might have resigned?

> **Todd:** Did General Kelly offer to resign or not? There's been a lot of confusion, with our own reporting, with other reporting, there seems to be—did he unofficially offer to write the resignation letter, but just not officially hand it to him?[21]

In other news about what Trump or those around him might conceivably do in the future, dissected endlessly on cable TV: After the president criticized a Parkland, Florida, sheriff's deputy for hiding outside during the February 2018 school shooting, MSNBC's Lawrence O'Donnell devoted nearly half his show to disputing Trump's claim that he would have run into the building. O'Donnell gave his own assessment, then invited a panel of guests to speculate on what Trump would have done.[22] It was the closest thing to blank TV you will find in modern life. MSNBC should have run a test pattern.

And here is everybody's favorite headline—and chyron—from CNN:

CNN: Trump gets 2 scoops of ice cream, everyone else gets 1[23]

America: We have to find them and kill their children.

Here's an actual front-page headline from *The New York Times*' Web site:

Trump Spoke to Witnesses About Matters They Discussed with Special Counsel

- The special counsel in the Russia inquiry has learned of two conversations in which President Trump spoke to key witnesses about the investigation.

- Experts said Mr. Trump's contact with the men most likely did not constitute witness tampering.

Trump Had Eggs for Breakfast

- The special counsel has learned that Trump had eggs for breakfast.

- Experts say eating eggs most likely did not constitute criminal behavior.

It's getting difficult to maintain the fiction that the *Times* is the gold standard of journalism.

If you were to ask any normal person what his top concerns

for the country are, the answers would be along the lines of jobs, schools, the drug epidemic, crime, immigration (i.e., all of the above), and so on. But our media go from station stop to station stop of irrelevancy. Imagine your typical day. You talk with your boss, meet a client, refinance your mortgage, go to lunch. In each situation, you begin with casual chitchat about the weather, sports, that sort of thing. But, eventually, you get to the point.

With the media, we never get to the point. There's no *Okay, this is why I'm here.* Instead it's just hours and hours of *It sure is windy today. Yes, and not only that, but it's windy down the street. I talked to my sister-in-law in Massachusetts and it's windy up there, too.*

Here is Jake Tapper interviewing Trump aide Kellyanne Conway on CNN's *State of the Union* on Sunday, February 11, 2018:

> **Tapper [look of extreme gravitas]:** But I do want to ask you about White House Communications Director Hope Hicks, who apparently is dating Robert Porter. Porter's second wife, Jennifer Willoughby, said she is worried about Hope Hicks. Take a listen.
>
> (BEGIN VIDEO CLIP)
>
> **Willoughby:** It worries me for a lot of reasons. I mean, it definitely worries me, because, if I'm being frank with you, if he has not already been abusive with Hope, he will.
>
> (END VIDEO CLIP)
>
> **Tapper:** Are you worried at all about Hope Hicks?

Imagine you're at home in Des Moines, Iowa, watching this.

C'mon, honey! It's time to go to church . . .

Just hang on one more second—the interview's almost over.
I need to know if I should be worried about Rob Porter
beating up Hope Hicks!

That's the audience! Jake Tapper thinks we, the American
public, should be in a state of wild suspense, wondering if someone
we've never heard of will beat up Hope Hicks. When the interview
was over, a minute later, you know CNN producers were rushing
up to Tapper, telling him, *That was GREAT. You turned it around.
You showed empathy. This is why they pay you $10 million a year.*

At the height of their powers, Monty Python could not have
done better.

THE ONE THING WE MIGHT
GET OUT OF TRUMP

An essential component of saving the country is absolutely destroying the press. Not a brick upon a brick should remain. Then it can
be rebuilt on more ethical lines. The days when the media were
entitled to a presumption of accuracy is long past. And they're getting worse all the time. *Democracy Dies in Darkness!*

The left is confused about what "fake news" means. It does not
mean saying sunset will be at 6:18 p.m., when it's actually at 6:23
p.m. It means reporting the diametric opposite of what is happening, sending people away with a false story, so that they cannot
function in a democracy. Fake news means reporting, for example,
that Trump colluded with Russia to sway the election when it was
the Democratic Party and the FBI that colluded with Russia to
sway the election. Things have been trending this way for a while,

but under Trump, the media's transformation into an enemy of democracy is complete.

The problem is, journalists don't get out enough. Everyone in the media thinks exactly the same way. If you didn't know anyone who thought Trump would win, maybe you want to step back and reconsider your connection to reality. Some members of the Resistance might even know, as an intellectual matter, that their best argument is to admit that Trump voters do have legitimate gripes—about unfair trade deals, the opioid crisis, guest workers, crime, and mass immigration.

But they can't do it. When journalists get together, they lose control and become a clique of mean girls dishing on the new girl at school. They have to call Trump the "short-fingered vulgarian" or construct absurd conspiracy theories about Russia. Try going to a burned-out company town in southern Ohio and saying the biggest problem with Trump is that he's an arriviste. To the media, that is the ultimate anti-Trump argument.

The country will be in very bad shape if Trump doesn't arise from his torpor and keep his campaign promises, but if we get nothing else from his presidency, at least the media will be totally discredited. He brings out the best in them! Trump may be shallow, narcissistic, disloyal, and the crudest kind of braggart, but he's like chemotherapy for the country: it's unpleasant to go through, you vomit, your hair falls out—but it kills cancer cells, and you live. Trump's presidency may be an unpleasant thing to go through, but everyone on *The New York Times'* editorial board will die.

And who knows? Maybe Trump will keep his promises and end up on Mount Rushmore, his granite hair impervious to the breeze. As he likes to say, we'll see.

NOTES

CHAPTER ONE

1. "Watch Stephen Colbert Fall Apart on Election Night 2016," Showtime-WOR 710, November 8, 2016, available at https://710wor.iheart.com/fea
tured/mark-simone/content/2018–05–05-watch-stephen-colbert-fall
-apart-on-election-night-2016.
2. McKay Coppins, "He Is Going to Test Our Democracy as It Has Never Been Tested," *The Atlantic*, January 17, 2017.
3. Sheri Berman, "Can It Happen Here?" *New York Times*, May 20, 2018.
4. *The 11th Hour*, MSNBC, April 6, 2017.
5. Albert R. Hunt, "For Blacks in the U.S., Much Work Remains," *New York Times*, March 16, 2015.
6. John Harwood, "Dissent Festers in States That Obama Forgot," *Honolulu Star-Advertiser*, June 20, 2013.
7. "Top GOP Priority: Make Obama a One-Term President," *National Journal*, October 23, 2010.
8. Thomas Friedman, "I Believe I Can Fly," *New York Times*, November 14, 2010.
9. "Try Something Hard: Governing" (editorial), *New York Times*, November 14, 2010.
10. "McConnell's Hope" (editorial), *Courier-Journal* (Louisville, Kentucky), October 29, 2010.
11. Owen Gleiberman, "Film Review: 'Chappaquiddick,'" *Variety*, September 10, 2017.
12. Jane Mayer and Ronan Farrow, "Four Women Accuse New York's Attorney General of Physical Abuse," *The New Yorker*, May 7, 2018.

13. See Brian Bandell, "Top Hispanic-Owned Businesses: At MCM, Six Brothers Build on Their Family's Construction Legacy," *South Florida Business Journal* (Fort Lauderdale/Miami, Florida), September 1, 2017; Press Release, "Munilla Construction Management (MCM) Wins $66M Contract to Build School at Guantanamo Bay Naval Base," press release, available at https://www.con structiondive.com/press-release/20160727-munilla-construction-manage ment-mcm-wins-66m-contract-to-build-school-at.

14. "Diversity Fail? All-Women Engineering Team Blamed for Collapse of Miami Pedestrian Bridge," SandraRose.com, March 18, 2018, available at http:// sandrarose.com/2018/03/diversity-fail-women-engineering-team-behind -collapse-miami-pedestrian-bridge. Although she later denied being on the project, days earlier Leonor Flores said of the bridge, "It's very important for me as a woman and an engineer to be able to promote that to my daughter, because I think women have a different perspective. We're able to put in an artistic touch and we're able to build, too." Clara-Meretan Kiah, "Community Gathers to Watch 950-Ton Bridge Move Across Southwest 8th Street," FIU News, 03/14/2018March 14, 2018, available at https://news.fiu.edu/2018 /03/community-gathers-to-watch-950-ton-bridge-move-across-southwest -8th-street/120395.

15. Patricia Mazzei and Stephanie Saul, "Bridge Collapse Saps Spirits and Research Efforts at Florida International University," *New York Times,* March 17, 2018, https://www.nytimes.com/2018/03/17/us/florida-international -university-bridge.html.

16. Rema Rahman, "Protesters Greet Inauguration Guests, Clash with Police in Streets," *Roll Call,* January 20, 2017, https://www.rollcall.com/politics /protesters-greet-inauguration-guests; Keith L. Alexander, "Judge Dismisses Lead Rioting Charge against Defendants in Inauguration Day Protest Trial," *Washington Post,* December 13, 2017, https://www.washingtonpost.com /local/public-safety/judge-dismisses-lead-rioting-charge-against-six -defendants-in-inauguration-day-rioting-trial/2017/12/13/38db9382-e020 –11e7–8679-a9728984779c_story.html; Ryan J. Reilly, "Inside the Trial That Could Determine the Future of Free Speech in America's Capital," *Huffington Post,* December 10, 2017, https://www.huffingtonpost.com/entry /protesting-dc-trump-inauguration-trial_us_5a1e1e84e4b0d724fed48d32.

17. Petula Dvorak, "Fiery Rhetoric a Close Relative of Violence," *Washington Post,* December 1, 2015.

18. *The Situation Room,* CNN, July 6, 2010.

19. See Mark Walsh, "Immigration's Next Chapter: Arizona Is Set to Tell Its Tale of How to Stop Illegal Immigrants," *ABA Journal,* April, 2012.

20. Cheryl K. Chumley, "Rep. Gutierrez: Obama Assured Me He'll 'Stop the Deportation of Our People,'" *Washington Times,* July 21, 2014, http://www .washingtontimes.com/news/2014/jul/21/luis-gutierrez-obama-assured -me-hell-stop-deportat.

21. *Countdown with Keith Olbermann* (guest-hosted by Lawrence O'Donnell), MSNBC, July 28, 2010.

CHAPTER TWO

1. *The Last Word with Lawrence O'Donnell,* MSNBC, June 18, 2012.
2. Rachel Hahn, "Meet the Futurist Designer Behind Björk's Iconic Vagina Dress," *Vogue,* June 1, 2018, available at https://www.vogue.com/article/micol -ragni-designer-vagina-dress-bjork-primavera-barcelona-festival-style -erykah-badu-kelela.
3. These were all from the show broadcast on March 2, 2016. "Trash-Talking Teens: Underage Characters' Use of Sex Talk and Profanity on Broadcast Network TV," Parents Television Council, http://w2.parentstv.org/Medi aFiles/PDF/Studies/TTTStudy.pdf.
4. Neil Genzlinger, "Each Person in a Family Is Grappling with Secrets," *New York Times,* March 2, 2016.
5. David Wiegand, "With the Luck of the Irish, 'O'Neals' Could Be Real Deal," *San Francisco Chronicle,* February 26, 2016.
6. Diane Werts, "'The Real O'Neals' Review: Perfect Family Image Crumbles," *Newsday,* March 1, 2016.
7. *The Last Word with Lawrence O'Donnell,* MSNBC, April 16, 2018.
8. *MTP Daily,* MSNBC, October 10, 2016.
9. See, e.g., *The Situation Room,* CNN, October 26, 2016; *Erin Burnett OutFront,* CNN, October 31, 2016.
10. Nexis search for "(trump or president)" w/s "(admit! or brag! or boast or acknowledge!)" w/s "sex!" w/s "assault!" in the two years preceding April 27, 2018: *Washington Post*: 240 documents; *New York Times*: 132 documents.
11. "The Sleaziness of Donald Trump" (editorial), *New York Times,* October 7, 2016.
12. *All In with Chris Hayes,* MSNBC, March 9, 2017.
13. *Anderson Cooper 360,* CNN, October 10, 2017.
14. *The Last Word with Lawrence O'Donnell,* MSNBC, October 10, 2016.
15. Dana Milbank, "The Religious Right Makes a Deal with the Devil," *Washington Post,* October 11, 2016.
16. *Anderson Cooper 360,* CNN, December 8, 2017.
17. Charles Blow, "G.O.P. Visions of Tectonic Realignment," *New York Times,* February 12, 2018.
18. *Fresh Air,* NPR, September 18, 2017.

CHAPTER THREE

1. "What Donald Trump Said About Russian Hacking and Hillary Clinton's Emails," *New York Times,* July 27, 2016.
2. *To the Contrary with Bonnie Erbé,* PBS, August 10, 2008.
3. *Countdown with Keith Olbermann,* MSNBC, August 5, 2008.

4. Jennifer Rubin, "Note to Trump and Thiel: The President Is Always Taken Literally," *Right Turn* blog, *Washington Post,* November 14, 2016 ("the world takes what the president of the United States says both seriously and literally").

5. "Statement by FBI Director James B. Comey on the Investigation of Secretary Hillary Clinton's Use of a Personal E-Mail System," FBI National Press Office, July 5, 2016, https://www.fbi.gov/news/pressrel/press-releases /statement-by-fbi-director-james-b-comey-on-the-investigation-of-secretary -hillary-clinton2019s-use-of-a-personal-e-mail-system. (The statement said that the missing e-mails were "now gone" and the devices cleaned "in such a way as to preclude complete forensic recovery.")

6. *The Five,* Fox News, April 8, 2015.

7. Gregory Roberts, "Jindal Gets Media Bounce from Announcement," *The Advocate* (Baton Rouge, Louisiana), July 5, 2015. Marco Rubio warned that "the biggest danger" from Hillary's private server was that sensitive information was stolen by the Russians, Chinese, or other foreign powers for "insight into our thinking and into our strategy"; Al Weaver, "Rubio: 'Reckless, Irresponsible' Clinton Left Email Vulnerable to Russia, China," *Washington Examiner,* August 12, 2015. Jeb! Bush said it was "probable" that China and Russia obtained classified information from Hillary's private server; Kimberly Railey, "Bush Faces a Squeeze on His Right and Left," *The Hotline* blog, *National Journal,* August 20, 2015.

8. "How the Republican Candidates Fared in Their First Encounter," *New York Times,* August 8, 2015; Kristen East and Isabelle Taft, "GOP Debate: Best Zingers, Laugh Lines and Trumpisms," *Politico,* August 7, 2015; Kieran Corcoran, "'I Would Say Obama's Incompetent . . . But That's Not Nice': Round-Up of the Best GOP Debate One-Liners," DailyMail.com, August 7, 2015.

9. Jonathan Lemire, "Continuing Battle with Media, Trump Avoids News Conference," Associated Press, December 23, 2016.

10. Michael Kranish, "For Decades, Trump Sought to Craft Relationships, and Deals, in Russia," *Washington Post,* January 12, 2017.

11. Austan Goolsbee, "The First 100 Days," Fox News, February 15, 2017.

12. Colbert I. King, "Would Trump Pass a Security Clearance?" *Washington Post,* February 18, 2017.

13. Michael Grunwald, "Rating Trump's Yuge Month One," *Politico,* February 22, 2017.

14. *Hardball with Chris Matthews,* MSNBC, March 3, 2017.

15. David Filipov, "The Message in Moscow: Anti-Russia Hysteria Is Behind Scrutiny of Sessions," *Washington Post,* March 5, 2017.

16. Amanda Carpenter, *State of the Union,* CNN, May 14, 2017.

17. Julie Hirschfeld Davis, "Trump Will Meet Putin on Sidelines of G-20," *New York Times,* June 30, 2017.

18. Juan Williams, *The Five,* Fox News, July 11, 2017.
19. Evan Pérez and Dan Merica, "DEA Leader Rebukes Trump Telling Officers to Be 'Rough' on Suspects," CNN Wire, August 1, 2017.
20. Chris Cillizza, "The Tragic Death and Horrible Politicization of Seth Rich, Explained," CNN Wire, August 2, 2017.
21. Heidi Stevens, "This Role Reversal Isn't All That Funny," *Chicago Tribune,* August 16, 2017.
22. *CNN Newsroom,* CNN, September 19, 2017.
23. Jay Bookman, "New Book on Trump No Surprise," *Atlanta Journal-Constitution,* January 7, 2018
24. *The Beat with Ari Melber,* MSNBC, February 26, 2018.

CHAPTER FOUR

1. "Racist Assault at a Child's Birthday Party Yields Long Prison Terms in Georgia," NPR, February 28, 2017, https://www.npr.org/sections/thetwo-way/2017/02/28/517688757/racist-assault-on-a-childs-birthday-party-yields-long-prison-terms-in-georgia.
2. David Neiwert, Darren Ankrom, Esther Kaplan, and Scott Pham, "Homegrown Terror: Explore 9 Years of Domestic Terrorism Plots and Attacks," Center for Investigative Reporting, June 22, 2017, https://apps.revealnews.org/homegrown-terror.
3. Thomas C. Reeves, *Gentleman Boss: The Life of Chester Alan Arthur* (New York: Knopf, 1975), 3–4.
4. David Leonhardt and Ian Prasad Philbrick, "Donald Trump's Racism: The Definitive List," *New York Times,* January 15, 2018.
5. For the full description of the guilt of the convicted Central Park rapists, see Ann Coulter, *Demonic: How the Liberal Mob Is Endangering America* (New York: Crown Forum, 2011), chap. 13.
6. Hunton & Williams, *Independent Review of the 2017 Protest Events in Charlottesville, Virginia* (Richmond, VA: Hunton & Williams, 2017). ("Let them fight," Chief Al Thomas allegedly said. "It will make it easier to declare an unlawful assembly.")
7. Michael Wolff, *Fire and Fury: Inside the Trump White House* (New York: Henry Holt, 2018).
8. *Hardball with Chris Matthews,* MSNBC, August 16, 2017.
9. Edna Friedberg, "Why They Parade by Torchlight," *The Atlantic,* August 21, 2017.
10. Franklin D. Roosevelt, "Remarks to the Torchlight Paraders on Election Night. Hyde Park, New York," November 7, 1944, American Presidency Project, http://www.presidency.ucsb.edu/ws/?pid=16472.
11. Tedd Levy, "Looking Back: Torchlight Parade: A Tradition That Harkens Back to Colonial Days," *Shoreline Times,* December 12, 2011.

CHAPTER FIVE

1. Frank Snepp, "Brenneke Exposed," *Village Voice*, September 10, 1991; Steve Emerson and Jesse Furman, "The Conspiracy That Wasn't," *The New Republic*, November 18, 1991; Frank Snepp, "October Surmise," *Village Voice*, February 25, 1992.

2. Gary Sick, "The Election Story of the Decade," *New York Times,* April 15, 1991.

3. Available at https://www.thenation.com/authors/stephen-f-cohen.

4. Kelly McLaughlin, "Exclusive: Bill and Hillary Clinton Have 'AT LEAST a One-Way Open Marriage' Claims Their Veteran Pollster, *Daily Mail,* April 7, 2018, http://www.dailymail.co.uk/news/article-5532631/Clintons-one -way-open-marriage-pollster-says.html.

5. "Full Transcript: FBI Director James Comey Testifies on Russian Interference in 2016 Election," *Washington Post,* March 20, 2017.

6. Christopher Andrew and Vasili Mitrokhin, *The Sword and the Shield: The Mitrokhin Archive and the Secret History of the KGB* (New York: Basic Books, 1999), 243.

7. W. Averell Harriman, "If the Reagan Pattern Continues, America May Face Nuclear War," *New York Times,* January 1, 1984, https://www.nytimes .com/1984/01/01/opinion/if-the-reagan-pattern-continues-america-may -face-nuclear-war.html. See also John Kenneth Galbraith, "Reagan vs. the Military," *New York Times,* February 5, 1984, https://www.nytimes.com /1984/02/05/opinion/reagan-vs-the-military.html, and every column by Anthony Lewis.

8. "The assessment was made by four intelligence agencies—the Office of the Director of National Intelligence, the Central Intelligence Agency, the Federal Bureau of Investigation and the National Security Agency." "Corrections: June 29, 2017," *New York Times,* June 29, 2017, https://www.nytimes .com/2017/06/29/pageoneplus/corrections-june-29–2017.html.
The "Director of National Intelligence" is not an agency. It is a man, specifically James Clapper—and he has repeatedly stated that only three agencies concluded that Russia leaked the e-mails to WikiLeaks. See videos of Clapper correcting the misimpression that "17 intelligence agencies" concluded that Russia hacked the DNC here: Matt Vespa, "The Myth That 17 Intelligence Agencies Were Involved in Russian Interference Analysis Will Not Die," *Townhall,* July 7, 2017, https://townhall.com/tipsheet/mattvespa/2017/07/07 /former-spy-chief-not-all-17-intelligence-agencies-were-involved-in-russian -interference-analysis-n2351676.
The New York Times throws Clapper into its "correction," counting him as an "agency" to get the numbers up.

9. Mary Beth Sheridan, "Zedillo Key to End of Prop. 187, Villaraigosa Says," *Los Angeles Times,* August 4, 1999, http://articles.latimes.com/1999/aug /04/news/mn-62514.

10. See Ann Coulter, *Adios, America! The Left's Plan to Turn Our Country into a Third World Hellhole* (Washington, DC: Regnery, 2015), chap. 13.

11. Philip Giraldi, "Israel's Dirty Little Secret," *Unz Review,* June 20, 2017, http://www.unz.com/pgiraldi/israels-dirty-little-secret.

12. See *Hannity,* Fox News, February 25, 2016 (Hannity: "A lot was made over the issue when you said that you would be neutral in the Israeli-Palestinian conflict. But you do see that Israel is the victim in this."); Armin Rosen, "Donald Trump just defended taking an atypical approach to the Israeli-Palestinian conflict," *Business Insider,* February 25, 2016, http://www.businessinsider.com/donald-trump-israel-stance-palestine-2016–2.

13. Michael Wilner, "Rubio Strikes Trump on Israel, Seeking Crucial Florida Win," *Jerusalem Post,* February 27, 2016 (noting that Trump opponent Marco Rubio was likely motivated by "the country's largest pro-Israel donors" when he went after Trump for saying he would be "neutral" in negotiations between Israel and the Palestinians, saying, "The position you've taken is an anti-Israel position.").

14. Peter Stone, "Sheldon Adelson to Give $25m Boost to Trump Super Pac," *The Guardian,* September 23, 2016, https://www.theguardian.com/us-news/2016/sep/23/sheldon-adelson-trump-super-pac-donation-25-million.

15. Alana Wise, "Trump Tells Netanyahu He Would Recognize Jerusalem as Israel's Capital," Reuters, September 25, 2016, https://www.reuters.com/article/us-usa-election-trump-netanyahu/trump-tells-netanyahu-he-would-recognize-jerusalem-as-israels-capital-idUSKCN11V0Q6.

16. David Horowitz and Richard Poe, *The Shadow Party: How George Soros, Hillary Clinton, and Sixties Radicals Seized Control of the Democratic Party* (Nashville, TN: Nelson Current, 2006); Stephen F. Cohen, *Failed Crusade: America and the Tragedy of Post-Communist Russia* (New York and London: W. W. Norton, 2001); Marshall I. Goldman, *The Piratization of Russia: Russian Reform Goes Awry* (London and New York: Routledge, 2003); Janine R. Wedel, "The Harvard Boys Do Russia," *The Nation,* May 14, 1998.

17. See Goldman, *Piratization of Russia* ("Without concern for the lack of such preconditions, the reformers plowed quickly ahead with privatization and prided themselves initially at least on the fact that 60 to 70 percent of Russian state enterprises were privatized in just three or four years").

18. See, e.g., John Lloyd, "The Russian Devolution," *New York Times,* August 15, 1999.

19. Michael Lewis, "The Speculator," *The New Republic,* January 10 and 17, 1994; Emily Tamkin, "Who's Afraid of George Soros?" *Toronto Star,* October 15, 2017. One measure of Soros's control of Russian assets is that in Russia's financial crash at the end of the decade, his Quantum Fund is said to have lost $2 billion.

20. Horowitz and Poe, *Shadow Party.* Historian Stephen F. Cohen calls it "the worst American foreign policy disaster since Vietnam," and the reformers "the biggest kleptocrats of the twentieth century"; Cohen, *Failed Crusade.*

21. See Tamkin, "Who's Afraid of George Soros?"; Lewis, "The Speculator."

22. See, e.g., Dr. Kamal Wickremasinghe, "Lessons for Lanka: Malaysia's Election

Story," *Daily News* (Colombo, Sri Lanka), May 27, 2013 (describing Soros's method of funding electoral "observers" and "exit polls" to lay the groundwork for phony claims of electoral fraud).

23. Tamkin, "Who's Afraid of George Soros?"

24. "Ukraine's Orange Revolution Echoes Uncertainly in Central Asia," Agence France Presse, December 5, 2004.

25. Yang Razali Kassim, "Tackling Asean's Currency Soros," *Business Times* (Singapore), July 30, 1997; "Malaysian leader Discusses Currency Crisis with ASEAN's partners," Agence France-Presse, July 28, 1997.

26. Jehangir S. Pocha, "Foreign-Funded Nonprofits under Investigation in China," *Boston Globe*, June 15, 2006.

27. Simon Saradzhyan, "President Lashes Out at the West," *Moscow Times*, December 24, 2004.

CHAPTER SIX

1. *This Week,* ABC News, July 24, 2016, https://abcnews.go.com/ThisWeek /week-transcript-live-philadelphia-democratic-national-convention/story ?id=40825144. See also *State of the Union,* CNN, July 24, 2016 (Mook to Jake Tapper: "Experts are telling us that Russian actors broke into the DNC and stole these e-mails. And other experts are saying that the Russians are releasing these e-mails for the purpose of helping Donald Trump").

2. David E. Sanger and Nicole Perlroth, "As Democrats Gather, a Russian Subplot Raises Intrigue," *New York Times,* July 24, 2016.

3. Amy Chozick, "Democrats Allege D.N.C. Hack Is Part of Russian Effort to Elect Donald Trump," *New York Times,* July 26, 2016. See also Nicholas Confessore, "Donald Trump Suggests He'd Expand His Plans to Limit Immigration," *New York Times,* July 25, 2016 ("Mr. Mook provided no evidence that the Russian government had directed the release of the emails, which were posted Friday by WikiLeaks. An internal D.N.C. audit conducted by the firm CrowdStrike indicated that the hack was perpetrated by two groups of hackers with ties to Russian intelligence").

4. William Goldschlag and Dan Janison, "On Convention Eve, Democrats Try to Bury New Email Embarrassment," *Newsday,* July 25, 2016.

5. Cameron Joseph, "Kremlin Gremlin FBI: Probes Russian Hack of Dems Putin Seen Aiding Pal Trump," *Daily News,* July 26, 2016.

6. Mark Z. Barabak, "Democrats Take On a Cold Warrior Role," *Los Angeles Times,* July 25, 2016.

7. Todd J. Gillman and Katie Leslie, "Clinton Aides Work to Dampen Email Uproar," *Dallas Morning News*, July 26, 2016.

8. Gillman and Leslie, "Clinton Aides Work."

9. Del Quentin Wilber, Tracy Wilkinson, and Brian Bennett, "FBI Probing Russian Links to DNC Leak," *Baltimore Sun,* July 26, 2016.

10. See, e.g., Glenn Garvin, "Were the Hackers Who Broke into the DNC's Email Really Russian?" *Miami Herald,* March 24, 2017, available at http://

www.miamiherald.com/news/nation-world/national/article140461978
.html ("This is a close-knit community and criticizing a member to the outside world is kind of like talking out of turn" [Jeffrey Carr of Taia Global
Inc.] said. "I've been repeatedly criticized for speaking out in public about
whether the hacking was really done by the Russians. But this has to be
made public, has to be addressed, and has to be acknowledged by the House
and Senate Intelligence Committees"). See also Michael J. Sainato, "Cybersecurity Firm That Attributed DNC Hacks to Russia May Have Fabricated
Russia Hacking in Ukraine," *Counterpunch,* March 23, 2017, available at
https://www.counterpunch.org/2017/03/23/cybersecurity-firm-that
-attributed-dnc-hacks-to-russia-may-have-fabricated-russia-hacking
-in-ukraine; Brian Krebs, "The Download on the DNC Hack," *Krebs on Security,* January 17, 2017, available at https://krebsonsecurity.com/2017/01/the
-download-on-the-dnc-hack; Matt Taibbi, "Something About This Russia
Story Stinks," *Rolling Stone,* December 30, 2016, available at https://www
.rollingstone.com/politics/features/something-about-this-russia-story
-stinks-w458439.

11. See, e.g., John Solomon, "Assange Meets US Congressman, Vows to Prove
    Russia Did Not Leak Him Documents," *The Hill,* August 16, 2017, available at
    http://thehill.com/policy/cybersecurity/346904-assange-meets-us
    -congressman-vows-to-prove-russia-did-not-leak-him.
12. Gillman and Leslie, "Clinton Aides Work."
13. Eli Lake, "Russians Hacked DNC, Cyber Experts Say," *Charleston Gazette-
    Mail,* July 26, 2016.
14. *CNN Newsroom,* CNN, July 25, 2016.
15. Gillman and Leslie, "Clinton Aides Work."
16. Gillman and Leslie, "Clinton Aides Work."
17. Lake, "Russians Hacked DNC."
18. *CNN Newsroom,* CNN, July 25, 2016.
19. Cory Bennett, "Democrats' New Warning: Leaks Could Include Russian Lies,"
    Politico, August 7, 2016, https://www.politico.com/story/2016/08/democrats
    -cyberhack-russia-lies-227080.
20. Bennett, "Democrats' New Warning."
21. *CNN Newsroom,* CNN, July 25, 2016.
22. *World News Tonight with Peter Jennings,* ABC, March 16, 1992.
23. "The Other Woman," *Primetime Live,* ABC, January 30, 1992 (interview
    with Sam Donaldson).
24. Katharine Q. Seelye and Julie Bosman, "Critics and News Executives Split
    over Sexism in Clinton Coverage," *New York Times,* June 13, 2008.
25. Clinton Claiming Sexism Harmed Her Campaign, *NBC Nightly News,* May
    20, 2008.
26. "The Linda Tripp Tapes: An In-Depth Analysis," *Inside Politics,* CNN,
    November 17, 1998. See also *All Things Considered,* NPR, September 23,
    1998 ("President Clinton linked Linda Tripp with Paula Jones' lawyers, who

he said were out to hurt him politically. WILLIAM J. CLINTON, PRES-IDENT OF THE UNITED STATES: They've been up all night with Linda Tripp, who had betrayed her friend Monica Lewinsky, stabbed her in the back").

27. That is the result of several search requests of *The New York Times* archives on Nexis, including: "hillary and (russia or putin or moscow) and clinton w/s (russia or putin or moscow)."

28. Jason Horowitz, "Here's What You Missed in the Debate," *New York Times,* January 18, 2016. See also Jo Becker and Scott Shane, "Hillary Clinton, 'Smart Power' and a Dictator's Fall," *New York Times,* February 27, 2016 (Clinton aides noting how Hillary had impressed Putin by "listening to his tales of tagging polar bears and tracking Siberian tigers"); Mark Landler, "Where Hillary Clinton's Heavy Attack Was Light on Specifics," *New York Times,* June 4, 2016 (in a major foreign policy address, Hillary "made no mention of steps she would take to counter Mr. Putin's aggression"); Amy Chozick and Mark Landler, "Returning Fire, Clinton Scorns Trump as Unfit," *New York Times,* June 3, 2016 (Hillary's scorching attack on Trump was: "He says he has foreign policy experience because he ran the Miss Universe pageant in Russia").

29. David E. Sanger and Nick Corasaniti, "D.N.C. Says Russian Hackers Penetrated Its Files, Including Dossier on Donald Trump," *New York Times,* June 14, 2016.

CHAPTER SEVEN

1. Jo Becker, Steven Erlanger, and Eric Schmitt, "How Russia Often Benefits When Julian Assange Reveals the West's Secrets," *New York Times,* August 31, 2016, https://www.nytimes.com/2016/09/01/world/europe/wikileaks -julian-assange-russia.html.

2. See, e.g., David E. Sanger, "Hillary Clinton's Email Was Probably Hacked, Experts Say," *New York Times,* July 6, 2016.

3. David E. Sanger and Charlie Savage, "U.S. Says Russia Directed Hacks to Influence Elections," *New York Times,* October 7, 2016.

4. Joint Statement from the Department of Homeland Security and Office of the Director of National Intelligence on Election Security, DHS Press Office, October 7, 2016, https://www.dhs.gov/news/2016/10/07/joint-statement -department-homeland-security-and-office-director-national.

5. David E. Sanger, "A Hawkish Role Reversal," *New York Times,* October 21, 2016.

6. Mark Landler and David E. Sanger, "Obama Says He Told Putin: 'Cut It Out' on Hacking," *New York Times,* December 16, 2016.

7. See also CNN's Reality Check Team, "The Final Debate: CNN's Reality Check Team Vets the Claims," CNN.com, October 19, 2016; Linda Qiu, "Fact-Checking Donald Trump and Hillary Clinton in the Las Vegas Debate," *Miami Herald,* October 20, 2016.

8. Lauren Carroll, "Hillary Clinton Blames High-Up Russians for WikiLeaks Releases," *PolitiFact,* October 19, 2016, http://www.politifact.com/truth-o -meter/statements/2016/oct/19/hillary-clinton/hillary-clinton-blames -russia-putin-wikileaks-rele.

9. Eliza Collins, "Yes, 17 Intelligence Agencies Really Did Say Russia Was Behind Hacking," *USA Today,* October 21, 2016, https://www.usatoday.com /story/news/politics/onpolitics/2016/10/21/17-intelligence-agencies -russia-behind-hacking/92514592.

10. Leonid Bershidsky, "Clinton Should Stop Blaming Russians and Focus on Cybersecurity," *Chicago Tribune,* October 27, 2016.

11. Nicole Perlroth and Michael D. Shear, "Private Security Group Says Russia Was Behind Hack of Clinton Campaign Chairman," *New York Times,* October 21, 2016.

12. Jonathan Allen and Amie Parnes, *Shattered: Inside Hillary Clinton's Doomed Campaign* (New York: Crown, 2017).

13. Eric Lipton, David E. Sanger, and Scott Shane, "The Perfect Weapon: How Russian Cyberpower Invaded the U.S.," *New York Times,* December 13, 2016.

14. Amy Chozick, "Clinton Says 'Personal Beef' by Putin Led to Hacking Attacks," *New York Times,* December 16, 2016.

15. Reid Wilson, "Final Newspaper Endorsement Count: Clinton 57, Trump 2," *The Hill,* November 6, 2016.

16. Matt Taibbi, "Something About This Russia Story Stinks," *Rolling Stone,* December 30, 2016, https://www.rollingstone.com/politics/features/some thing-about-this-russia-story-stinks-w458439.

17. Office of the Director of National Intelligence, "Assessing Russian Activities and Intentions in Recent US Elections," ICA 2017–01D, January 6, 2017, https://www.dni.gov/files/documents/ICA_2017_01.pdf.

18. See, e.g., James Downie, "Obama Should Fire John Brennan," *Washington Post,* July 31, 2014, https://www.washingtonpost.com/blogs/post-partisan /wp/2014/07/31/obama-should-fire-john-brennan/?noredirect=on&utm _term=.6d0a69e52e41.

19. Mark Landler and Helene Cooper, "New U.S. Account Says Bin Laden Was Unarmed During Raid," *New York Times,* May 3, 2011, https://www .nytimes.com/2011/05/04/world/asia/04raid.html.

20. "CIA Director Denies Spying on Senate Intel Committee," NBC News, March 11, 2014, https://www.nbcnews.com/storyline/cia-senate-snooping /cia-director-denies-spying-senate-intel-committee-n49916.

21. Mark Mazzetti and Carl Hulse, "Inquiry by C.I.A. Affirms It Spied on Senate Panel," *New York Times,* July 31, 2014, https://www.nytimes.com/2014/08 /01/world/senate-intelligence-commitee-cia-interrogation-report.html.

22. See, e.g., Downie, "Obama Should Fire John Brennan."

23. John O. Brennan (@JohnBrennan), Twitter, March 17, 2018, 5:00 a.m., https://twitter.com/JohnBrennan/status/974978856997224448.

24. Derek Chollet, former assistant secretary of defense, *CNN Newsroom*, CNN, May 23, 2017 ("John Brennan . . . is one of the finest public servants we have . . . He is a straight shooter. He calls it as he sees it . . . I think we have to take him at his word").

25. Brianna Keilar, *CNN Newsroom*, CNN, May 24, 2017 ("People [are] saying that [Brennan is] someone who is a straight shooter. He has a long career").

26. Joy Reid, *Meet the Press*, May 28, 2017 ("Are you telling me that the now-elected Trump administration didn't trust John Brennan . . . these straight arrow guys in our intelligence services?").

27. See, e.g., Glenn Kessler, "James Clapper's 'Least Untruthful' Statement to the Senate," *Washington Post*, June 12, 2013; Jonathan Turley, "James Clapper's Perjury, and Why DC Made Men Don't Get Charged for Lying to Congress," *USA Today*, January 19, 2018.

CHAPTER EIGHT

1. Office of the Director of National Intelligence, "Assessing Russian Activities and Intentions in Recent US Elections," ICA 2017–01D, January 6, 2017, https://www.dni.gov/files/documents/ICA_2017_01.pdf.

2. Amy Chozick, "Clinton Says 'Personal Beef' by Putin Led to Hacking Attacks," *New York Times*, December 16, 2016.

3. Julia Ioffe (@juliaioffe), Twitter, January 6, 2017, https://twitter.com/search?l=&q=report%20from%3AJuliaIoffe%20since%3A2017–01–05%20until%3A2017–01–13&src=typd&lang=en.

4. Alexandra King, "Glenn Greenwald Urges Press to Be Skeptical of Intel Report," CNN, January 8, 2017, https://www.cnn.com/2017/01/08/us/greenwald-intel-report-reliable-cnntv/index.html.

5. David A. Graham, "An Intelligence Report That Will Change No One's Mind," *The Atlantic*, January 6, 2017, https://www.scribd.com/article/335890773/An-Intelligence-Report-That-Will-Change-No-One-S-Mind.

6. Susan Hennessey (@Susan_Hennessey), Twitter, January 6–12, 2017, https://twitter.com/search?l=&q=report%20from%3ASusan_Hennessey%20since%3A2017–01–05%20until%3A2017–01–20&src=typd&lang=en.

7. Walter Pincus, "Tenet Defends Iraq Intelligence," *Washington Post*, May 31, 2003 (citing VIPS favorably); William Raspberry, "Failures of the Sept. 11 Commission," *Washington Post*, July 26, 2004 (admiring profile of McGovern); Dave Kehr, "Revisiting the Road to Iraq War, Step by Step," *New York Times*, August 20, 2004 (describing McGovern as "an articulate and dryly funny former C.I.A. analyst"); Ray McGovern, letter to the editor, "Answering 'What if Cheney's Right?'" *Washington Post*, May 17, 2009; Ray McGovern, letter to the editor, "C.I.A. Torture and the Issue of Blame," *New York Times*, February 25, 2015.

8. "A Demand for Russian 'Hacking' Proof," *Yerepouni Daily News*, January 18, 2017.

9. Michael D. Shear and David E. Sanger, "Putin Led a Complex Cyberattack Scheme to Aid Trump, Report Finds," *New York Times,* http://www.nytimes.com/images/2017/01/07/nytfrontpage/scannat.pdf.

10. *This Hour with Kate Bolduan,* CNN, May 22, 2018.

11. Richard Harwood, "A Question of Loyalty: U.S. Intelligence in the Year of the Spy," *Washington Post,* December 8, 1985.

12. Jim Hoagland, "CIA-Shah Ties Cloud Iran Data," *Washington Post,* December 17, 1978.

13. That was the summary given by Rep. Henry S. Reuss (D–Wisc.), who had commissioned the analysis; quoted in Bernard Gwertzman, "U.S. Survey Shows a Steady Growth In Soviet's G.N.P.," *New York Times,* December 26, 1982.

14. Associated Press, "C.I.A. Sees Stagnation in Soviet," *New York Times,* May 31, 1983.

15. Michael R. Gordon, "C.I.A.'s Report Revives Soviet-Growth Debates," *New York Times,* March 29, 1987.

16. George Lardner Jr. and R. Jeffrey Smith, "CIA Shared Data," *Washington Post,* April 28, 1992.

17. White House, briefing by Deputy Press Secretary for Foreign Affairs (August 1, 1990) ("I can't get into details because this involves intelligence matters, sources and methods . . . But we do look forward to the Arab neighbors of those two countries to continue the mediation efforts and to continue urging dialogue.")

18. Central Intelligence Agency, "Iraq's Weapons of Mass Destruction Programs, October, 2002, https://www.cia.gov/library/reports/general-reports-1/iraq_wmd/Iraq_Oct_2002.htm#iraq-s-weapons-of-mass-destruction-programs.

CHAPTER NINE

1. See, e.g., Josh Gerstein, "In Texts, FBI Agents on Russia Probe Called Trump an 'Idiot.' Messages Could Fuel GOP Claims That Bias Tainted Clinton and Trump Investigations," *Politico,* January 12, 2017; "Read FBI's Strzok, Page Texts About Trump," Fox News, January 21, 2018, http://www.foxnews.com/politics/2018/01/21/ex-mueller-aides-texts-revealed-read-them-here.html.

2. Eric Levitz, "DOJ Report Confirms That the President Is a Dishonest Conspiracy Theorist," *New York,* June 14, 2018.

3. Aaron Blake, "Peter Strzok's 'Insurance Policy' Text Message Looks Bad. but It Doesn't Look Like a Smoking Gun," *Washington Post,* December 18, 2017.

4. Anna Dubenko, "Right and Left: Partisan Writing You Shouldn't Miss on the Robert Mueller Investigation," *New York Times,* December 20, 2017 (quoting *The Wall Street Journal*). *The Times'* version is: "But officials have told the inspector general something quite different. They said Ms. Page

and others advocated a slower, circumspect pace, especially because polls predicted Mr. Trump's defeat." Matt Apuzzo, Adam Goldman, and Nicholas Fandos, "Code Name Crossfire Hurricane: The Secret Origins of the Trump Investigation," *New York Times*, May 16, 2018.

That isn't something "quite different." In fact, it's exactly how normal people understood and why they were appalled.

5. Scott Shane, Adam Goldman, and Matthew Rosenberg, "Trump Received Unsubstantiated Report That Russia Had Damaging Information About Him," *New York Times*, January 10, 2017.

6. Shane, Goldman, and Rosenberg, "Trump Received Unsubstantiated Report."

7. Apuzzo, Goldman, and Fandos, "Code Name Crossfire Hurricane."

8. Jane Mayer, "Christopher Steele, the Man Behind the Trump Dossier," *The New Yorker*, March 12, 2018.

9. "The Russia House: Trump Blusters, America Suffers" (editorial), *Daily News*, March 6, 2018.

10. "Transcript of Mitt Romney's Speech on Donald Trump," *New York Times*, March 3, 2016, https://www.nytimes.com/2016/03/04/us/politics/mitt -romney-speech.html.

11. *All In with Chris Hayes*, MSNBC, March 5, 2018.

12. *MTP Daily*, MSNBC, March 5, 2018.

13. *The Rachel Maddow Show*, MSNBC, March 5, 2018. ("[Russia] reportedly did not want to Mitt Romney, so they put the kibosh on him from Russia. That, of course, in turn implies that Russia did want Rex Tillerson, who is the person we all ended up with.")

14. *The 11th Hour*, MSNBC, March 5, 2018 (quoting Jane Mayer, "Christopher Steele, the Man Behind the Trump Dossier," *The New Yorker*, March 12, 2018).

15. Shane, Confessore, and Rosenberg, "How a Sensational, Unverified Dossier."

16. Shane, Goldman, and Rosenberg, "Trump Received Unsubstantiated Report."

17. David Wallis, "For Your F.B.I. File, Take a Number (15,001)," *New York Times*, August 11, 1996, https://www.nytimes.com/1996/08/11/weekinre view/for-your-fbi-file-take-a-number-15001.html.

18. "Filegate Scandal Begins to Develop a Strong Odor" (editorial), *Atlanta Journal-Constitution*, July 9, 1996.

19. Hearing on FBI Background Files, before the House Comm. on Government Reform and Oversight, chaired by Rep. William F. Clinger (R-Pa.), 104th Cong. (August 1, 1996) (Chairman Clinger: "The FBI reviewed the file and came upon the interview notes which state that Mr. Nussbaum claimed that Craig Livingstone came, quote, 'highly recommended by the First Lady,' Hillary Clinton").

20. See Office of the Inspector General, *Special Report: A Review of the FBI's Handling of Intelligence Information Prior to the September 11 Attacks*, November 2004, chap. 3, https://oig.justice.gov/special/0506/chapter3 .htm; "Bush Opposes 9/11 Query Panel," CBS News, May 23, 2002, http://

www.cbsnews.com/news/bush-opposes-9-11-query-panel/; Eric Licht-blau, "Report Details F.B.I.'s Failure on 2 Hijackers," *New York Times,* June 10, 2005.

21. Massimo Calabresi, "Why the FBI Dropped Its Previous Orlando Shooter Investigations," *Time,* June 14, 2016, http://time.com/4368439/orlando-shooting-omar-mateen-fbi-investigation-dropped.

CHAPTER TEN

1. Hearing on Oversight of the Federal Bureau of Investigation, before the Senate Comm. on the Judiciary, 115th Cong. (May 3, 2017).
2. Hearing on Oversight of the Federal Bureau of Investigation, before the Senate Comm. on the Judiciary, 115th Cong. (May 3, 2017).
3. Peter Baker, "In Trump's Firing of James Comey, Echoes of Watergate," *New York Times,* May 9, 2017.
4. *Anderson Cooper 360,* CNN, May 9, 2017.
5. *CNN Tonight,* CNN, May 9, 2017.
6. *Anderson Cooper 360,* CNN, May 9, 2017.
7. *CNN Tonight,* CNN, May 9, 2017.
8. *Hardball with Chris Matthews,* MSNBC, May 9, 2017.
9. "Full transcript: Acting FBI Director McCabe and Others Testify before the Senate Intelligence Committee," *Washington Post,* https://www.washingtonpost.com/news/post-politics/wp/2017/05/11/full-transcript-acting-fbi-director-mccabe-and-others-testify-before-the-senate-intelligence-committee/?noredirect=on&utm_term=.666bea831669.
10. See, e.g., "The (In)Complete (and Growing) List of Ridiculous Trump Superlatives," Mugsy's Rap Sheet, http://mugsysrapsheet.com/2017/07/03/the-incomplete-and-growing-list-of-ridiculous-trump-superlatives; "Language Expert: Donald Trump's Way of Speaking Is 'Oddly Adolescent,'" *The 11th Hour,* MSNBC, September 15, 2017, https://www.youtube.com/watch?v=phsU1vVHOQI.
11. Lester Holt, interview with President Donald Trump, *NBC Nightly News,* May 11, 2017.
12. Hearing on Russian Interference in the U.S. 2016 Elections, before the Senate Comm. on Intelligence, 115th Cong. (June 8, 2017).
13. *The Situation Room,* CNN, June 7, 2017.
14. Chris Cillizza, "Giuliani's Other Big Admission May Be Even Worse," CNN, May 3, 2018, https://www.cnn.com/2018/05/03/politics/donald-trump-rudy-giuliani-james-comey/index.html.
15. William Saletan, "Rudy Giuliani Can't Reconcile Donald Trump's Explanations for Firing James Comey," *Slate,* May 5, 2018, https://slate.com/news-and-politics/2018/05/rudy-giuliani-also-made-a-mess-of-trumps-explanation-for-firing-james-comey.html.
16. Amber Phillips, "Republicans Have a New Comey Problem, Thanks to Rudy Giuliani," *Washington Post,* May 3, 2018, https://www.washingtonpost.com

/news/the-fix/wp/2018/05/03/republicans-have-a-new-comey-problem
-thanks-to-rudy-giuliani.

CHAPTER ELEVEN

1. *All In with Chris Hayes*, MSNBC, December 5, 2017.
2. *The Rachel Maddow Show*, MSNBC, January 29, 2018.
3. In 1995, President Clinton directed attorney general Janet Reno to form local task forces on clinic violence that would respond to threats and criminal acts. Reno formed the National Task Force on Violence Against Health Care Providers, making it a permanent body in 1998. It was still not enough for the abortion ladies. See Annette Fuentes, "Clinic Crimes: Lots of Talk, Little Action," *In These Times*, December 27, 1998.
   See also Hearing on the Threat Posed to the United States by Terrorists, before the Senate Comm. on Appropriations, 106th Cong. (February 4, 1999) (statement by Louis J. Freeh, Director, Federal Bureau of Investigation) ("The FBI continues to vigorously investigate various bombings of abortion clinics and incidents of violence targeting abortion providers across the country").
4. *The Situation Room*, CNN, January 23, 2018.
5. *MTP Daily*, MSNBC, December 11, 2017.
6. *All In with Chris Hayes*, MSNBC, May 17, 2017.
7. "Witch-Hunt in American Politics; Tested by Challenges," *CNN Tonight*, CNN, May 18, 2017.
8. *Anderson Cooper 360*, CNN, June 9, 2017.
9. *The Last Word with Lawrence O'Donnell*, MSNBC, July 20, 2017.
10. *MTP Daily*, MSNBC, December 11, 2017.
11. Kenneth Starr, *The Starr Report: The Findings of Independent Counsel Kenneth W. Starr on President Clinton and the Lewinsky Affair* (New York: PublicAffairs, 1998).
12. As the former administrative aide to White House counsel Bernard Nussbaum, Tripp was not only the last person to see deputy White House counsel Vince Foster alive before he committed suicide—and thus was already a witness in Starr's Whitewater investigation—but the first person to see Kathleen Willey emerge from Clinton's office after he'd allegedly groped her—and thus was a probable witness in Jones's lawsuit. Lewinsky was pressuring Tripp to perjure herself, conforming her story to the one she and the president planned to tell.
13. "A Crisis from Petty Sources" (editorial), *New York Times*, January 22, 1998.
14. Chitra Ragavan, "Kenneth Starr Details," *Morning Edition*, NPR, January 26, 1998.
15. "A Crisis from Petty Sources," *New York Times*.
16. Susan Schmidt, Peter Baker, and Toni Locy, "Clinton Accused of Urging Aide to Lie," *Washington Post*, January 21, 1998.

17. "President Clinton's Deposition," *Washington Post,* March 13, 1998, https://www.washingtonpost.com/wp-srv/politics/special/clinton/stories/clintondep031398.htm.

18. Alabama congressman H. L. "Sonny" Callahan. See, e.g., John Kass, "Sure Clinton's Tryst Is a Private Matter—Just Like War Is," *Chicago Tribune,* September 15, 1998, http://articles.chicagotribune.com/1998–09–15/news/9809150157_1_callahan-white-house-bosnia.

19. "President Clinton's Deposition," *Washington Post.*

20. "Trump's Firing of Comey Is All About the Russia Inquiry" (editorial), *New York Times,* May 9, 2017.

21. Peter Baker, "In Trump's Firing of James Comey, Echoes of Watergate," *New York Times,* May 9, 2017; Matthew Haag, "Flashback to F.B.I. Chief's '93 Firing, and to Saturday Night," *New York Times,* May 9, 2017.

22. Dana Milbank, "Trump, Like Nixon, Will Fail," *Washington Post,* May 10, 2017.

23. RichardNixonLibrary (@NixonLibrary), Twitter, May 9, 2017, 4:15 p.m.

24. "Updates and Reactions to F.B.I. Director Comey's Firing," *New York Times,* May 9, 2017.

25. "James McCord's Letter to Judge John Sirica," March 19, 1973, Watergate.info, http://watergate.info/1973/03/19/mccord-letter-to-judge-sirica.html.

26. John M. Crewdson, "Gray Testifies That Dean 'Probably' Lied to F.B.I.," *New York Times,* March 23, 1973, https://www.nytimes.com/1973/03/23/archives/gray-testifies-that-dean-probably-lied-to-fbi-reports-nixon-aide.html.

27. Walter Rugaber, "Gray Says He Destroyed Files from Hunt Given Him as He Met Ehrlichman and Dean," *New York Times,* April 27, 1973, https://www.nytimes.com/1973/04/27/archives/gray-says-he-destroyed-files-from-hunt-given-him-as-he-met-ehrlichn.html.

28. Paul Johnson, *Modern Times: The World from the Twenties to the Nineties* (New York: HarperCollins, 2001), 649.

29. See, e.g., Johnson, *Modern Times,* 647–49.

CHAPTER TWELVE

1. Matt Zapotosky, "Former Attorney General, a Critic of Clinton, Argues Against Prosecution," *Washington Post,* October 11, 2016; Charlie Savage, "Trump's Pledge to Jail Clinton Gets Experts Thinking of 'Tin-Pot Dictators,'" *New York Times,* October 11, 2016.

2. Michael Cottone, "Rethinking Presumed Knowledge of the Law in the Regulatory Age," *Tennessee Law Review* 82, no. 137 (March 24, 2015).

3. See, e.g., Tim Graham, "Another Late Hit: The Media at Work" *National Review* Online, November 3, 2000; Mike Rappaport, "Lawrence Walsh and the Abuse of Power," *Law & Liberty,* March 24, 2014, http://www.libertylawsite.org/tag/abuse-of-power.

4. Among other things, the government's chief cooperating witness, Bill Allen, had contradicted his most damning testimony in previous statements. He

had also been accused of suborning the perjury of a fifteen-year-old hooker, Bambi Tyree. Another witness, who said Stevens had paid the full amount due, was flown back to Alaska just before the D.C. trial began, preventing him from testifying.

5. See FBI agent Chad Joy's whistleblower document, http://legaltimes.type pad.com/files/whistleblower-2.pdf; Henry F. Schuelke III, Report to Hon. Emmet G. Sullivan of Investigation Conducted Pursuant to the Court's Order, dated April 7, 2009, http://www.emptywheel.net/wp-content/uploads/2012 /03/stevens_report.pdf; Rob Cary, "Recalling the Injustice Done to Sen. Ted Stevens," *Roll Call*, October 28, 2014, https://www.rollcall.com/news/recalling _the_injustice_done_to_sen_ted_stevens_commentary-237407–1.html.

6. David Willman, *The Mirage Man: Bruce Ivins, the Anthrax Attacks, and America's Rush to War* (New York: Bantam, 2011), 200.

7. David Freed, "The Wrong Man," *The Atlantic*, April 13, 2010.

8. David Willman, "How Anthrax Case Stalled," *Los Angeles Times,* June 29, 2008.

9. See, e.g., David Snyder and Marilyn W. Thompson, "Md. Pond Drained for Clues in Anthrax Probe," *Washington Post,* June 10, 2003.

10. See, generally, Freed, "Wrong Man."

11. David Willman, *The Mirage Man,* 197–201; Carl M. Cannon, "When Comey and Mueller Bungled the Anthrax Case," RealClearPolitics, May 21, 2017, https://www.realclearpolitics.com/articles/2017/05/21/when_comey_and _mueller_bungled_the_anthrax_case_133953.html.

12. Willman, *The Mirage Man,* 198.

13. See, generally, Freed, "Wrong Man."

14. William J. Broad and Scott Shane, "For Suspects, Anthrax Case Had Big Costs," *New York Times,* August 10, 2008.

15. James Barrett, "Report: How Many Lawyers on Mueller's Team Are Democrats, Republicans?" *The Daily Wire,* February 22, 2018, https://www.dai lywire.com/news/27442/report-how-many-lawyers-muellers-team -are-james-barrett; Chuck Ross, "Newest Mueller Prosecutor Donated to Hillary Clinton," *The Daily Caller,* May 3, 2018, http://dailycaller.com/2018 /05/03/mueller-lawyer-hillary-clinton.

16. Hearing on Russian Interference in 2016 Election, before the House Comm. on the Judiciary, 115th Cong. (December 13, 2017) (statement by Congressman Steve Chabot).

17. Hearing on Russian Interference in 2016 Election, before the House Comm. on the Judiciary, 115th Cong. (December 13, 2017) (statement by deputy attorney general Rod Rosenstein). See also *Anderson Cooper 360,* CNN, December 20, 2017 (Jeffrey Toobin: "They are allowed to have political opinions . . . that is not a disqualifying factor to work in a criminal investigation"; Michael Zeldin: "There's a difference between having a political opinion and having a bias impact the outcome of your investigation").

18. *The Last Word with Lawrence O'Donnell*, MSNBC, March 22, 2017.

CHAPTER THIRTEEN

1. Eric Swallwell, "FBI Chief Hours from Testifying on Russia," CNN, March 19, 2017.

2. Hearing on Russian Active Measures Investigation, before the House Permanent Select Committee on Intelligence, 115th Cong. (March 20, 2017) (statement by Representative Jim Himes).

3. *All In with Chris Hayes,* MSNBC, March 27, 2017.

4. Byron York, "In Trump-Russia Probe, Was It All About the Logan Act?" *Washington Examiner,* December 3, 2017, http://www.washingtonexam iner.com/byron-york-in-trump-russia-probe-was-it-all-about-the-logan -act/article/2642434.

5. "Big Dupes at Big Peace: Ted Kennedy—Part 2," Big Peace, October 10, 2010 (interview with Dr. Paul Kengor about his book *Dupes: How America's Adversaries Have Manipulated Progressives for a Century* [Intercollegiate Studies Institute, 2010], which reprints the KGB memo discussing Kennedy's letter), http://bigpeace.com/stzu/2010/10/10/big-dupes-at-big-peace-ted -kennedy-part-2; "Text of KGB Letter on Senator Ted Kennedy" (citing Kengor at p. 317), Free Republic, http://www.freerepublic.com/focus/f-news /1760564/posts.

6. See, generally, Lydia Dennett, "The 'Foreign Agents' Law Paul Manafort Is Charged with Breaking Is Wildly Underenforced," *Vox,* November 3, 2017, https://www.vox.com/the-big-idea/2017/11/3/16596484/fara-foreign -agents-registration-manafort-enforcement-scandal.

7. Peter Schweizer, *Do as I Say (Not as I Do): Profiles in Liberal Hypocrisy* (New York: Doubleday 2006), 164–66.

8. "Flacking for Dictators in the 21st Century," Freedom House, March 13, 2012, https://freedomhouse.org/blog/flacking-dictators-21st-century.

9. James Harding, *Alpha Dogs: The Americans Who Turned Political Spin into a Global Business* (New York: Farrar, Straus and Giroux, 2008).

10. Ben Smith and Kenneth P. Vogel, "Obama Consultants Land Abroad," *Politico,* November 18, 2009.

11. Helene Cooper and Eric Lichtblau, "American Lobbyists Work for Ivorian Leader," *New York Times,* December 22, 2010, https://www.nytimes.com /2010/12/23/world/africa/23coast.html.

12. Celia Dugger, "African Leader Hires Adviser and Seeks an Image Change," *New York Times,* June 28, 2010, https://www.nytimes.com/2010/06/29 /world/africa/29obiang.html.

13. Eric Lichtblau, "Arab Unrest Puts Their Lobbyists in Uneasy Spot," *New York Times,* March 1, 2011, https://www.nytimes.com/2011/03/02/world /middleeast/02lobby.html.

14. Lichtblau, "Arab Unrest Puts Their Lobbyists."

15. Alexandra Jaffe, "Obama Advisers Coming Up Short in Campaigns Abroad," CNN Wire, May 9, 2015.

16. Anshel Pfeffer, "Forget About Bibi and Shelley, It's Really Finkelstein

vs. Greenberg," *Haaretz,* December 13, 2012, https://www.haaretz.com
/.premium-israel-s-election-america-s-strategists-1.5272294.

17. Lichtblau, "Arab Unrest Puts Their Lobbyists."
18. Patrick Temple-West, "Democrats Working Both Sides of Nigeria's Presidential Election," *Politico,* February 14, 2015, https://www.politico.com/story
/2015/02/nigeria-presidential-election-goodluck-jonathan-muhammadu
-buhari-115190.
19. Ken Silverstein, "I've Covered Foreign Lobbying for 20 Years and I'm Amazed Manafort Got Busted," *Politico,* https://www.politico.com/maga
zine/story/2017/10/30/paul-manafort-indictment-foreign-lobbying-russia
-probe-215764.
20. Alan Rappeport, "Top Experts Confounded by Advisers to Trump," *New York Times,* March 22, 2016.
21. Rappeport, "Top Experts Confounded."
22. Ellen Nakashima, Devlin Barrett, and Adam Entous, "Court Let FBI Monitor an Adviser to Trump," *Washington Post,* April 12, 2017.
23. *The Situation Room,* CNN, April 12, 2017.
24. *The Last Word with Lawrence O'Donnell,* MSNBC, April 11, 2017.
25. *The Last Word with Lawrence O'Donnell,* MSNBC, April 11, 2017.
26. *All In with Chris Hayes,* MSNBC, March 2, 2017.
27. "Unnecessary Harm" (editorial), *New York Times,* February 13, 2008.

CHAPTER FOURTEEN

1. *The Rachel Maddow Show,* MSNBC, September 12, 2017.
2. Hearing on the nomination of Sen. Jeff Sessions, R-Ala., to be attorney general, before the Senate Comm. on the Judiciary, 115th Cong. (January 10, 2017).
3. Claire McCaskill (@clairemc), Twitter, March 2, 2017, 7:06 a.m., https://
twitter.com/clairecmc/status/837272862432104448.
4. "Sessions Undisclosed Conversations with Russian Official," *CNN Tonight,* CNN, March 1, 2017.
5. "Sessions Undisclosed Conversations with Russian Official," *CNN Tonight.*
6. "Attorney General Jeff Sessions, When Still Senator and an Adviser to the Trump Campaign, Had Meetings with Russia's Ambassador to the U.S. but He Did Not Disclose Them During His Confirmation Hearings," *CNN Tonight,* CNN, March 1, 2017.
7. "Attorney General Jeff Sessions, When Still Senator," *CNN Tonight.*
8. *The Rachel Maddow Show,* MSNBC, March 2, 2017.
9. *The Rachel Maddow Show,* MSNBC, March 9, 2017.
10. Aaron Blake, "Six Times Jeff Sessions Talked About Perjury, Access and Recusal—When It Involved the Clintons," *Washington Post,* March 2, 2017.
11. Michelle Ye Hee Lee, "Nancy Pelosi's Claim That Bill Clinton Was Impeached for 'Something So Far Less' than Jeff Sessions," *Fact Checker* blog, *Washington Post,* March 2, 2017.

12. "Sessions Speaks Out on Conversations with Russian Ambassador," *CNN Tonight,* CNN, March 2, 2017.

13. Kristine Phillips, "23 People Ask the Justice Department to Launch a Criminal Inquiry into Its Chief, Jeff Sessions," *Washington Post,* March 27, 2017.

14. "Top Democratic Leaders Call for Attorney General to Resign," *CNN Newsroom,* CNN, March 2, 2017.

15. Hearing on Fiscal Year 2017 Department of Defense Budget Request, before the Senate Comm. on Appropriations, 114th Cong. (April 27, 2016) (statement by Sen. Dick Durbin, D-Ill.).

16. Hearing on Fiscal Year 2017 State Department Budget Request, before the Senate Comm. on Foreign Relations, 114th Cong. (February 23, 2016) (statement by Sen. Barbara Boxer, D-Calif.).

17. John Hudson, "P5+1 Nations Press Senate Democrats to Support Iran Deal," *Foreign Policy,* August 6, 2015, http:// http://foreignpolicy.com/2015/08/06 /p51-nations-press-senate-democrats-to-support-iran-deal. See also "Manchin Urges West Virginians to Read Iran Nuclear Deal on His Website," press release, States News Service, August 19, 2015 ("Manchin spoke with Sergey Ivanovich Kislyak, Russian Ambassador [July 24]").

18. Kaitlin Collins, "Russian Ambassador Sergey Kislyak Appeared as Obama White House Visitor at Least 22 Times," *The Daily Caller,* March 2, 2017, http://dailycaller.com/author/kcollins.

19. See, e.g., *All In with Chris Hayes,* MSNBC, June 6, 2017 (Democratic representative Ted Lieu: "You've got the attorney general lying before Congress, that's perjury"); *All In with Chris Hayes,* MSNBC, June 8, 2017 (Chris Hayes: "Jeff Sessions, under oath, before his colleagues in the Senate, appears to have forgotten or lied about his contacts with Sergey Kislyak"); *The Last Word with Lawrence O'Donnell,* MSNBC, June 12, 2017 (Lawrence O'Donnell: "Jeff Sessions may already be a subject of the special prosecutor's investigation, possibly for perjury in testifying to the Senate, or possibly for involving his possible Russian connections").

20. Laura Jarrett and David Shortell, "DOJ Releases Portion of Sessions' Security Clearance Form Sought in FOIA Lawsuit," CNN, July 13, 2017.

21. *The Rachel Maddow Show,* MSNBC, September 12, 2017.

22. See also Julia Manchester, "FBI Told Sessions He Didn't Need to Disclose Foreign Contacts for Clearance: Report," *The Hill,* December 10, 2017, http:// thehill.com/homenews/administration/364200-fbi-told-sessions-he-didnt -have-to-disclose-foreign-contacts-for; Danika Fears, "CNN Goofed on Sessions," *New York Post,* December 12, 2017.

CHAPTER FIFTEEN

1. "Read the Emails on Donald Trump Jr.'s Russia Meeting," *New York Times,* July 11, 2017, available at https://www.nytimes.com/interactive/2017/07 /11/us/politics/donald-trump-jr-email-text.html.

2. "Read the Emails on Donald Trump Jr.'s Russia Meeting," *New York Times.*

3. *All In with Chris Hayes,* MSNBC, October 30, 2017.

4. *MTP Daily,* MSNBC, July 10, 2017.

5. Hearing on the Nomination of Christopher A. Wray to Be Director of the Federal Bureau of Investigation, before the Senate Comm. on the Judiciary, 115th Cong. (July 12, 2017).

6. Matt Apuzzo, Michael S. Schmidt, Adam Goldman, and Eric Lichtblau, "Comey Tried to Shield the F.B.I. from Politics. Then He Shaped an Election," *New York Times,* April 22, 2017. See also Tom Hamburger & and Rosalind S. Helderman, "FBI Once Planned to Pay Former British Spy Who Authored Controversial Trump Dossier," *Washington Post,* February 28, 2017, https://www.washingtonpost.com/politics/fbi-once-planned-to-pay-former-british-spy-who-authored-controversial-trump-dossier/2017/02/28/896ab470-facc-11e6–9845–576c69081518_story.html.

7. Michael Isikoff, "Clinton Team Works to Deflect Allegations on Nominee's Private Life," *Washington Post,* July 26, 1992; Michael Isikoff and Mark Hosenball, "Snooping for Pols," *Newsweek,* September 5, 1994.

8. Glenn Kessler, "Did Hillary Clinton Collude with the Russians to Get 'Dirt' on Trump to Feed It to the FBI?" *Fact Checker* blog, *Washington Post,* February 9, 2018, available at https://www.washingtonpost.com/news/fact-checker/wp/2018/02/09/did-hillary-clinton-collude-with-the-russians-to-get-dirt-on-trump-to-feed-it-to-the-fbi.

9. Jo Becker, Mark Mazzetti, Matt Apuzzo, and Maggie Haberman, "Mueller Zeros In on Story Put Together About Trump Tower Meeting," *New York Times,* January 31, 2018.

10. Adam Entous, Devlin Barrett, and Rosalind S. Helderman, "Clinton Campaign, DNC Paid for Research That Led to Russia Dossier," *Washington Post,* October 24, 2017 (quoting Brian Fallon:) ("I would have had no problem passing it along and urging reporters to look into it. Opposition research happens on every campaign, and here you had probably the most shadowy guy ever running for president, and the FBI certainly has seen fit to look into it. I probably would have volunteered to go to Europe myself to try and verify if it would have helped get more of this out there before the election.").

CHAPTER SIXTEEN

1. Adam Entous, Devlin Barrett, and Rosalind S. Helderman, "Clinton Campaign, DNC Paid for Research That Led to Russia Dossier," *Washington Post,* October 24, 2017.

2. Scott Shane, Nicholas Confessore, and Matthew Rosenberg, "How a Sensational, Unverified Dossier Became a Crisis for Donald Trump," *New York Times,* January 11, 2017.

3. Scott Shane, "What We Know and Don't Know about the Trump-Russia Dossier," *New York Times,* January 11, 2017.

4. See chart in "Cruz Moving to Suspend His Campaign with Indiana Loss Today? Here's Why," *Virginia Right!* May 3, 2016, http://www.varight.com /news/cruz-moving-to-suspend-his-campaign-with-indiana-loss-today -heres-why.

5. *All In with Chris Hayes,* MSNBC, March 20, 2017.

6. *The Last Word with Lawrence O'Donnell,* MSNBC, March 22, 2017.

7. *Erin Burnett OutFront,* CNN, April 18, 2017.

8. *New Day,* CNN, April 19, 2017.

9. "Source: FBI Used British Dossier for Trump Associate FISA Warrant," *At This Hour,* CNN, April 19, 2017.

10. *Hardball with Chris Matthews,* MSNBC, April 20, 2017.

11. *The Rachel Maddow Show,* MSNBC, May 3, 2017.

12. Hearing on Oversight of the Federal Bureau of Investigation, before the Senate Comm. on the Judiciary, 115th Cong. (May 3, 2017). Senate Judiciary committee Chairman Chuck Grassley said he wanted to know "where did the money come from and what motivated the people writing the checks?" Director Comey refused to answer. "I don't want to say," was Comey's boilerplate response.

13. Nicholas Fandos, "Hopes Dim for Congressional Russia Inquiries as Parties Clash," *New York Times,* October 22, 2017.

14. *The Rachel Maddow Show,* MSNBC, October 24, 2017. She did briefly mention that Elias had paid for the dossier on "behalf" of the Clinton campaign and the DNC, but if you coughed at the right moment, you would not know that the dossier that launched the Russia investigation was a Hillary Clinton–funded opposition research project.

15. *CNN Tonight,* CNN, November 2, 2017.

16. *New Day,* CNN, January 3, 2018.

17. *Erin Burnett OutFront,* CNN, January 19, 2018.

CHAPTER SEVENTEEN

1. Ezra Klein (@ezraklein), Twitter, December 30, 2017, 10:00 a.m., https:// twitter.com/ezraklein/status/947165455256637441.

2. Erik Wemple, "New NYT Scoop on Russia Raises Questions About Old NYT Story On Russia," *Washington Post,* January 1, 2018.

3. Sharon Lafraniere, Mark Mazzetti, and Matt Apuzzo, "How the Russia Inquiry Began: A Campaign Aide, Drinks and Talk of Political Dirt," *New York Times,* December 30, 2017.

4. Lafraniere, Mazzetti, and Apuzzo, "How the Russia Inquiry Began: A Campaign Aide, Drinks and Talk of Political Dirt.".

5. Evan Pérez and Shimon Prokupecz, "Sources: State Dept. Hack the 'worst ever,'" CNN Wire, CNN, March 10, 2015.

6. "Democrats Sorely Need a Plan B Instead of a Clinton Coronation," *Washington Examiner,* March 10, 2015.

7. "Even Hackers Are Concerned Obama's and Clinton's Emails Remain Vulnerable," *The Guardian,* April 27, 2015, https://www.nytimes.com/2016/07/28/us/politics/trump-conference-highlights.html.

8. Lisa Lerer and Eric Tucker, "New Inquiry into Clinton Emails Fuels Political Questions," Associated Press, July 25, 2015.

9. Michael S. Schmidt and David E. Sanger, "F.B.I. Is Tracking Path of Classified Email From the State Dept. to Clinton," *New York Times,* August 14, 2015.

10. Aarti Shahani, "Did Clinton Camp Delete Emails or Wipe Server? The Difference Matters," *All Things Considered,* NPR, September 14, 2015.

11. See, e.g., "Emails Show Russia-Linked Hackers Tried at Least 5 Times to Break into Clinton Private Server," Associated Press, September 30, 2015; "Hillary Hacked?" *Good Morning America,* ABC News, October 1, 2015.

12. *The View,* ABC, October 1, 2015.

13. Hugh Hewitt radio show, "Robert Gates, 'Odds Are Pretty High' That Russia, China and Iran Have Compromised Hillary's Server," *Hugh Hewitt Show,* January 21, 2016, https://www.youtube.com/watch?v=JtjTAnTup0M.

14. Matt Apuzzo, "Security Logs of Clinton's Email Server Are Said to Show No Evidence of Hacking," *New York Times,* March 4, 2016.

15. Nicholas Kristof, "Is Hillary Clinton Dishonest?" *New York Times*, April 23, 2016, available at https://www.nytimes.com/2016/04/24/opinion/sunday/is-hillary-clinton-dishonest.html.

CHAPTER EIGHTEEN

1. *All In with Chris Hayes,* MSNBC, February 20, 2018.

2. "Schumer Floor Remarks on the First Year of the Mueller Investigation, the Deficit, and Net Neutrality," Senate Democrats, May 17, 2018, https://www.democrats.senate.gov/news/speech/schumer-floor-remarks-on-the-first-year-of-the-mueller-investigation-the-deficit-and-net-neutrality.

3. *Anderson Cooper 360,* CNN, May 17, 2018.

4. Mueller also got a plea bargain from a guy in California, Richard Pinedo, who sold fake bank account numbers to people who wanted to circumvent the verification procedures at Web sites like Amazon, eBay, and Facebook. He was caught up in the Mueller dragnet because among his customers were the indicted Russians. Pinedo is like the California videographer Nakoula Basseley Nakoula, whose short film "Innocence of Muslims" was blamed for the 2012 Benghazi attack. The Obama administration pursued Nakoula to the ends of the earth, sending him back to prison on a parole violation, to continue the charade that it was his video, and not the Obama administration's incompetence, that caused Benghazi. Pinedo and Nakoula are roadkill in a liberal fantasy.

5. See, e.g., Brooks Jackson, "Ask Factcheck: More Money Doesn't Guarantee Nomination," FactCheck.org, January 11, 2008, https://www.factcheck.org/2008/01/more-money-doesnt-guarantee-victory.

6. Evan Osnos, "Reading the Mueller Indictment: A Russian-American Fraud,"

The New Yorker, February 16, 2018, https://www.newyorker.com/news/news-desk/reading-the-mueller-indictment-a-russian-american-fraud.

7. See e.g., Jon Markman, "The Amazon Era: No Profits, No Problem," *Forbes,* May 23, 2017; Melanie Pinola, "Can I Really Make a Living by Blogging?" *Lifehacker,* March 6, 2014.

8. David Pierson and Tracey Lien, "The Goal Was Espionage. The Tactics Were Social Media 101," *Los Angeles Times,* February 16, 2018.

9. Christopher Ingraham, "Somebody Just Put a Price Tag on the 2016 Election. It's a Doozy," *Washington Post,* April 14, 2017, https://www.washingtonpost.com/news/wonk/wp/2017/04/14/somebody-just-put-a-price-tag-on-the-2016-election-its-a-doozy.

10. Brian Williams on *The 11th Hour,* MSNBC, February 16, 2018.

11. Chris Hayes on *All In with Chris Hayes,* MSNBC, February 16, 2018.

12. Matt Miller, MSNBC justice and security analyst, on *All In with Chris Hayes,* MSNBC, February 16, 2018.

13. Noam Cohen, "Facebook Isn't Just Violating Our Privacy," *New York Times,* March 29, 2018.

14. "The Latest: 13 Russians Accused of Plot to Disrupt Election," Associated Press, February 17, 2018.

15. *CNN Newsroom,* CNN, February 18, 2018.

16. *Wolf,* CNN, February 16, 2018.

17. *The Last Word with Lawrence O'Donnell,* MSNBC, February 16, 2018.

18. *Erin Burnett OutFront,* CNN, February 16, 2018.

19. See, e.g., Robert Semple, "Nixon Calls Manson Guilty, Later Withdraws Remark," *New York Times,* August 4, 1970, https://www.nytimes.com/1970/08/04/archives/nixon-calls-manson-guilty-later-withdraws-remark-refers-to-coast.html; "Manson Shows Headline to Jury; Mistral Bid Fails," *Washington Post,* August 5, 1970, http://jfk.hood.edu/Collection/Weisberg%20Subject%20Index%20Files/N%20Disk/Nixon%20Richard%20M%20President%20Watergate%20Files/Manson%20Charles/Item%2004.pdf.

20. David D. Kirkpatrick, "As Clinton Runs, Some Old Foes Stay on Sideline," *New York Times,* February 19, 2007.

21. U.S. v. Internet Research Agency (indictment), paragraph 57.

22. Ann Coulter, "True Grit," *Jewish World Review,* June 12, 2003, http://www.jewishworldreview.com/cols/coulter061203.asp.

23. Rob Goldman (@robjective), Twitter, February 16, 2018; see Goldman's tweets about the thirteen Russians indictments here: https://twitter.com/robjective/status/964680122006581248.

24. Kevin Roose, "On Russia, Facebook Sends a Message It Wishes It Hadn't," *New York Times,* February 19, 2018, https://www.nytimes.com/2018/02/19/technology/russia-facebook-trump.html.

25. *New Day,* CNN, February 19, 2018.

26. Cohen, "Facebook Isn't Just Violating."

27. *Hardball with Chris Matthews,* MSNBC, February 16, 2018.

28. "New Black Panther Leader Quanell X: Trump Is Right About Democrats Exploiting Black Votes," YouTube, posted by The AntiCoIntelPro Show, August 26, 2016, https://www.youtube.com/watch?v=NbKEwS8mLQc.

29. Jim Hoft, "Reuters Cameraman Risks Demotion by Showing Donald Trump's Blessing by Black Detroit Preacher," September 4, 2016, http://www.thegate waypundit.com/2016/09/reuters-cameraman-risks-demotion-showing -donald-trumps-blessing-black-detroit-preacher-video.

30. Matt Apuzzo and Sharon LaFraniere, "13 Russians Indicted as Mueller Reveals Effort to Aid Trump Campaign," *New York Times,* February 16, 2018, https://www.nytimes.com/2018/02/16/us/politics/russians-indicted -mueller-election-interference.html.

31. Jack Goldsmith, "The Downsides of Mueller's Russia Indictment," *Lawfare* blog, February 19, 2018, https://www.lawfareblog.com/downsides-muellers -russia-indictment.

32. Thomas Frank, "Everyone Thought the Russians Wouldn't Bother to Defend Themselves Against Mueller's Charges. Then This Happened," *BuzzFeed News,* April 11, 2018, https://www.buzzfeed.com/thomasfrank/a-russian -company-that-mueller-has-accused-of-election.

33. See, e.g., Josh Gerstein, "Judge Rejects Mueller's Request for Delay in Russian Troll Farm Case," *Politico,* May 4, 2018.

34. See e.g., Sarah N. Lynch, "Russian Firm Tied to 'Putin's Cook' Pleads Not Guilty in U.S.," Reuters, May 9, 2018.

CHAPTER NINETEEN

1. Jerry Seper, "FBI Agents Say Justice Blocked Probe," *Washington Times,* September 23, 1999; Editorial, "See No Evil," *Washington Times,* September 24, 1999.

2. Michael Kranish, "GOP Eyes Policy Link to China Funding," *Boston Globe,* May 19, 1998.

3. "Text of the Attorney General's Letter Sent to the House Judiciary Chairman," *New York Times,* October 4, 1997.

4. See, e.g., Kranish, , "GOP Eyes Policy Link to China Funding."

5. "Discovery of 44 Tapes Exposes Vulnerabilities of 2 Institutions," *New York Times,* October 12, 1997.

6. "America's Stolen Secrets" (editorial), *New York Times,* May 26, 1999.

7. "Weekend Update with Norm Macdonald," *Saturday Night Live,* season 23, episode 5 (November 8, 1997), NBC, http://snltranscripts.jt.org/97/97eup date.phtml.

8. "Sen. John Edwards Caught with Mistress and Love Child!" *National Enquirer,* July 22, 2008.

9. Beth Reinhard and Emma Brown May, "Probe of Leaked Banking Records Related to Michael Cohen Expands After New Yorker Report," *Washington Post,* May 17, 2018.

10. The leaker came forward to *The New Yorker*'s Ronan Farrow, in a CYA admission to get ahead of the inspector general's report. Farrow did all he could to prettify this outrageous illegal leaking, focusing the article on the leaker's pure "motive," which makes absolutely no sense:
"There has been much speculation about who leaked the confidential documents, and the Treasury Department's inspector general has launched a probe to find the source. That source, a law-enforcement official, is speaking publicly for the first time, to *The New Yorker,* to explain the motivation: the official had grown alarmed after being unable to find two important reports on Cohen's financial activity in a government database." Ronan Farrow, "Missing Files Motivated the Leak of Michael Cohen's Financial Records," *The New Yorker,* May 16, 2018, https://www.newyorker.com/news/news-desk/missing-files-motivated-the-leak-of-michael-cohens-financial-records.
11. "What You're Really Worried About Tonight If You're Donald Trump," *The Last Word with Lawrence O'Donnell,* MSNBC, May 30, 2018, http://www.msnbc.com/the-last-word/watch/lawrence-what-you-re-really-worried-about-tonight-if-you-re-donald-trump-1245090371771.

CHAPTER TWENTY

1. Asha Rangappa, "The FBI Didn't Use an Informant to Go After Trump. They Used One to Protect Him," *PostEverything* blog, *Washington Post,* May 18, 2018.
2. Eric Lichtblau and Steven Lee Myers, "Investigating Donald Trump, F.B.I. Sees No Clear Link to Russia," *New York Times,* October 31, 2016.
3. Denton L. Watson, "Thurgood Marshall's Red Menace," *New York Times,* December 10, 1996.
4. David J. Garrow, *Bearing the Cross: Martin Luther King, Jr., and the Southern Christian Leadership Conference* (New York: William Morrow, 1986); David J. Garrow, "The FBI and Martin Luther King," *The Atlantic,* July–August 2002, https://www.theatlantic.com/magazine/archive/2002/07/the-fbi-and-martin-luther-king/302537. See also John Barron, *Operation Solo: The FBI's Man in the Kremlin* (Washington, DC: Regnery, 1996).
5. David J. Garrow, *The FBI and Martin Luther King, Jr.* (New York: Penguin, 1983), 61.
6. Arthur M. Schlesinger, *Robert Kennedy and His Times* (Boston: Houghton Mifflin, 1978), 359.
7. See David J. Garrow, "When Martin Luther King Came Out Against Vietnam," *New York Times,* April 4, 2017, https://www.nytimes.com/2017/04/04/opinion/when-martin-luther-king-came-out-against-vietnam.html.
8. David J. Garrow, "An Awkward Alliance," review of *Lyndon Baines Johnson, Martin Luther King Jr., and the Laws That Changed America,* by Nick Kotz, *Washington Post,* January 16, 2005.
9. David J. Garrow, "The FBI and Martin Luther King," *The Atlantic.*
10. See, e.g., Schlesinger, *Robert Kennedy and His Times,* 359. ("The Bureau kept

up its pressure" to place taps on King's phone, which "had been on Hoover's agenda for some time." Until "Kennedy finally assented.") See also every newspaper or magazine article on the King wiretaps ever written.

11. See, e.g., Andrew Ferguson, *Fools' Names, Fools' Faces* (New York: Atlantic Monthly Press, 1996).

12. Eileen Sullivan, "Trump Pushes Possibility of Campaign Informant as 'Really Bad Stuff,'" *New York Times,* May 18, 2018.

13. Anthony Lewis, "Ford Campaign for CIA Could Harm the Agency," *Nevada State Journal,* January 13, 1976, https://www.newspapers.com/newspage /78783692 (saying the murder of Welch was being "manipulated in order to arouse a public backlash against legitimate criticism").

14. Julie Hirschfeld Davis and Adam Goldman, "Trump Demands Inquiry into Whether Justice Dept. 'Infiltrated or Surveilled' His Campaign," *New York Times,* May 20, 2018, https://www.nytimes.com/2018/05/20/us/politics /trump-mueller.html.

15. David Leonhardt, "Trump's Attacks on the Rule of Law Reach a New Level," *New York Times,* May 21, 2018.

16. "Obama Orders Investigation into Cyberattacks during Election Campaign," Radio Free Europe, December 9, 2016.

17. Devlin Barrett, "Obama Orders Review in al-Qaida Sleeper Case," Associated Press, January 22, 2009.

18. "Bush Orders Documents Seized by FBI Sealed for 45 Days," *The Frontrunner,* May 26, 2006.

19. "Clinton Orders Investigation into Waco Tragedy," *Morning Edition*, NPR, April 21, 1993.

20. Steven A. Holmes, "Clinton Orders Investigation on Possible Racial Profiling," *New York Times,* June 10, 1999.

21. "Excerpts from Senate Panel's Summary of Findings on Abscam Operations," *New York Times,* December 17, 1982; see, generally, Leslie Maitland, "At the Heart of the Abscam Debate," *New York Times,* July 25, 1982, https://www .nytimes.com/1982/07/25/magazine/at-the-heart-of-the-abscam-debate .html.

CHAPTER TWENTY-ONE

1. Office of the Director of National Intelligence, "Assessing Russian Activities and Intentions in Recent US Elections," ICA 2017–01D, January 6, 2017, https://www.dni.gov/files/documents/ICA_2017_01.pdf; Anders Corr, founder, Corr Analytics, interviewed on Bloomberg Radio, Financial Markets Regulatory Wire, February 24, 2016.

2. Clifford J. Levy and Ellen Barry, "For Jaded Russians, Obama's Star Power Does Not Translate," *New York Times,* July 8, 2009.

3. Steven Lee Myers and David M. Herszenhorn, "Clinton Tells Russia That Sanctions Will Soon End," *New York Times,* September 9, 2012.

4. Peter Baker, "Pressing 'Reset,' Even If the Computer May Be Hacked" (editorial), *New York Times,* July 1, 2010.

5. Peter Baker, "Republicans Hint at Hope for Arms Pact with Russia," *New York Times,* December 1, 2010.

6. "Russia Offers Kind Words, but Its Fist Is Clenched," *New York Times,* February 6, 2009.

7. Ellen Barry, "Mr. Obama and Russia," *New York Times,* February 12, 2009.

8. Stephen Sestanovich, "Cold War Leftovers," *New York Times,* May 20, 2009.

9. Geoffrey Wheatcroft, "Let's Just Be Friends . . . ," *New York Times,* October 30, 2011.

10. "Mr. Obama and Mr. Medvedev" (editorial), *New York Times,* July 4, 2009.

11. "Pressing 'Reset,' Even If the Computer May Be Hacked," *New York Times.*

12. Peter Baker, "The Never-Ending Cold War," *New York Times,* March 29, 2012 ("Two decades after the end of the cold war, Mitt Romney still considers Russia to be America's 'No. 1 geopolitical foe.' His comments display either a shocking lack of knowledge about international affairs or just craven politics. Either way, they are reckless and unworthy of a major presidential contender").

13. Byron York, "How Pundits Got Key Part of Trump-Russia Story All Wrong," *Washington Examiner,* March 18, 2017, https://www.washingtonexaminer .com/byron-york-how-pundits-got-key-part-of-trump-russia-story-all -wrong.

14. Byron York, "What Really Happened with the GOP Platform and Russia," *Washington Examiner,* November 26, 2017, https://www.washingtonex aminer.com/byron-york-what-really-happened-with-the-gop-platform -and-russia.

15. "Russia's Motives for Meddling," *Washington Post,* July 26, 2016.

16. *The Rachel Maddow Show,* MSNBC, March 8, 2017.

17. "Full Transcript: FBI Director James Comey Testifies on Russian Interference in 2016 Election," *Post Politics* blog, *Washington Post,* March 20, 2017.

18. Mark Hosenball, "Mueller Probing Russia Contacts at Republican Convention: Sources," Reuters, March 29, 2018, https://www.reuters.com/article/us -usa-trump-russia-convention/mueller-probing-russia-contacts-at -republican-convention-sources-idUSKBN1H52VT. See also Kyle Cheney, "Mueller Interested in 2016 Convention Episode Dismissed by House GOP," *Politico,* May 1, 2018.

19. *The Rachel Maddow Show,* MSNBC, March 29, 2018.

20. Raphael Crystal, letter to the editor, in "The Messages of the Mueller Inquiry," *New York Times,* October 31, 2018.

21. *Hardball with Chris Matthews,* MSNBC, December 4, 2017.

22. Alison Smale, "German Chancellor Rules Out Weapons Aid to Ukraine," *New York Times,* February 3, 2015.

23. Albert R. Hunt, "Confronting Russia Holds Peril for U.S.," *New York Times,* June 15, 2015.

24. Jennifer Steinhauer and David M. Herszenhorn, "Defying Obama, Many in Congress Press to Arm Ukraine," *New York Times,* June 12, 2015.

25. See, e.g., Tony Patterson, "Angela Merkel's Unlikely Journey from Communist East Germany to the Chancellorship," *The Independent* (UK), November 17, 2015, https://www.independent.co.uk/news/world/politics/angela-merkels -unlikely-journey-from-communist-east-germany-to-the-chancellorship -a6738271.html.

26. Judith Bergman, "Europe: Illegal to Criticize Islam," Gatestone Institute, December 12, 2016, https://www.gatestoneinstitute.org/9525/europe-illegal -criticize-islam.

27. David E. Sanger, "Putin's Hopes for Relief Under a Trump Presidency Back-fire Spectacularly," *New York Times,* July 31, 2017.

28. See, e.g., Marc Thiessen, "The 10 Best Things Trump Has Done in His First Year in Office," *Washington Post,* December 27, 2017.

29. Scott Shane, Nicholas Confessore, and Matthew Rosenberg, "How a Sensational, Unverified Dossier Became a Crisis for Donald Trump," *New York Times,* January 11, 2017.

30. "Transcript: Republican Presidential Debate," *New York Times,* December 16, 2015 (transcript of the "undercard" Republican debate, as transcribed by the Federal News Service).

31. "Fox Business Network Holds a 2016 Republican Presidential Candidates Debate" (second panel), Federal News Service, November 11, 2015.

CONCLUSION

1. In a Harvard-Harris poll that was provided exclusively to *The Hill,* 65 percent of voters believe there is a lot of fake news in the mainstream media. That number includes 80 percent of Republicans, 60 percent of independents, and 53 percent of Democrats. See Jonathan Easley, "Poll: Majority Says Mainstream Media Publishes Fake News," *The Hill,* May 24, 2017, http://thehill.com/homenews/campaign/334897-poll-majority-says -mainstream-media-publishes-fake-news (citing the Harvard-Harris poll of 2,006 registered voters in May 2017).

2. Michael B. Marois, "White House Buries Controversial News Under Hurricane Harvey Watch," *Time,* August 26, 2017, http://time.com/4917040/white -house-buries-controversial-news-under-hurricane-harvey.

3. Jeremy Diamond, "3 Headlines the White House Hopes You'll Miss as Hurricane Harvey Hits," CNN, August 26, 2017, https://www.cnn.com/2017 /08/25/politics/white-house-three-headlines-during-hurricane-friday /index.html.

4. Abby Phillip, "Trump Gives New Meaning to the Friday Night News Dump, Enraging His Critics," *Washington Post,* August 26, 2017, https://www.wash

ingtonpost.com/politics/trump-gives-new-meaning-to-the-friday-night
-news-dump-enraging-his-critics/2017/08/26/001f75d6–8a7b-11e7–9ce7
–9e175d8953fa_story.html.

5. Dana Bash, "Trump's Ratings Comment Was Abhorrent," *The Situation Room*, CNN, August 28, 2017, https://www.cnn.com/videos/politics/2017/08/28/bash-trump-arpaio-pardon-high-ratings-abhorrent-sot.cnn.

6. Glenn Thrush and Julie Hirschfeld Davis, "Trump Eyed 'Far Higher' Ratings in Pardoning Joe Arpaio as Hurricane Hit," *New York Times,* August 28, 2017.

7. Noor al-Sibai, "'One Big Reality Sh*tshow': Internet Pounds Trump for Heartless 'Ratings' Excuse for Arpaio Pardon During Harvey," *Raw Story*, August 28, 2017, https://www.rawstory.com/2017/08/one-big-reality-shtshow-internet-lambastes-trump-for-heartless-ratings-excuse-for-arpaio-pardon-during-harvey.

8. Thomas L. Friedman, "What Trump Is Doing Is Not O.K.," *New York Times,* February 14, 2017, https://www.nytimes.com/2017/02/14/opinion/what-trump-is-doing-is-not-ok.html ("We were attacked on Dec. 7, 1941, we were attacked on Sept. 11, 2001, and we were attacked on Nov. 8, 2016").

9. Hearing on Russian Interference in the U.S. 2016 Election, before the Senate Comm. on Intelligence, 115th Cong. (June 8, 2017).

10. Hearing on Russian Interference in the U.S. 2016 Election, before the Senate Comm. on Intelligence, 115th Cong. (June 8, 2017).

11. Matt Apuzzo and Emmarie Huetteman, "Comey Bluntly Raises Possibility of Trump Obstruction and Condemns His 'Lies,'" *New York Times,* June 8, 2017.

12. Michael S. Schmidt, Mark Mazzetti, and Matt Apuzzo, "Disputing Times Article About Inquiry into Russia," *New York Times,* June 9, 2017.

13. See, e.g., Dave Moniz, Kevin Johnson, and Jim Drinkard, "CBS Backs Off Guard Story," *USA Today*, September 21, 2004 ("[CBS source for National Guard documents Bill] Burkett's emotions varied widely in the interviews. One session ended when Burkett suffered a violent seizure and collapsed in his chair"); Howard Kurtz, Michael Dobbs, and James V. Grimaldi, "In Rush to Air, CBS Quashed Memo Worries," *Washington Post,* September 19, 2004 ("[Burkett] has told reporters that he suffered from depression and had a nervous breakdown after the military declined to treat him for a tropical disease he contracted while on assignment in Panama").

14. See, e.g., Rachel Kapochunas, "Foley Name to Stay on Ballot, Complicating Prospects for New GOP Contender," *Congressional Quarterly Today*, September 29, 2006.

15. "Ex-CIA Boss Says Russian Meddling Is an Attack," *CNN Newsroom*, CNN, December 12, 2016.

16. "McCain Calls for Senate Hearing on Russian Cyber Threats," *CNN Newsroom,* CNN, December 31, 2016.

17. Paul Krugman, "To Recover After Trump, the American People Must Stop Being Useful Idiots," *Las Vegas Sun,* December 25, 2016.
18. *Hardball with Chris Matthews,* MSNBC, June 21, 2017.
19. Evan McMullin, "Republicans, Protect the Nation," *New York Times,* February 17, 2017.
20. "Transcript of Pelosi, Ranking Democrats Press Conference Reacting to Resignation of National Security Advisor Michael Flynn," press release, Congresswoman Nancy Pelosi, February 14, 2017.
21. See, e.g., Chuck Todd, *Meet the Press,* NBC, February 11, 2018.
22. "Trump's Superhero Fantasy World," *The Last Word with Lawrence O'Donnell,* MSNBC, February 26, 2018, https://www.msnbc.com/the-last-word/watch/lawrence-trump-s-superhero-fantasy-world-1171297859671.
23. This was all over the news, but CNN can probably claim ownership. Dan Merica, "Trump gets 2 scoops of ice cream, everyone else gets 1—and other top lines from his *Time* interview," CNN.com, May 11, 2017, https://www.cnn.com/2017/05/11/politics/trump-time-magazine-ice-cream/index.html; Ellie Shechet, "Here's a Real Chyron That Appeared on CNN Today," *Jezebel,* May 11, 2017, https://theslot.jezebel.com/heres-a-real-chyron-that-appeared-on-cnn-today-1795143837.

INDEX